The Life and Music of John Field
1782 – 1837

A portrait of John Field, *c.* 1800, attributed to James Lonsdale

The Life and Music of
JOHN FIELD
1782–1837

Creator of the Nocturne

Patrick Piggott

UNIVERSITY OF CALIFORNIA PRESS

Berkeley and Los Angeles 1973

University of California Press
Berkeley and Los Angeles, California

ISBN: 0–520–02412–5
Library of Congress Catalog Card Number: 72–97741

Printed in Great Britain

To Phyllis and Terry de Valera

Contents

Contents

Illustrations

Preface

So little is generally known about John Field that it has been, and still is, only too easy for writers to indulge in guess-work about his life and music without arousing the suspicions of the average reader. As recently as 1970 there appeared, in an important symposium devoted to Liszt,[1] various inaccurate references to Field, one of which, from the distinguished pen of Sacheverell Sitwell, states that he died in Vienna, instead of in Moscow; while the 'Register of Persons' in the same book not only places Spohr's solitary meeting with Field in London, instead of St. Petersburg, but moves his death back to Moscow, and in conditions of 'pitiful privation' for which there is no documentary evidence.

It was perhaps a printer's error, in a recent article in *The Listener*, which caused the name of the Russians who have always been credited with the 'rescue' of Field in Naples in 1835—the Rakhmanovs—to appear as Romanov (the name of the Russian imperial family); but the transformation of A. Y. Bulgakov, from one of whose letters an anecdote is quoted, into 'a young lady' cannot be explained so easily. Such minor slips— and they are very numerous in most writings about Field—could easily be avoided; but somehow, where Field is concerned, a reliance on vague memories of what has been read in the past has too often been thought enough by writers who are otherwise carefulness itself. Thus Eric Blom, in what was, at the time (1930), a fairly stimulating article about Field, faced, perhaps, with the contradictory evidence of an eye-witness who maintained that Field was married in 1807 and the fact that the registration of the wedding is dated 1810, cheerfully split the difference (more or less) and married him off to 'a young French actress' (she was certainly young and French, but not an actress) in 1808.

[1] Alan Walker (ed.) *Franz Liszt the Man & His Music*, Barrie & Jenkins, London, 1970.

Blom relied for many details of his essay (such as the possible, but quite unproven meeting of Field with the Irish actress, Harriet Smithson, in Paris, in 1833) on the statements of W. H. Gratton Flood, whose short memoir, *John Field of Dublin*, came out in 1920. Gratton Flood, an enthusiastic nationalist but a most incautious researcher, jumped hurriedly to a great many wrong conclusions; and though he did quite useful work in bringing to light facts about Field's childhood in Dublin his memoir is, in the main, inaccurate and misleading.

Much of Flood's little book seems to be based on a not always perfect understanding, or perhaps an inaccurate translation, of Heinrich Dessauer's *John Field, sein Leben und seine Werke*, which was submitted as a thesis for a Doctorate in Philosophy at the University of Leipzig in 1912, and which remains the most important study of Field so far produced. Though Dessauer did not go to Russia, he received great assistance from the celebrated St. Petersburg music historian, N. F. Findeisen, who sent him a large amount, indeed the greater part, of what was then available about Field in Russian.

The publication, in 1960, of A. Nikolayev's interesting study of Field proved how very thorough had been Findeisen's researches in the early years of the century; for Nikolayev, to whom all Russian sources of information were presumably open, was not able to add much of importance to Dessauer, to whose work he is greatly indebted, as must be all later writers on Field.

Dessauer's sources, supplied by Findeisen, included two important biographical sketches, one by Field's life-long friend, F. A. Gebhard, and the other by his favourite pupil, Alexander Dubuk.[1] Gebhard's memoir first came out in a Russian journal, *Sevyernaya Pchela* ('The Northern Bee'), shortly after Field's death, and it was used as the basis of the long obituary notice which appeared in the *Allgemeine Musikalische Zeitung* in July, 1837. Dubuk's memories of Field were written many years after the death of his beloved master: though by no means free from error, they are still of great interest and importance to the student of Field.

It is impossible to over-estimate the value of Cecil Hopkinson's remark-

---

[1] The Russian vowel ю(yuh), which occurs twice in the name Дюбюк, has a clumsy look when reproduced phonetically in English. The French 'Dubuque' is often used (non-Russian editions of Tchaikovsky's early *Mazurka de Salon*, Op. 9 No. 3 are dedicated to 'Alexandre Dubuque') but this seems out of place in a book written in English. The spelling, Dubuk, is used here, but readers are asked to imagine something more like Dyuhbuke.

able *Thematic Catalogue of John Field* (1961), the result of many years of Holmesian detective work. Mr. Hopkinson's bibliography is much more than a catalogue; it is both a monument of erudition and a mine of information filled with richly promising seams, many of them still awaiting development.

I am aware of the danger of calling attention to errors in earlier publications about Field; such things have a disagreeable habit of returning, like boomerangs, to the point from which they were launched; but it is a risk that must be taken. At the same time, it must be conceded that when writing about Field mistakes can easily be made. Even Tolstoy teeters precariously on the edge of a blunder in his well-known reference to Field in *War and Peace*. Count Rostov's 'house pianist', Dimmler (he was a real person, a successful Moscow piano teacher, and himself a pupil of Field) is asked by the Countess, 'Monsieur Dimmler, please play my favourite Field Nocturne.' Unfortunately at the time in which the scene is set (about 1810) Field had not yet chosen this title for the pieces in what was to become his nocturne genre, and if he had written any of them (there is no evidence that he had) he would then have called them romances. If the great Tolstoy, with all his care and attention to the most minute detail, can make mistakes, however small, we infinitely lesser mortals cannot hope to avoid them entirely. But we can at least collect and compare all the available information, returning whenever possible to the original sources, and this I have tried to do to the best of my ability.

As for Field's music—this, too, has often been subjected to strange misunderstandings and sometimes to very rough handling. One had hoped that such insensitive productions as the fantastically overloaded *Transkription zum Konzertgebrauch* of the Fifth Nocturne, by Ignaz Friedman, or Alec Rowley's 'revision', with 'new' harmonies and elaborated passage-work, of the early Rondo in E major (surely the poor thing had suffered enough after going through most of its life weighed down by the nocturnal cloak thrown round it by Schlesinger in 1833) were things of the past. Not so, however: a recent transcription, for harp, by a gifted British composer (who should know better) of the Eleventh Nocturne—one of Field's most poetic and serenely beautiful pieces—in which the performer is instructed to play 'in the style of an Irish jig', leaves one gravely doubtful whether matters have improved. Perhaps the increased attention now being given to Field's best music by professional pianists will make it more familiar and better understood, and so save it from such coarse maltreatment in the future.

I should like to express my thanks to Mr. C. F. Colt for permission to reproduce photographs of his Pape and Tischner pianos; to the British Museum for James Malton's engraving of Dublin's Rotunda and for the Kiprensky portrait of Field; to the National Portrait Gallery for the Engelbach engraving of Field; to the Radio Times Hulton Picture Library for the pictures of Moscow and St. Petersburg; to Mr. David McKenna, C.B.E., for the reproduction of the painting by Alexander Martin Shee which is in his possession; to the Library of Congress, Washington, and the Gesellschaft der Musikfreunde, Vienna for permission to reproduce pages from Field manuscripts; to the Bibliothèque Publique et Universitaire, Geneva, for permission to reproduce Field's letter to J. A. Galliffe; to the Osterreichische Nationalbibliothek for the profile portraits of Field and Clementi.

It remains for me to thank all those who have assisted me in the preparation of this book. I am particularly indebted to my friend Mr. T. de Valera, a dedicated Field scholar whose advice and generously given information have proved invaluable; to Dr. Martin Carey, another equally erudite Field devotee, who drew my attention to many previously unknown facts concerning Field's later years; to Mr. Cecil Hopkinson, Dr. Gerald Abraham, the late Arthur Hedley, Madame Pierre Leyris (of Paris) and Professor A. Nikolayev (of Moscow), all of whom have provided me with valuable facts, and to Mr. Vladimir Shibayev for his kind help in the matter of the transliteration of Russian words and titles. I am also grateful for the ready help given to me by the staffs of the libraries of the Conservatoires of Moscow and Leningrad, the Saltikov-Shchedrin Library in Leningrad, the Lenin Library in Moscow, the libraries of the Leningrad Philharmonic Society, the Brussels Conservatoire, the Gesellschaft der Musikfreunde in Vienna and many other European libraries and museums. Finally I wish to offer my most sincere thanks to my friends Laurella Matthews and Mantle Childe for their unfailing help, advice, criticism and encouragement, and to the Leverhulme Trust fund for making possible my visit to Moscow and Leningrad.

Talycoed PATRICK PIGGOTT
September 1971

I

A Child Prodigy in Dublin

❧

No PERIOD in Dublin's history before the proclamation of the Irish Republic is more interesting than the eighteen years which immediately followed the establishment of Ireland's first independent parliament in 1782.

The city had been getting bigger and growing in international importance throughout the eighteenth century; but now, with the political aims of the great Irish patriot, Henry Gratton, finally achieved, and an Irish parliament freed from English dominance no longer a dream but a reality, Dublin began to assume, for the first time, the outward appearance of a capital.

Not only were the city's grandiose building schemes given an added impetus, but in both public and private life there was a new confidence and animation which was reflected in the bustle and excitement of the streets. There were more hackney coaches to be seen about Dublin than in London, and at least as many sedan chairs as around St. James's; and now the former absentee leaders of the Irish fashionable world, attracted by the glitter and prosperity resulting from the city's changed status, were returning home to enjoy the brilliant social life of the Irish metropolis.

Even the lot of the poorer classes, though still deplorable, was gradually beginning to improve, thanks to a greatly increased demand for their labour, and to the various welfare services which were introduced about this time, some of them (such as the Lying-in Hospital and public bathing establishments in which the poor were given medical attention) surprisingly in advance of those of other European capitals.

Not that Dublin was by any means free from the dirt, cruelty, squalor and want which were common to all great cities in the eighteenth century; quite the reverse, in fact: but the violence and excess which had always characterised Irish life, even among the ruling classes, were at last beginning to give way to the civilising influence of culture and to the manners of polite society.

It was a period of great promise, one in which the emergence of outstanding personalities, not only in the fields of politics, religion and arms (these Ireland had always produced in plenty) but in the arts and sciences might legitimately be expected. Many such figures did eventually appear, but except perhaps in the field of architecture their talents were, in almost every case, brought to fruition far from Ireland's shores; for the brilliant era ushered in by the foundation of Gratton's parliament proved to be a false dawn. In the year 1800, the notorious Act of Union put an end to Ireland's political freedom for more than a century, and with the departure for Westminster of the Irish members, many of them bitter and broken-hearted at what they rightly regarded as a betrayal of their hopes, the city became dark and deserted, the candles in a thousand glittering Waterford chandeliers were snuffed for the last time, and the music and laughter of the fashionable world were stilled into silence. Very soon it was as if the unforgettably colourful hey-day of Gratton's Dublin had never been.

Among those gifted Dubliners who might, perhaps, have enjoyed brilliant careers in their native city, had Ireland's independence and prosperity continued into the nineteenth century, was a child born in the very year that the country's status as a separate kingdom was established. John Field was born in July 1782,[1] and on September 5th[2] he was christened in St. Werburgh's church, one of the finest of Dublin's many beautiful Georgian churches.

[1] W. H. Gratton Flood, in his *John Field of Dublin*, London, 1920, confidently gives July 26th as the date of Field's birth. He undoubtedly copied this date from Dessauer, who however, was less convinced of its accuracy, having failed to obtain official confirmation of it from the Recorder's Office. Dessauer found the date in the various Russian memoirs of Field published by his friends and former pupils. But an article published in the Russian journal *Son of the Fatherland*, gives July 16th as the date of Field's birth; the author of the article claimed that the information was given to him by one of Field's pupils, though he does not say which one. Neither Dubuk nor Gebhard, Field's closest associates among those who wrote of him after his death, mentions the date of his birth.

[2] Not September 30th, the date given by Flood. At a first glance, the date of the registration of Field's christening in the records of St. Werburgh's church does look rather like September 30th, but a closer inspection reveals that it really is September 5th. An interval of about two months between birth and christening was quite usual among Irish Protestants in the eighteenth century.

In the same church, only twenty-six years earlier, the marriage of a certain John Fields to a girl named Ann Hearne had been solemnised. It is possible that these were the child's grandparents and that John was named according to the old Celtic tradition whereby a grandfather's Christian name is passed on to his eldest grandson (it is relevant that John's eldest sister, born four years after him, was named Ann), but this remains a matter of conjecture. The church register tells us, however, that the child's parents were named Robert and Grace,[1] and if Robert really was the son of that John Fields who was married in St. Werburgh's in 1756 (the alteration of the name from Fields to Field is not a serious objection, the orthography of names being a very fluid matter in those days) he must have been several years younger than his wife, who is known to have been about twenty-eight when her eldest son was born.

In most accounts of John Field's origin, the few facts recorded about the place of his birth and the date of his christening are given correctly: but not in all. In several of the various memoirs which appeared after his death (notably in Russia, but also in other countries) it was suggested that he was born, not in Dublin, but in Strasbourg, and that he was the son of a French violinist named Duchamp (sometimes spelled Dechamp). The story usually runs that in a fit of jealousy provoked by the flirtatious behaviour of his wife, always described as 'tall and beautiful', the boy's father violently attacked a certain canon of Strasbourg cathedral who had been paying her too much attention, and, as a result, was obliged to leave the country in a hurry; that he fled to England, and after playing for a while in the London theatres, set out to exploit the talents of his prodigy son in the fashionable city of Bath, where Duchamp *fils* (his name now Anglicised to Field) attracted much attention and was lucky enough to be noticed by the celebrated Muzio Clementi, who at once offered to take the boy under his wing.

This romantic rhapsody would be hardly worth repeating were it not unquestionably the invention of John Field himself, who varied it on occasion by placing the venue of Clementi's meeting with the young 'Duchamp' in Paris: 'We met on the boulevards' was his vague description of the imaginary encounter, though when pressed for more details he would smile and say that it had all happened too long ago for him to remember much about it.

[1] An exhaustive search has, so far, revealed no trace of the registration of their marriage, which may, of course, have taken place elsewhere than in Dublin.

An inveterate *blagueur* who was also an ardent Francophile, Field probably first invented this fictitious account of his origin for the benefit of his many friends among the large coteries of French emigrés in Moscow and St. Petersburg, in whose society he delighted. Some of them evidently found it easy to believe him, for his unreserved, Bohemian nature and liberal political views accorded very ill with their stereotyped ideas about the English. That Field was in fact not English but Irish would be insufficient in their eyes to account for his strikingly 'un-English' manners. To this day it can sometimes be difficult to persuade people of other races that the Celts of the British Isles are not the blood brothers of the English, or even that the Celtic languages are not mere dialects of Anglo-Saxon.

Field's romancing about his birth may also have been partly inspired by his undoubted Anglophobia—'ils sont des bêtes sauvages' he once said of the English; and it must have gone against the grain with him to have had to admit to British nationality on his wedding day (he was married in Moscow in 1810), for, apart from the bridegroom himself, all else concerned in the ceremony, the priest, the principal witnesses, and even the bride were French. In the marriage register of Moscow's French Catholic Church, he was described as 'Johann [*sic*] Field, born in Dublin, son of Robert Field, artist, living in London, and of Grace Marsh.' This is the first hint we have that Marsh was probably his mother's maiden name.

John's mother may indeed have been tall and beautiful (no portrait of her exists) and his father was undoubtedly a violinist, but they were both natives of Ireland and their name had never been Duchamp.[1] At the time of John's birth, they were living in Golden Lane, a street of terraced houses in an unfashionable, but quite respectable, middle-class part of Dublin. Most of the Golden Lane of those days has long since disappeared, but at least one two-storied eighteenth-century house remains standing,[2] and

---

[1] Much time and paper has been wasted on pointless speculations about the origin of Field's name. In 1895, a short biography of Field was included in *Famous Composers and their Works*, edited by K. Paine and K. Klauser, and in this the name was 'traced' back to the de la Felds, Huguenot emigrants who are said to have landed in England in the fourteenth century. There is absolutely no possibility of proving John Field to have been descended from these de la Felds, but most of his later biographers have continued to debate the matter (not, however, Gratton Flood, whose strong Irish nationalist sentiments did not permit him to consider the possibility, even in order to reject it, that the Dublin Fields might have had a non-Irish origin, however remote). In fact Field, like Hill, Lane, Brook, Lea, Marsh and many others, is one of the commonest of topographical names in all parts of the British Isles, and there is no point in trying to credit it with an obscure Huguenot origin.   [2] 1971.

it was in such a house that the Field family not only lived in 1782 but, if we are to believe Gratton Flood, also ran a small music school in which Robert taught the violin and his father the pianoforte. Flood gives no evidence to support this statement, and he seems to have been unaware that Robert Field and his ever-increasing family moved several times during the course of the next twelve years.

It is possible to trace some of the Field family's peregrinations through the registrations of the christenings of their younger children: Robert (1784) born in Aungier Street; Isaac and Robert Mark (1785 and 1786) born in Golden Lane; Ann (1788) born in Chancery Lane; Grace Marsh (1790) also born in Chancery Lane, and finally Grace (1791) born in Camden Street.

The use of the parents' names, Robert and Grace, for more than one child is probably an indication that the high rate of infant mortality in eighteenth-century Dublin took its periodical toll of the Field family. It will also be noted that the movements of the Fields included a return to Golden Lane, which was perhaps the home of the grandparents, where the young family looked for shelter when Robert's fortunes were at a low ebb. Whether Robert and his father really carried on a small music academy in Golden Lane remains conjectural, like so much else that concerns the period of John Field's childhood, but it seems more probable that, according to the custom of the time, they would have visited most of their pupils in their own homes. Undoubtedly they had other sources of income, for we know, on the authority of John himself, that his father was a theatre violinist and his grandfather an organist in one of the city churches.[1] But even when father and son shared the same roof their combined earnings can never have been large.

It was natural that as soon as young John showed signs of exceptional musical talent he should be regarded as a potential early contributor to the family purse. The poor child must indeed have possessed an unusually intense love of music, for the harsh treatment which he received from his grandfather, who took charge of his training, and his father, who superintended his practice, could easily have turned him against music for ever. Towards the end of his life, Field confided to Fétis, the celebrated

---

[1] There is some slight evidence that John Field's paternal grandfather was not the only organist in his family. A 'thumbnail' biography of Field, written on the back of one of his few extant letters (presumably in the hand of the recipient, the Swiss historian Galiffe-Pictet) states that his mother was the sister of a Dublin organist.

French critic, that the frequent beatings inflicted on him in childhood finally induced him to run away from home, but that hunger eventually drove him back to his relentless taskmasters. Whatever were his subsequent sufferings (and one likes to think that the fright occasioned by his temporary disappearance may have moderated their severity) his love of music survived them, and he continued to make such remarkable progress in piano playing that when he had reached the age of nine he was considered ready for a course of 'finishing' lessons with Tommaso Giordani, who was then a leading figure in the musical life of Dublin.

Giordani, one of a large family of versatile musicians, was born in Naples, but divided his career between London and Dublin, finally settling in the latter city in 1783. His operas were regularly given in Dublin's theatres (Robert Field must often have played under his direction) and he was in great demand as a teacher. A tall and elegant figure, he was one of the several distinguished Italian musicians, among them Castrucci and Geminiani, who have periodically dominated the Dublin musical scene, even into the twentieth century. It is a tradition which ended only with the death of Michele Esposito in 1929.

The eighteenth-century novelist, Sydney Owensen (better remembered today as the diarist, Lady Morgan), tells us that she knew Giordani, whom she described as 'bewitched with the musical sympathies of the Dublin people'. Lady Morgan does not mention, however, that Giordani, as we shall see, sometimes had reason to complain of their lack of support for his more ambitious ventures, though his prestige and his success as a teacher were great enough for him to have no regrets about his decision to settle in the Irish capital. No doubt Robert Field thought that the easiest way to launch his prodigy son would be to place him in the care of this very influential musician, and certainly Giordani lost little time in presenting the boy to the Dublin public.

We have only Gratton Flood's authority for the statement that Master Field first appeared in Dublin on February 14th, 1792, as one of the 'Musical Children' in a benefit concert for Master Tom Cooke (another of Giordani's pupils who was soon to make some mark in the musical world), for there is no mention of John in any press announcement or report connected with this concert. Perhaps Flood did not realise that the 'Musical Children', so-called, were not just a series of solo items played by Giordani's best pupils, but a highly-trained 'act', in which a number of little musicians gave polished performances of ensemble music for various combinations of instruments. They were having a great success with the Dublin musical public during the season of 1792.

There is, however, no doubt about the date of Master Field's official debut, which took place on March 24th, 1792, at the first of three Lenten 'Spiritual Concerts' arranged by his new master at the Rotunda Assembly Rooms, a popular resort at the north end of magnificent Sackville Street, reputed at that time to be the widest street in Europe. The pleasure gardens attached to the Rotunda were Dublin's answer to London's Vauxhall and Ranelagh, and there, for an entry fee of sixpence, the public could enjoy a wide variety of entertainments, musical and otherwise.

Giordani's concerts, in imitation of the celebrated *Concerts Spirituels* of Paris, were a new kind of entertainment for Dublin, and their organiser did everything possible to make his programmes varied and attractive. He advertised them in the leading Dublin papers (one guinea admitted to all three concerts) and he followed up the initial announcement of the series with full details of the first programme: it included a 'New Overture' by Haydn, arias sung by two leading Dublin vocalists, and 'Madam Krumpholtz's difficult pedal harp concerto . . . performed on the Grand Piano Forte by Master Field.' The star of the evening, however, was 'the celebrated Madam Gautherot', who played a violin concerto; and the concert finished with some new sacred choral pieces by Giordani himself. As a finishing touch, the 'Musical Children' trooped on to perform a *quartetto* by Pleyel.

One of the few newspapers in which Giordani did not advertise, the *Dublin Evening Post*, was the only one to publish an account of this concert. It is, despite its literary shortcomings, of exceptional interest, containing as it does the first known description of John Field's playing. It deserves quotation in full:

> On Saturday last was given, at the public rooms, Rutland Square,[1] the first of Signor Giordani's Spiritual Concerts: a species of entertainment with peculiar propriety adapted to the present season, and degree of pleasure to a polished audience [*sic*].
> In the first act the overture from Hayden [*sic*] was well and correctly given, Wayman's song had that energy and force which his extensive powers of voice are so well adapted to express, and Small's was distinguished by that correctness of tone that eminently mark that excellent

[1] The Rotunda Assembly Rooms and Pleasure Gardens were situated in Rutland Square. The rooms still exist, but since early in the present century the famous Round Room has been sadly reduced in status: it is now a cinema.

singer. The pedal harp concerto on the Piano Forte by Master Field was really an astonishing performance by such a child, and had a precision and execution far beyond what could have been expected.

Madam Gautherot's first appearance this season closed the first act, and her concerto on the violin did credit to her established reputation, for brilliancy of finger, rapidity of execution, and elegance of tone. The second act was entirely formed of two new pieces of sacred music composed by Signor Giordani, which reflected high honour on the abilities of that eminent master, and were capitally executed, but obviously would have been improved by a more powerful choir. The company was perfectly fashionable; but either from the want of proper notification or from some other untoward circumstance, by no means numerous. This is justly to be lamented; as it must now throw a damp on an elegant kind of entertainment much wanted in this city, and discourage a master whose professional merit strongly claims the warmest public patronage. (March 27th, 1792)

Giordani's disappointment over the size of the audience at his first concert did not deter him from going ahead with his plans for the others, at both of which John also played. The advertisements for the second concert described him as 'The Much-Admired Master Field, a youth of eight years [he was really ten] who will perform on the Piano Forte a new concerto composed by Signor Giordani'—and for the third he was announced to play both a concerto and a sonata, though the names of the composers were not given.

Three appearances at the most important concerts of a single season, as well as an unusual amount of press publicity, must have aroused considerable interest in the little virtuoso. It is surprising therefore that neither the boy's father nor his teacher appear to have done anything to develop this initial success, and that no further public appearances were arranged for him during what was to prove to be the last year of his life in Dublin.

It is not known what decided Robert Field to emigrate with his family to England in 1793. A few years later, and reasons would not have been far to seek; but signs of serious economic or political deterioration in Dublin life did not appear until after the abortive rising of the United Irishmen in 1798. In 1793 there was still local patronage available for the promotion of promising native talent.

Robert's belief that his son was destined to become a great musician, perhaps even another Mozart, must certainly have been one of his principal motives for the taking of such a drastic step. In London, as everyone knew, lived some of the world's greatest pianists and piano teachers—greater even than Giordani, though their fees were likely to be proportionately higher than his. It is curious, therefore, that the immediate destination of the Field family in England was not London but Bath.

Gratton Flood's statement that Robert Field was invited by Venanzio Rauzzini, the director of Bath's musical entertainments, to lead the orchestra in Bath's elegant New Assembly Rooms will not bear close investigation. While it is possible that Robert may, at one time, have been in touch with Rauzzini through the latter's brother, Matteo, a popular Dublin singing teacher who had died in 1791, there is no evidence that he ever led an orchestra in Bath, or that his playing was equal to such a responsible position. Some now forgotten circumstance (was it nothing more than the impression made on him by a remarkable scale model of the famous West-country spa which was fascinating all Dublin in 1792?) decided the matter, and led to the uprooting of the Fields from their last Dublin home in Camden Street, a better address than any they had previously occupied, in the summer of 1793. As the packet bearing him to Bristol[1] sailed out of Dublin harbour, little John Field must have looked back for a long time at the receding shores of Ireland. Had he but known it, he was bidding his native land a last farewell.

[1] A regular packet service sailed between Dublin and Bristol in the eighteenth century. It was much used by the fashionable world, as it provided the quickest route both to Bath and to London.

II

In London with Clementi

⁓ᙓᙡᖇᖇ⁓

THERE IS no record that Robert Field found any opportunity of publicly
displaying John's talents in Bath. It is even possible that if he had tried to
do so he might have met with opposition, for the name of Field was
already known in that city's musical life. Thomas Field, the future
organist of Bath Abbey,[1] then aged seventeen, was a regular performer, as
pianist, at the fashionable concerts given in the New Assembly Rooms, and
he is hardly likely to have welcomed a rival who was not only a namesake
but an infant prodigy of exceptional brilliance.

Though the Dublin Fields arrived in Bath during the summer of
1793, they remained there for only a few months, and we have no means
of knowing whether the shortness of their stay was due to the fact that
Robert regarded Bath, from the first, as a mere stepping-stone to London,
or whether his playing was not good enough for the sophisticated international society which attended the Assembly Rooms. He may have been
a useful theatre violinist, but the fact that he left Bath before the start of
the winter season and took a seemingly inferior post in the orchestra of
London's little Haymarket Theatre suggests at least the possibility that
his playing did not measure up to the high standards of Venanzio
Rauzzini.

One of Field's biographers[2] has suggested that the elegance and luxury
of Bath at the height of its prosperity gave the boy a sense of inferiority
from which he never recovered; but it is difficult to believe that a mere

[1] Thomas Field was appointed organist of Bath Abbey only two years later. His
son, Henry Field (born 1797), also became an infant prodigy pianist. In later years, he
made several appearances at the London Philharmonic Society's concerts and was sometimes called 'Field of Bath' to distinguish him from his more celebrated namesake,
'Russian Field'.

[2] Eric Blom, 'John Field', *The Chesterian*, 1930, 201-7 and 233-8.

child, and one, moreover, who had been brought up in a capital city, could have received such an overpowering and psychologically disfiguring impression from a six months' stay in an English spa, however glittering its social life.And what is the evidence that he suffered from a sense of inferiority? His stuttering speech might perhaps be regarded as a symptom of some emotional flaw in his personality, though such an impediment is not necessarily the result of an inferiority complex; but in later life he certainly possessed a very clear idea of his worth, and he showed a disregard for convention and for the opinion of others which suggests a careless confidence rather than the opposite. In any case, a single summer season in Bath cannot have made a very lasting impression on a boy of eleven.

As soon as the Field family had settled into new quarters in London, the question of John's future became of the first importance. He was now eleven, and it is surprising that his father still seems to have had no thought of making quick money out of the boy's precocious talent. On the contrary, he strained his financial resources very considerably by apprenticing John to Muzio Clementi, the most important piano teacher of the day, for the then large premium of one hundred guineas.

It is difficult to assess the exact value of the guinea at the end of the eighteenth century, but certainly such a sum represented a lot of money to a humble theatre violinist, probably something like two thousand pounds today, and it is remarkable that Robert Field was able to spare so much out of his savings. Evidently he was prepared to stake everything he had on John's career, and it is with this generous action, perhaps the most important of his life, that we lose sight of him. Though John's mother makes a brief reappearance on the scene many years later we know nothing more of his father—not even the year of his death. Once John had been apprenticed to Clementi, his parents relinquished most of their claims on him, and his new master became the dominant influence on him throughout the next ten years.

There were many celebrated pianists living in London in 1793, among them the great Dussek, Gyrowetz, and also J. B. Cramer, himself a former pupil of Clementi, who was then in the process of establishing his immense pedagogic reputation. But it was with good reason that the French called Clementi *le Pape des musiciens*, for to study with him set a seal on one's career; he could command what fees he chose and he was equally in demand among wealthy amateurs and aspiring virtuosi. At the very moment of John's arrival in London, his future rival, Johann Nepomuk Hummel, who had been Mozart's favourite pupil, was completing a year's study with Clementi; and it says much for John's talent, and for the excellent training he had received in Dublin, that Clementi not only accepted him willingly as a pupil (plus the hundred guineas) but within four months was presenting the boy at public concerts as the product of his own teaching.

It was in April, 1794, that the first mention of 'Master Field, the talented ten-year-old pupil of Clementi' appeared in the London press. It will be noticed that, as in Dublin, his age was reduced by two years: he is said to have been small as a child, and of course the younger he appeared to be the greater would be the *réclame* of his teacher. The following month, he played in public a concerto by his new master, and also one by Dussek, a composer who was to influence him considerably in later years.

Clementi was evidently very proud of John, for he talked of him frequently, telling his friends that the boy's quick perceptiveness and ability to remember anything accurately and perform easily were so great that he seldom needed to be told anything twice. John made several other concert appearances during his first year in London, but the highlight of the season for him, as for every other musician, must have been the final visit to London of Joseph Haydn. Haydn heard John play, probably at one of Barthelmon's concerts in May, 1784, and noted in his diary (in English —of a kind) that he had heard 'Field a young boy, which plays the pianoforte extremely well.' Such praise from the greatest musician of the day, if it reached his knowledge (Haydn and Clementi were well acquainted and it is likely that John's playing was mentioned between them), must have given immense encouragement to the young virtuoso and heartfelt satisfaction to his family.

But to be apprenticed to Clementi involved other things besides lessons, long hours of study, and general artistic development stimulated by constant association with a teacher who was among the greatest musicians of his time. Clementi was certainly that, but he was also an active business man, with interests in the worlds of music publishing and piano manufacture. This is not the place to embark on an account of Clementi's business career, but the fact that he was, in more than one sense, John's master meant that the youth was obliged to display his great pianistic talent in Clementi's piano warehouse more often than on the concert platform.

Clementi required him, as he had required Cramer, to work as a salesman-demonstrator, showing off Clementi pianos to prospective customers. John's career as an infant prodigy was soon over, for after 1795 we hear of no more concert appearances until 1799. But it was during these years that his creative talent began to develop.

It is possible that John had been trying his hand at composition before he left Dublin, but of this we have no proof.[1] Some rondos and variations on popular airs of the day which were, at one time, thought to belong to those years are now known to be of later date, and the themes of some of them, once believed to be by Giordani, are by other composers. The year 1795 has been suggested as the date of publication of some brilliant variations on 'Fal lal la, the much admired air in *The Cherokee*', and of a rondo based on 'Signora Del Caro's Hornpipe', and, if this date is correct, these are the earliest pieces to have been printed under Field's name. But 1796 is the date of the first authentic specimen of his original composition, and also of his penmanship. It consists of a single page, containing a fragment of thirty-one bars, apparently the beginning of a Rondo in A major, which once belonged to a Mrs. Alpe of Hardingham Hall, near Attleborough, Norfolk. Mrs. Alpe left an account of the circumstances in which it was written, inserting it both above and below the music:

Composed by John Field (aged twelve years) afterwards pianiste [*sic*] to the Emperor of Russia and given to me by him, in the presence of

[1] The New York Public Library possesses an interesting manuscript volume on the fly-leaf of which is written, in a careful copperplate hand, 'John Field Junr. 1789. Duets'. The name is inscribed twice elsewhere on the same page, apparently by different hands. One of these signatures has a childish look, and may be the earliest known writing of John Field. It is dated 1790: Field was then eight.

Cecil Hopkinson wrongly describes the contents of the volume as 'a collection of contemporary songs arranged for four hands'. In fact the duets are for two single-line treble parts, mostly moving in thirds and sixths, and are probably intended for violins. They are followed by a few songs, their texts carefully written out, but with the airs left unaccompanied. In the later part of the book there are some very simple keyboard arrangements of such well-known tunes as 'Drink to me only with thine eyes', and the first of these is preceded by a C major scale covering four octaves and with every note letter-named and fingered.

It is impossible to believe that the infant prodigy who was performing difficult concertos and sonatas in public in 1792 can have had anything to do with these primitive writings of the previous year. But the two-part duets may well have been used for his violin lessons. Hopkinson thought it possible that the volume might contain some childish efforts at original composition, but there is no evidence to support this theory.

Mr Clementi in the year 1796. This fragment was merely intended as a specimen of his manuscript powers at that early age, and I believe was never published or completed. The passage in semitones originally terminated on D sharp, but on Mr Clementi's suggestion that it was harsh, Field immediately altered it as above.

There are points of interest both in the fragment of music and in Mrs. Alpe's note about it. It will be seen that John was still thought to be two years younger than his actual age (he was then fourteen, but Mrs. Alpe believed him to be twelve), and Clementi's correction implies that the music was genuinely improvised for the occasion and not a reproduction of something already composed.[1]

The musical fluency and the remarkably confident and professional-looking hand shown in this little manuscript suggests much previous practice in both composition and pencraft. It is probable that, supervised by Clementi, John wrote a great deal during these years (Clementi was responsible for his entire education, not merely his piano playing) but, if so, most of these early works have disappeared.

Not quite all, however, for in addition to the two little pieces already mentioned, a similar effusion, 'The two favourite Slave Dances in Black-beard, arranged as a Rondo', was published by Longman and Broderip (a firm in which Clementi had a business interest) in 1798, and there is evidence that some variations on the song 'Since then I'm doomed', and a rondo on another popular air, 'Speed the Plough', also date from this time. In addition, it is possible that certain other pieces of the same type, published anonymously, may also be by the young Field; for while it cannot yet be proved that these pieces are his work, they do in fact contain passages which are even more characteristic of his later music than anything in the accredited early pieces. The whole question of these anonymous pieces has been exhaustively discussed by another writer.[2]

These early works, however, are never based on original material, nor can they be regarded as any sort of preparation for the Piano Concerto in E flat which was performed by its seventeen-year-old composer on February 7th, 1799, at a concert given by 'The New Musical Fund established for the relief of decayed musicians, their widows and orphans

---

[1] It must also be mentioned that Field never held the honorary post of Court Pianist in Russia. He was offered the title but refused it.

[2] Cf. Alan Tyson, 'John Field's earliest compositions', *Music and Letters*, July 1966, 239–48.

residing in England', and which won Field his first success as a composer, as well as enhancing his reputation as a pianist. This concert took place in the King's Theatre, a very large building which had been opened a few years previously. Shortly afterwards, Field repeated the concerto at a concert in the much smaller Haymarket Theatre, and in one, if not in both of these performances his proud father probably sat among the violins of the accompanying orchestra.

It is difficult to believe that this successful and engaging concerto, with its clear texture, its simple but adequate scoring, and its effective solo part was preceded by nothing but a few trifling pieces based on borrowed themes; but in the absence of any evidence to the contrary we must regard it as Field's first serious work. It was, of course, composed under Clementi's watchful eye, and perhaps Robert Field, with his long practical orchestral experience, may have given helpful advice about the scoring.

The concert in the Haymarket Theatre, which took place on May 27th, was a benefit night for a prodigy violinist, G. F. Pinto, then aged thirteen, and the favourite pupil of Johann Peter Salomon. Field was himself a capable violinist, though in later years he preferred playing the viola in quartets, and (again, if we are to believe Gratton Flood) he may have studied the instrument under Pinto's guidance. That the two boys were well acquainted is certain, for Pinto, who was also a composer, published a piano sonata dedicated 'to my friend, John Field' in 1800; but it seems curious, to say no more, that a boy in his teens, the son of a professional violinist, should be instructed by a child four years his junior.

Ten days after the concerto's first performance, Clementi took Field with him to a dinner party given by his friend, Thomas Holcroft. Holcroft noted in his diary that after dinner 'Field played a concerto and other things of his own composition.' One wonders what those 'other things' were. Holcroft continued: '[He] is a youth of genius, for which Clementi loves, admires, and instructs him; highly to his own honour'; which leaves us with an agreeable impression of the relations between master and pupil at this time. Unfortunately, in later years they were greatly to deteriorate.

Field's first concerto was not published until many years later, despite its continued success at subsequent performances. But the young composer's next serious work, a set of three piano sonatas, Op. 1, dedicated to Clementi, achieved publication soon after its completion in 1801. By this time, John's apprenticeship was at an end (the *Morning Post* for

February 21st, 1801, refers to him as 'the late pupil of Clementi'), though their association continued. He still worked in Clementi's warehouse, but now his master paid him a small wage, and his new freedom, coupled with his rising fame, would probably have allowed him to make a brilliant career in London had he remained there. He had already made a start as a teacher, and the successful début of his pupil, Charles Neate (only two years his junior), at the Covent Garden Oratorio Concerts in 1800 must have been a valuable advertisement for him.[1]

The measure of his growing prestige is indicated by the fact that he was beginning to be in demand among portraitists. An interesting medallion engraving of Field's and Clementi's profiles, side by side, was published in London in 1801, as part of a collection of twenty-seven portraits, by Loutherbourg, of the leading musicians of the day. Another interesting, though rather idealised portrait of the time shows the young composer, pen in hand, apparently in the very act of composing his Second Sonata in A major, the opening bars being clearly discernible in the painting. Even more significant is a remarkable portrait, attributed to Alexander Shee, who was later to become the president of the Royal Academy. This striking picture, much more realistic than any other portrait of Field, gives an impression of his personality which is quite unlike that of the calm, handsome man who gazes at us from the portraits of his maturity, though it bears some resemblance to Loutherbourg's likeness in profile. Alexander Shee was young and ambitious when he painted Field at the turn of the eighteenth century, and he had no time to waste on sitters who were neither rich nor important. As Field was certainly not rich, it is significant that Shee nevertheless considered it worthwhile to paint his portrait.

There must have been numerous discussions and preparations before it was decided that John should leave England with Clementi in 1802. He was no longer bound by the contract of apprenticeship signed by his father (an eighteenth-century apprentice usually served his master for a term of seven years, in return for which he was taught his trade), but Clementi evidently thought that a wider experience of life and music in Paris and

---

[1] Charles Neate was equally accomplished as a pianist and a 'cellist. He studied the 'cello with William Sharp, with whom (according to W. H. Hadow) Field also had some lessons in 'cello-playing. Field was certainly a capable violinist and viola-player but it is not known from where Hadow obtained the information that he also played the 'cello. (See Grove, *Dictionary of Music & Musicians*, 3rd ed. (1927), III, 609.)

Golden Lane, Dublin, a woodcut by Fergus O'Ryan

The Rotunda Assembly Rooms, Dublin

An engraving by Landseer from a cameo by H. de Janvrey after original portraits by P. J. Loutherbourg of the young Field with his master, Clementi

Detail from portrait of John Field, c. 1798, attributed to A. M. Shee

Vienna (he intended to leave John in Vienna while he travelled on to St. Petersburg) would be of great benefit to the young musician.

Biographers of Field usually take an unkind view of Clementi, describing him as a sort of amalgam of Scrooge and Svengali, and laying great emphasis on what Spohr called his 'truly Italian parsimony'. Undoubtedly he was 'careful', but he was certainly not always close-fisted. Thomas Holcroft's diary, already referred to, contains the following entry for Christmas Day, 1798: 'Mr Clementi surprised me much by a very liberal and friendly offer of a loan of two or three hundred pounds: thinking it might be want of money that induced me to sell my effects and go abroad'. Holcroft refused the offer, but he felt that it 'was a strong testimony to the goodness of his [Clementi's] own heart'. A few days later, however, (January 3rd, 1799), we read that 'Mr Clementi brought me a hundred pounds as a loan. Seems very desirous that I should not quit the kingdom', and this time Holcroft appears to have accepted the money. There is surely nothing parsimonious about such behaviour, and though there was probably an *arrière pensée* to Clementi's suggestion that John should accompany him on what was, primarily, a business trip (his brilliant pupil was of great value to him as an advertisement), he undoubtedly had a genuine wish to promote the young man's career;[1] and he was evidently prepared to pay his travelling expenses, at least as far as Vienna.[2]

That John should be his travelling companion was in Clementi's mind for some time before their departure, because in December, 1801, he wrote to Ignaz Pleyel (a once-famous composer and favourite pupil of Haydn, who owned a music publishing firm in Paris which was Clementi's most valued business connection in that city) offering new publications by various composers, including Field (the three sonatas), and adding that Pleyel was likely to see Field in Paris very soon. Six months later, however, the date of their departure was still uncertain, and in June Clementi wrote again to Pleyel:

Mon Cher Ami, Mes affaires dans ce pays me retiennent encore quelque temps, et, pour dire la verité, je ne sais quand je pourrai partir pour

---

[1] Cf. Evangeline Lehman, 'John Field, an Irishman, the Grandfather of Russian music', *The Etude* LVIII (March, 1940), 154.

[2] Gebhard stated that Field's father paid Clementi a hundred guineas for the expenses of the tour. This may be, and probably is a mistake arising out of the hundred guineas which Robert Field is known to have paid Clementi for John's apprenticeship. See *Allgemeine Musikalische Zeitung*, 19 July 1837, no. 29, 463.

la France. Je suis très sensible à votre politesse et honnêteté en m'offrant un lit dans votre maison; mais je vous prie de ne plus le garder pour moi, n'etant pas sûr du tout de mon voyage . . .

It is almost certain that Pleyel's invitation to Clementi to be his guest was subsequently extended to Field as well, and it is perhaps relevant that about this time Clementi & Co. published Pleyel's Concertante in F, 'arranged for the Piano Forte by John Field, under the immediate direction of Mr Clementi'.

We catch a glimpse of the two musicians, very shortly before their departure for Paris, in the pages of William Gardiner's autobiography, *Music and Friends*, published in London in 1838.[1] Gardiner first met Clementi while passing through London on his way to Paris in July, 1802, and Clementi kindly offered him a place in his carriage for the journey: but Gardiner wanted to reach Paris in time for the Bastille Day celebrations (July 14th) and so declined the offer. While he was in London, he dined frequently at Clementi's house and was immensely impressed by his host's powers as a linguist: 'The peace [of Amiens] had brought many foreigners to England and I sat down at his [Clementi's] table with French, Spanish, Germans, Italians, Russians, Turks, and Arabs, and with every one of these Clementi held a conversation, generally in their own language . . . while we were at table a young gentleman named Field, an *élève* of Mr. Clementi, sat down to the pianoforte and gratified the company by playing one of Bach's Fugues, in which, by force of touch, he maintained a clear distinction in the four different parts. This extraordinary young performer accompanied him on his travels . . .'

Clementi and his protégé met with a warm reception from the musical world of Paris on their arrival at the beginning of August, 1802, and Pleyel evidently lost no time in arranging soirées at which John's brilliant playing was admired by the assembled connoisseurs. At these he doubtless played his three sonatas, for their publication in Paris shortly after his visit suggests that a demand for them had been created.[2] Probably he also played his concerto, as well as works by Clementi, Dussek, etc., but he made his greatest effect in music which he might not have ventured to include in public concerts—that of Bach and Handel, composers who were virtually unknown in Paris at that time. John's performances from memory of Bach's '48' astonished the French musicians and were long remembered

---

[1] Pages 243–4.
[2] Surprisingly, the French edition of these sonatas was not brought out by Pleyel.

in Paris (one recalls William Gardiner's enthusiastic account of his Bach playing), and Clementi must have been highly gratified by the deep impression made by his pupil.

But it was time to leave Paris. His business arrangements completed, Clementi was soon ready to set off for Vienna, armed with a special safe-conduct pass provided by First Consul Napoleon himself. The fatigues and difficulties of travel in those troubled times were enormous, and though Clementi, according to Gardiner, travelled in his own carriage, there were numerous hazards to face daily—horses to be changed, couriers to be engaged, and, above all, there was the havoc caused to the roads of Europe by the Napoleonic wars. It is recorded that a journey between Berlin and Vienna at that time could take as long as twenty days, and it is not surprising, therefore, that the two musicians did not reach Vienna from Paris until the autumn was nearly upon them.

In Vienna, as in Paris, they received the hospitality of one of Clementi's business colleagues: this time it was the publisher Artaria. Here Clementi intended that he and John should part company. John was now twenty— old enough, surely (so Clementi must have reasoned), to fend for himself without his master's guidance and protection. And Clementi had a particular reason for wishing the youth to remain in Vienna: himself one of the most highly-skilled composers of his time, he knew very well that John's grasp of counterpoint was weak, and that even his feeling for the basic formal principles of composition was insecure; that though his pupil's playing was the greatest credit to his teaching he still had a lot to learn as a composer. Clementi may have had an uneasy conscience about the matter. Perhaps he had somewhat neglected this side of John's education. Undoubtedly he must, at times, have been exasperated by John's tendency to avoid academic disciplines, and by his love of day-dreaming.[1] He intended, therefore, that John should undergo a course of lessons with the great contrapuntist, Albrechtsberger, who lived in Vienna, and who numbered Beethoven among his pupils. How the lessons were be to paid for we do not know, nor how John was to live once Clementi had left him; but to John, the prospect of being on his own in Vienna, now that the moment of parting was upon him, seemed infinitely alarming. He disliked Albrechtsberger's teaching, and, having no friends in Vienna, little money, and no knowledge of German he must have felt that, at all costs, he had to

[1] A few years later, in a letter to his partner, Collard, we find Clementi referring to Field as 'a lazy dog' (quoted in E. Lamburn, *A Short History of a Great House*, 34).

persuade Clementi to change his mind and include him in the forthcoming journey to St. Petersburg.

We shall never know what were the arguments he used to get his way. According to Clementi himself,[1] John had seemed to like the idea of studying with Albrechtsberger when it was first suggested. When, however, he had come to Clementi, 'with tears trembling in his eyes', begging to be allowed to stay with his master, the latter had felt so touched that he had been obliged to capitulate. But it had been an unwilling capitulation, for the expense of taking John to St. Petersburg and paying for his keep during what he expected to be a fairly long stay (it lasted in fact several months) was something he cannot have expected, and the alterations to his plans must have annoyed him very much. Severe economies would certainly have to be made, and John would have to work hard in the pianoforte warehouse which Clementi intended to open once they had reached the Russian capital.

It was at this moment that what seems to have been a fairly happy relationship began to deteriorate; and it must have been a silent and uneasy youth who followed the frowning Clementi into his coach for the start of their long, sometimes dangerous, and always increasingly cold journey to the great northern capital of the Tzar.

[1] Cf. 'Memoirs of Clementi', *Quarterly Music Magazine and Review*, 11/7 (1820), 313.

III

Arrival in Russia

❧❧

VERY LITTLE is known about the long journey of the two musicians from Vienna to St. Petersburg, but it must have been an exciting, if exhausting, experience for such an unsophisticated young traveller as Field, and one which would have left lasting impressions on him. Even the well-seasoned Clementi, used as he was to such journeyings, must have felt considerable relief when, eventually, the wide avenues and immense squares of St. Petersburg were to be seen dimly through the swirling mists of the Northern autumn.

The one small and unimportant fact recorded about the journey is that, as it neared its end, John somehow lost his hat. This episode, which occurred between Narva and St. Petersburg, the last lap of the journey, tells us that the travellers passed through Courland, as the Baltic States were then called, and that their route probably lay through Prague and Berlin, rather than through Poland. But however they travelled, they must have taken two or three weeks over the journey, and they can have arrived in St. Petersburg only just in time to escape the first severe frosts of the Russian winter.

Clementi went at once to the Hôtel de Paris, where he chose two of the least expensive rooms—those overlooking the hotel's inner courtyard. Here he and John were to live for several months, and Clementi intended that their stay should cost him as little as possible. The celebrated Clementi can never have been short of money for long, but on his first arrival in St. Petersburg, with John still on his hands, it is possible that his resources were temporarily reduced. But, wherever he travelled, he was soon in demand as a teacher, and, though his first object in going to Russia was to establish depots for his pianos and publications, it cannot have been long before he was beset by wealthy applicants for lessons, and was amassing roubles in plenty—certainly more than enough for a few to be spared for the comfort of his young companion. He continued, however, to practise rigid economies, and poor John undoubtedly went through a bad time during the next few months.

It is from this, the final period of their relationship, that Clementi's reputation for stinginess has grown. Most of the tales illustrating the harsh treatment John received from him were, naturally, told by the victim himself. The memoirs of his friend, the German actor-singer F. A. Gebhard, inform us that Field used to become quite agitated, in later years, at the very mention of Clementi's name, and the complaints which he poured into sympathetic ears were not forgotten when the time came for John's own life story to be told.

The affair of the lost hat, for instance, seems to have rankled for a long time. It is not related whether it was carried off by the wind, or whether John left it behind at an inn, but Clementi evidently considered the matter to be a typical example of John's carelessness, and more than a month went by before the young man was again equipped with suitable headgear for the extreme rigours of the St. Petersburg winter.

Even worse than the hat episode was Clementi's conviction that it would be a needless expense to buy thick clothing which might never be needed again after they had left Russia. He was prepared to endure the cold himself and he expected John to do the same. In an article printed in a Russian journal of 1834 we read the following: 'Even now there are people who remember Field walking through the streets without an overcoat, wearing Nanking underwear while the weather was at twenty-five degrees below zero, suffering from a cold and being obliged to blow his nose in the lining of his hat' (here the writer of the article inserts an apologetic 'I beg your pardon', as if fearful that he has been a little indelicate). Field had evidently acquired his new hat by this time, if not a handkerchief; but though we no longer appreciate the full significance of 'Nanking underwear'[1] it is clear that he must have been quite inadequately dressed for the extremely harsh climate.

[1] Nanking = Nankeen: a calico stuff, usually dyed buff by a tanning solution. Originally made in Nankin(g), China. It must have been made in a variety of weights, ranging from the (obviously very thin) material used for under-linen to something very much thicker. In Jane Austen's unfinished novel, *The Watsons*, Lord Osborne, advising Emma Watson how she should be shod for walking in muddy lanes, says, 'You should wear half-boots . . . Nothing sets off a neat ankle more than a half-boot; nankeen, goloshed with black, looks very well.'

One assumes that it must have been Field himself who made this one among his numerous discomforts common knowledge in musical circles, but there was someone else in St. Petersburg whose sharp eyes may have noticed the unsuitability of his underwear. The German violinist and composer, Louis Spohr, then still young and unknown, called on Clementi one day at the Hôtel de Paris and found both master and pupil, their arms up to their elbows in soapsuds, dealing with their weekly wash. Spohr was much amused, and, describing the scene in his diary, mentioned that Clementi, quite unconcerned at being discovered at such a menial task, advised him to follow his example, as the St. Petersburg washer-women charged far too much and ruined one's clothes into the bargain.

This anecdote, and Spohr's comments about the 'remarkable avarice of the rich Clementi', as well as his mention of 'a general report that Field was kept on a very short allowance from his master, and was obliged to pay for the good fortune of having his instruction by many privations' give an unfavourable impression of Clementi's treatment of Field at this time. Perhaps the most unkind aspect of his behaviour was the way in which he left the young man entirely to himself during the first weeks after their arrival. Giving him a mere pittance with which to buy simple provisions at the local market (he would have been horrified at the idea of John enjoying the hotel's *table d'hôte*), Clementi occupied himself with his business affairs and his new aristocratic pupils, often returning to the hotel very late at night. John, knowing no language but English, and suffering too much from the climate to explore the city, hardly left his room except for his daily foraging expedition. He soon became so lonely and depressed that it was almost a relief when, with the arrival of the first consignment of pianos from England, Clementi at last opened his showroom and John was able to resume his old duties as a salesman-demonstrator. It was while he was engaged in this drudgery that Spohr first heard him play. Deeply touched by John's wonderful artistry, the violinist could only press his hand in silent appreciation, for the two young men had no common language in which to talk. Spohr was greatly struck by the grotesque impression made by John's physical appearance at this time—his long, thin, ungainly body and ill-fitting clothes, the sleeves of his jacket reaching only to his elbows. 'But', he noted, 'all these defects were forgotten the moment he began to play.'

Clementi's social gifts, his brilliant command of languages and his 'extremely lively disposition and engaging manners',[1] quickly made him a popular member of several St. Petersburg clubs, among them the Citizens' Club, which was frequented by all the leading artists of the city. He was also much at the English Club, an aristocratic institution (English only in that it was run on the lines of such famous London clubs as White's or Brooke's) which possessed ample financial resources, and presented regular private concerts at which Clementi frequently played, receiving a fee of 500 roubles whenever he did so. Here Field, too, was first heard by a more attentive audience than the casual listeners at Clementi's warehouse; for Clementi, not always being free to attend the soirées at the English Club, sometimes sent John as his deputy. Master and pupil were paid the same fee, but Clementi always claimed the whole of the money intended for John, whose only benefit from these performances was the privilege of being allowed, for once, to dine at the hotel's *table d'hôte*. His growing resentment against Clementi was much increased by this treatment, and finally it led him to act in a manner which seems rather out of character—not in accord with the impression which we have so far received of a withdrawn, almost timid personality.

On the last occasion when Clementi sent him to deputise at the English Club, John, infuriated by the prospect of being obliged, once more, to surrender his fee, determined to take his revenge. He had made numerous acquaintances on his visits to the Citizens' Club and he now invited them all to dine with him at the Hôtel de Paris. Then, with considerable address, he cunningly tricked Clementi into giving the hotel manager the idea that the dinner was to be given at his expense. The frightful scene which occurred the following day, when Clementi was faced by a bill for a dinner of twenty covers, almost resulted in a complete rupture between him and his pupil; and it really is surprising that John, after a whole decade of subservience, was capable of hitting Clementi so hard on what seems to have been his tenderest spot. This episode, usually related with glee by Field's biographers, is typical of its period—a time when practical jokes were greatly relished by all but their victims. One's first reaction to it today is to observe that a certain independence of spirit, suppressed during John's youth, though perhaps hinted at in the unidealised, almost sullen face that gazes at us from Alexander Shee's portrait, was now beginning to emerge.

---

[1] Louis Spohr, *Selbstbiographie*, G. H. Wigand, 1860, 42.

The episode of the dinner party occurred very near the end of Clementi's visit to St. Petersburg, when John was already beginning to see the possibility of a life free from dependence on his former teacher. In the meantime, he had found a new friend, and, through him, an opportunity of occasionally enjoying better fare than the iron rations allowed him by Clementi. During his daily visits to the food market, he often chatted with a young footman who was employed in one of the great aristocratic households. In what language they conversed we have no idea; perhaps by now John had begun to pick up a little French (he never learned more than a smattering of Russian), though this hardly tallies with Spohr's report that, at this time, he could only speak English. The footman, taking John to be a servant like himself, befriended the young foreigner, and, whenever he could, invited him to dine in the kitchen of the great house he served, and in which his wife worked as a cook. Their acquaintance prospered for some time, unknown to Clementi, who, as the moment for his departure from St. Petersburg drew near, suddenly altered his treatment of Field and introduced him to some of his wealthy and aristocratic pupils.

Clementi began by taking John with him one evening to a soirée at the palace of Prince Demidov, whose daughter he had been teaching throughout his stay in St. Petersburg. As they entered the vestibule of the Demidov mansion they were ushered in by the very footman who had so frequently entertained John in the kitchen. In later years Field loved to tell this story and to describe the footman's evident anxiety at his young friend's apparently 'forward' behaviour in following his 'master' into the salon, the lackey's whispered warnings, his conviction that John had lost his wits, and finally his amazement when the young man was led forward to the piano and played more wonderfully than any artist who had been heard there before.[1]

But it was not only the humble footman who was overcome by the beauty of John's playing. The young Princess Demidova herself, and all the other connoisseurs present, were entranced by his art, and at once invitations and applications for lessons were showered upon him. It may be said that his brilliant career in Russia was launched from that moment, and the shrewd Clementi must have known very well that it would be so. Probably it was his intention that John should stay in St. Petersburg

---

[1] A. Nikolayev, *John Field*, 16.

after his own departure; for it was one of his favourite business practices to establish a brilliant pupil in an important cultural centre, and thus to create a new market for the spread of his publications and his pianos. Having kept John very much in subservience throughout his own stay in the city, he saw him successfully established as a popular performer with a promising teaching connection before he left it.

Among the valuable patrons to whom Clementi introduced Field was General Marklovsky, a rich and powerful music-lover who was in command of the regiment stationed at Narva. Clementi had a high opinion of the General, whose order for 'a grand pianoforte (with additional keys)' he sent home, with the strict injunction to 'be most particular, for the General minds no expense, and is a warm, good fellow'. Clementi also stated that 'John Field is in his [General Marklovsky's] house on my recommendation', which makes it quite clear that Field's entrée into society took place before Clementi's departure from St. Petersburg in June 1803, and with his concurrence. Unfortunately, the advantages which John gained from his long association with Clementi, and they were very considerable, were far outweighed in his mind by the memory of the discomforts, both physical and mental, which he had endured during their last year together; and when Clementi, having achieved the object of his journey to Russia by the establishment of a new outlet for the sale of his wares, moved on to Berlin, his next scene of action, John saw him go without regret and turned happily to the new and exciting prospect of freedom and affluence which lay before him.

IV

Lionised by St. Petersburg Society

❧

SOON AFTER Clementi left St. Petersburg, General Marklovsky, in whose house John was living, moved for the summer to his official residence at Narva, taking the young pianist with him. This enthusiastic amateur, who was extremely hospitable to all artists, was sometimes not above making use of his power as the commandant of Narva to ensure that no celebrated musicians passed through the town without giving him an opportunity of hearing them play. When travelling to St. Petersburg during the previous winter, Spohr, and his teacher, the violinist Eck, had found themselves forced to appear at one of the General's musical parties immediately on their arrival in Narva; and later, during a chance encounter with Spohr in St. Petersburg, the General had jocularly threatened to retain him for a whole week during his return journey to Germany. The General's threat was never put to the test because Spohr travelled home by sea; but had he passed through Narva he would have found Field luxuriously established there, a very willing prisoner in Marklovsky's house.

The warm months passed quickly. The brief northern summer neared its end: the sky became heavy and dark and a sharp wind began to blow over the Baltic. Back in St. Petersburg, the fashionable world was beginning to return from the country, planning its winter pleasures and discussing the new productions announced by the French and German theatres. Very soon the Marklovsky household was also on its way back to the capital, and Field's long residence in the General's house (ostensibly as a guest, but really as a kind of superior domestic musician) came to an end. He now took an apartment of his own and began to prepare for the busy winter season which lay ahead of him.

The most important event of his career in Russia was to take place early in 1804; this was to be his public début at a great concert in the Philharmonic Hall, which stood on the Nevsky Prospect. This beautiful concert room was then owned by Prince Galitzin, and was leased by him to concert promoters. Since 1790, all artistic events of any importance had taken place there, and Field's first public appearance (he had played, so far, only at private soirées) was to be another occasion of great significance in the artistic life of St. Petersburg.

He had among his supporting artists the ageing, but still celebrated soprano, Madame Mara, once one of the world's greatest singers, but now past her best.[1] As a boy, Field had appeared at Mara's concerts in London, and it was perhaps a memory of those events which led to her participation in his St. Petersburg début. Mara, who had also left London in 1802, was on her way to Moscow, where she was to remain, teaching her art to aspiring singers until the Napoleonic invasion of 1812 forced her to move elsewhere. Despite the great reputation which preceded her, she was completely overshadowed by Field because of the sensation which his playing created. He played his First Concerto, the same work which had won him his early successes in London (he had not yet found time to write a second), and he played it in such a way that he had the enormous audience at his feet. 'No other pianist can compare with him in mastery of technique and sincerity of feeling . . . He makes the instrument sound with unsurpassed sweetness and depth of tone . . . His art is inspired . . . He gives listeners unprecedented enjoyment'; all this praise, and much more, was poured into his ears, and printed in newspapers and journals, in whose columns it can be read to this day. Overnight Field became a great, an unparalleled success, and his name was soon a symbol of the highest quality in art. 'Not to have heard Field,' wrote Gebhard, 'was regarded as a sin against art and good taste', and, extravagant though this may sound, it suggests something of the Field 'fever' which raged in St. Petersburg after that memorable concert of March 1804.

The most important outcome of the concert was the great demand in which Field now found himself as a teacher. Public concerts in Russia were still very few (they were usually given in Lent, when, owing to the power of the Orthodox Church, theatrical performances were forbidden), and though there were many private concerts in the great houses of the nobility it was from teaching that most artists derived their livelihood. Field, as the most fashionable celebrity, could ask the highest fees; and the great and the wealthy were fully prepared to pay them in order that their daughters, and occasionally their sons, could claim to be his pupils. Had

[1] See Max Unger, *Muzio Clementis Leben*, 91–2.

he wished, he could have taught all day and every day, and made large sums of money; but, at this period, he made it a rule to begin each morning with his own practice, often devoting four or five hours to technical exercises before seeing his first pupil.[1] His evenings were sometimes given up to amusements, of which there were plenty in St. Petersburg, but he also had many engagements in private houses, for which he usually received not less than 500 roubles, paid in advance.

He did not achieve his uniquely privileged social position in a moment. At first he had to encounter some of the boorishness with which artists of his time were so often treated by their social superiors. There were one or two incidents, such as the occasion when, after some grandee had publicly handed him a mere hundred-rouble note for playing at a party, Field used the money to light his cigar; and another when he was reported to have passed on what he considered to be an unsuitably low fee to the footman who brought him his coat. But very soon he had no further annoyances of this kind, and was given privileges and respect accorded to few artists of his time.

It must be assumed that Field was composing during his earliest years in Russia, but there is nothing to prove that any work of importance dates from 1803; for his début in St. Petersburg was made, as we have seen, in what was still his only major work—the First Concerto, written five years previously. It is curious that this concerto was not published outside Russia until many years later, and then not by the firm of Clementi-Collard, but by the Leipzig firm of Breitkopf & Härtel. In a letter, dated 1805, Clementi instructed his London representative to arrange with Field for its publication: 'Has he [Field] sent you his Concerto in E flat? Get it soon, and pay him well, for I think 'twill sell.' What went wrong we do not know, but the concerto remained unpublished for many years. It is evident, however, that the first of Field's several works for piano with string quartet must have been composed during these early years, for another letter of Clementi's, written from Berlin in 1806, enquires: 'Has Field sent you the Concerto, the Quintetto and something more, as I had agreed with him, for his grand piano?' Clementi seems to have been the loser in this interesting piece of barter, for Field never kept his side of the bargain, and the works in question were never published by Clementi-Collard.

The Quintetto referred to was not the Quintet in A flat, published by

[1] See F. A. Gebhard's article in *Severnaya Pchela*, 1839, no. 180/176.

Breitkopf & Härtel in 1816, but one of the two *Divertissements* for piano and string quartet which were first published in Russia in 1810 or 1811. It is clear that one at least of these works must have been in existence when Clementi revisited St. Petersburg during the summer of 1806, but whether the concerto to which he refers was still the first, or whether Field had by now completed another concerto, we do not know. Apart from the fact that Clementi sold Field a piano and looked over his new manuscripts, nothing is known about their encounters during Clementi's last visit to Russia. Certainly Clementi must have been impressed by his former pupil's success, though he will have shaken his head over the mixture of luxury and chaos which were already the main characteristics of Field's way of life.

But before Clementi reappeared in St. Petersburg, Field, wisely deciding not to be satisfied only with the successes he had already won in the northern capital, had visited and conquered several other important cities in Russia, including Moscow, the old capital.

Early in 1805, he received an invitation from the Governor of Mittau to make a long visit to that city during the following autumn; and, remembering with pleasure his first visit to Courland during the summer of 1803, he accepted Governor Arsenyev's invitation, and prepared for another trip to the Upper Baltic.

Field went first to Riga, where he played with great success on the 7th October. He then moved on to Mittau. This old city (now called Yelgava) was at that time a place of very considerable importance. Not only was it the capital of the former Dukes of Courland, but, at the time of Field's visit, the old ducal palace was in use as a residence for the exiled Louis XVIII of France. Louis had been established there by the Emperor Paul I, in 1797, and provided with a pension of 200,000 roubles from the Russian Treasury. The city teemed with French exiles and seethed with rumours about the possible return to the French throne of Louis, who, a few months before, had published a declaration in which he promised to forget the past, to recognise liberty and equality, and to secure existing interests if he were recalled. Obviously, a possible future King of France was a patron worth having, and though the power of Napoleon was to keep Louis out of France for many more years, it must, in 1805, have seemed a clever and far-sighted action for Field to seek the patronage not only of the Baltic aristocracy, but also of the exiled French King.

Field's playing had the same effect on the Mittau connoisseurs as it had in St. Petersburg, and his visit was remembered there for many years. Other pianists who followed him fared badly. A local journal, criticising the performance of a pianist called Stiemer, who played in Mittau some weeks after Field had left, declared bluntly: 'The musical public is still so much in love with the playing of Mr Field . . . and the memory of him is still so alive among his pupils, that now only the most distinguished talent would be able to attract any attention. It was hardly worthwhile for Mr Stiemer to come [here].'[1]

Though Field first went to Mittau as the guest of Governor Arsenyev, he moved later to the house of Baron von Berner, another of those cultured dilettantes who were, in those days, the mainstay of the arts, and particularly of musicians. Von Berner is known to us from the autobiography of Spohr, where we learn that he was a 'Collegiate-Assessor' (one holding a high-ranking position in the Russian Civil Service), and that in his house Spohr often met a young pianist named Fräulein Brandt. This young girl was evidently outstandingly gifted, and she became one of Field's favourite pupils. She played to him; he played to her; and he is said to have written music which he dedicated to her, though her name does not appear as the dedicatee of any of his known compositions. All seemed set fair for a romantic relationship on the lines of that between Liszt and Caroline de Saint-Cricq; but though Field was in a highly romantic state of mind at the time, Fräulein Brandt lacked what almost always was, for him, an essential attraction: she was not a Frenchwoman.

There was, however, someone else in von Berner's household who had that qualification—the French governess provided by the Baron for his daughters' education; and this lady, who is said to have been no longer in her first youth, convinced Field that he was in love with her. Acting on impulse, he sat down and, in his still very uncertain French, dashed off what must be one of the shortest and most ill-composed proposals on record. The text of the letter has somehow been preserved; treasured, perhaps, by the lady in question. It was nothing if not laconic:

> Madamoiselle! Je vous aime. Au mois de Mai, quand j'aurai deux mille ecux je vous mariarai. Dites si vous voulez. F.[2]

But it was all that Mademoiselle required. She took him at his word and accepted him.

[1] See J. F. Recke (ed.), *Wöchentlichen Unterhaltungen für Liebhaber deutscher Lektüre in Russland*, 1806, 93.

[2] See Heinrich Dessauer, *John Field, sein Leben und seine Werke*, 21.

Almost at once, Field realised that he had made a terrible blunder, and he became so distracted with anxiety that his friends feared for his reason. Finally Baron von Berner himself intervened and somehow persuaded the governess to release Field from his engagement. Very wisely, John decided not to prolong his visit to Mittau and returned, as soon as possible, to Riga.

Poor nameless Mademoiselle! Her hopes of an honourable release from that 'Governess Trade', which Jane Austen's Miss Fairfax compared, with such bitter irony, to the Slave Trade, were frustrated. John's guilty feelings about the matter, once he had been rescued from his predicament, can only be guessed at; though it is perhaps significant that some years later he told a friend that he had originally left England to escape an entanglement with a young woman; and though this was no more than one of his romantic inventions on the lines of his tales about his 'French' origin, it may well have been suggested by his narrow escape from matrimony in Mittau.

On his return to Riga, Field gave two more concerts, on 22nd and 27th January. These took place in a hall belonging to the Chornogolovka Club,[1] and were apparently given in private as they do not appear to have been reviewed in the local press. But Field did not linger in Riga; very soon he was again on the move, bound this time for a much more important place—for Moscow, which was to become his favourite home for many years, and in which he was to enjoy successes at least equal to those which he had won in St. Petersburg.

---

[1] The Russian word *chornogolovka* can be used for various plants and birds of the far North, and it is tempting to believe that, in this case, it refers to the blackcap, the most mellifluously-voiced singing bird outside the migratory range of the nightingale. It is almost certain, however, that the club in question was that of the *Schwarzköpfe*, a powerful merchant guild in the Northern seaports which was descended from the medieval Hanseatic League. The patron saint of the *Schwarzköpfe* was St. Mauritius (a Moor); hence the name of the guild. In Field's time a magnificent *Schwarzkopfhaus* stood in Riga's *Hauptstadtplatz*, and it was probably in this building that his concerts took place. The *Schwarzkopfhaus* was destroyed during the Second World War.

'The Place of St. Isaac', engraved by J. C. Sadler, c. 1800, after a drawing by R. K. Porter

An autograph of a page from the Pastorale in A major

V

Moscow and Marriage

~⚬~

Fɪᴇʟᴅ's ꜰɪʀꜱᴛ concert in Moscow, which took place on March 2nd, 1806, was as brilliantly successful as had been his début in St. Petersburg two years before. He was at once besieged by applicants for lessons, and he received numerous invitations to perform in their salons from the richest and most distinguished families. It was a repetition of the enthusiasm for Field which took hold of St. Petersburg in 1804, but this time it occurred in an atmosphere which suited him even better.

St. Petersburg was, and still is, one of the world's most magnificent cities, but it can be rather overpowering, and in Field's day the grandiose splendour of its granite quays and marble palaces was mirrored in the rigid formality of the social structure imposed on it by the presence of the Emperor and his court. Moscow, on the other hand, was still a fascinating semi-Eastern city; a place full of ancient traditions, where life was a mixture of luxury, squalor and indolence, and where time seemed to move more slowly than elsewhere. Nothing could be more essentially Russian than Moscow's outward appearance—the walls and towers of its famous Kremlin, and the gilded, Byzantine domes of its innumerable churches. But the world of its high society looked towards far-off Paris for its fashions, its culture and its pleasures, and ignored the existence, as far as it could, of the rival capital in the North. French was the language heard in the elegant salons; the principal theatre was French; and a large French colony—mostly artists and political emigrés—lived in the vicinity of the French church and around the fashionable shopping district of the Kuznetsky Most (the Bridge of the Smiths). The charm of this Russo-Gallic world was extremly attractive to Field, who would have been as happy to remain in it indefinitely as the Muscovites would have been glad to keep him among them had he not felt obliged to return to the friends, pupils (and perhaps amours) who awaited him impatiently in St. Petersburg. In the summer of 1806, therefore, he left Moscow for a time, though with the definite intention of eventually returning there.

He did not wait long: the *St. Petersburg Record* for April 19th, 1807, contains an announcement of his departure for Moscow; and, though no details of it now survive, it is known that he gave another concert there in the latter part of the Spring season of that year.

Although he had not yet given up his apartment in St. Petersburg he now took one in the older capital with the intention of leading a divided life, moving periodically from one city to the other. But though it is impossible to trace all his movements between 1807 and 1812, such evidence as exists indicates that he spent most, if not the whole of this time in Moscow.

The dominating figure of Clementi having disappeared from his life, Field now emerges as a very distinctive and interesting personality. It is a great pity that extant letters in his hand are so few (a mere handful, of which the absurd proposal to the von Berner governess is almost the only one which reveals anything of its writer), but the impression of his character which one receives from the pages of various memorialists is sufficiently striking and unusual to make up for the lack of an epistolary self-portrait.

As a boy, he had remained a somewhat shadowy figure, principally notable for the intensity of his musical urge and the quasi-Dickensian miseries of his early childhood. Later, while under Clementi's wing, he occasionally steps out of the background, as if for some brief appearance on the concert stage; but always the thin, awkward, rather forlorn youth of those days fails to compete in interest with the brilliant personality of his witty, sardonic and untiringly energetic master. But with Clementi out of the way, the adult Field is suddenly before us; metamorphosed, apparently overnight, into an amusingly absent-minded and thoroughly hedonistic Bohemian; often feckless, but full of charm, and always surrounded by a circle of admirers who felt for him something very like hero-worship. According to Gebhard, whose memoirs relate mostly to Field's early life in St. Petersburg, the young virtuoso gloried in his new freedom and popularity, but continued to work hard at his art, and soon made enough money to live in style. He dressed well, rented magnificent rooms, kept servants to wait on him, and, the most important status symbol of all, possessed his own carriage. Once his daily practice and teaching were over he liked to relax among congenial companions,

34

usually at a restaurant; and there, smoking the best Havana cigars, drinking his favourite champagne, listening to the artistic and social gossip of the town and laughing at his own appalling puns (the habit of punning he probably picked up from Clementi, who was much given to this substitute for wit) he would remain there until the early hours of the morning.

Gebhard and his young wife were Germans, actors employed in the German Theatre in St. Petersburg, and Field, who by this time spoke French easily, tried to learn some German too. Gebhard recalled that 'he understood every word, and rarely kept out of the conversation. His accent greatly amused us, as it was a kind of Anglo-German, exactly like the German translation of *Fra Diavolo*.' One suspects that Field was not really a very talented linguist. French he could hardly avoid learning; but though he spoke the language fluently, his French accent seems to have been little better than his German, for another writer, a Frenchwoman, remembered that he spoke French with a strong English (or perhaps Irish?) accent. Russian he never attempted to master: it was not necessary in the circles in which he moved. Spelling was an awkward business for him in any language.

Though he never gambled at cards, he spent money freely, and gave away more than he spent. By lavishly treating his friends at restaurants he ran up enormous bills, which he paid periodically when he was in funds. He saw no point in saving money when all he had to do was to announce a concert and collect 6,000 roubles from the sale of the tickets: and if he threw his takings on the floor when he returned home after a post-concert carousal, waking up later to find that his dogs had chewed the banknotes to pieces, he only laughed. Why agitate oneself over anything so easily replaced as money?

Agitation of any kind was something quite foreign to him; complete calm of mind and body were as essential to his art as to his way of life. But, though he gave way too easily to a certain innate laziness, he did not allow it to ruin his playing. Whatever else he left undone, he never during these years neglected his technical practice, but always strove for an ever greater perfection of style and detail.

Composing, however, was another matter. Though the creative spark in him was never actually extinguished, it glimmered very feebly for long periods, and he only settled down to the labour of putting his ideas on paper when he absolutely had to have new material for an important concert.

Madame Louise Fusil, who knew him well during his earlier visits to Moscow, published, in 1842, a brilliant volume of memoirs which contains one of the most valuable accounts we have of Field, his circle, and his way of life in Moscow: it also describes how, in those days, he set about composing when he could no longer put off doing so.

According to Madame Fusil, 'Field did not work until forced to do so by the approach of his concerts . . . but it was necessary for him to be urged by his friends for a long time before he decided to sit down to the piano and begin. First he had a bowl of "grog" brought to him—to which he had frequent recourse, though without getting drunk—and he rolled up his sleeves in readiness. Then he was no longer the lazy man but the artist, the inspired composer; he wrote; he threw his pages to the winds, like the Sybil of the Oracles, and his friends gathered them together and put them in order. One had to be clever to decipher what he wrote, for he took no trouble to form the notes carefully; but his friends were used to it. As he advanced in his work his genius glowed to such a point that his copyists were almost unable to keep up with him . . . At three or four in the morning he felt exhausted and fell on his divan and slept. While he was sleeping his papers were put in order. The next morning, when he awoke, he would take several cups of black coffee and begin afresh. It was advisable, however, not to speak to him, even about the most urgent matter. His friends, who were all people of merit, understood him and kept a religious silence, for they appreciated his talent at its true value.'

Louise Fusil was a member of the French theatre company in Moscow. She was a clever actress, an able singer of light French songs, and a very valuable and popular member of the French community. She lived through the Napoleonic invasion and the burning of Moscow, but decided to leave when the French troops retreated. She even survived that appalling experience, and was one of the few French residents of Moscow who eventually returned to France. Years later she wrote a very interesting account of those extraordinary days; and though she is not always reliable, particularly about dates, her memoirs are still worth reading.

She knew Field well, and was obviously fond of him. She tells us that 'he had much wit, and . . . his stuttering speech made his repartee, filled with finesse, infinitely comic.[1] He had an agreeable face, and his counten-

---

[1] Was Field really a wit? Louise Fusil offers no evidence to support her statement that he was. Although Russian memoirs make much of his rather awful French puns (example: Count Orlov—'Monsieur Field, aimez-vous le Théologie?' Field—'Non, mais j'aime le

ance radiated genius; but . . . he was the most disorganised person . . . sleepy, vague; it was difficult to imagine how genius survived in the midst of such disorder. His laziness and carelessness were such that it was a penance for him to have to go into society, where it was necessary to consider one's appearance . . . or to the homes of friends. When Field was forced to go out in the evening to a salon or a concert, or to hear a pupil, he arrived with his stockings all wrinkled, or put on inside out, a white tie, of which the two ends pointed at the earth and the Heavens respectively, his waistcoat buttoned wrongly and his hat stuck on the top of his head, '*à la Colin*',[1] but everybody was so accustomed to his fantastic manners that nobody took any notice.'

Louise was extremely interested in Field's love life, and particularly in his affair with a young French girl, Mademoiselle Percheron, who was later to become his wife. How this young woman came to be living in Moscow in 1807 is not clear. She was not an actress, a *modiste* or a governess —in those days almost the only professions which could have brought her to Russia on legitimate business. We know only that on her arrival in Moscow she had been recommended to the protection of an old emigré Frenchman, named d'Ysarn (Madame Fusil mis-spells his name Disarn), who, it appears 'took a paternal interest in her'. Her Christian names were Adelaide Victoria, but everyone called her 'Percherette'.

Percherette was evidently very musical, and she became a pupil of Field soon after his arrival in Moscow in 1807. Many years later, during his last visit to London, in 1832, Field shocked the ladies assembled to meet him at Moscheles's house by his cynical remark that he had only married his wife because she never paid for her lessons, and it seemed the best way

---

thé au logis'), the only recorded remarks of his which might be called genuine *bons mots* are those concerning a third-rate Moscow painter named Robineau. Robineau, who fancied himself as an amateur musician, had composed an 'Elegy on the death of Mozart', which he hoped to persuade Field to play in public. Field refused, and added 'I should have been happy to have played it had it been an elegy by Mozart on the death of Robineau.' Not a very nice thing to say. Field must surely have had a particular dislike for Robineau, for he summed up his work with something very like a genuine aphorism: 'Only musicians care for Robineau's paintings, and as for his music, it only pleases painters.' Perhaps it was this sort of remark which earned him a reputation as a wit.

[1] A locution derived from a successful Opera-Comique, *Jeannot et Colin*, by the Maltese composer, Nicholas Isouard, known to Parisians as Nicolo. The work was produced at the Salle Feydeau, Paris, in 1806, and thereafter articles of dress (costume, cravate, chapeau) were often described as being '*à la Colin*'. One could also talk of '*jouer les Colins*', meaning to play the part of a young lover or rustic swain.

for him to get some return for his trouble. It is pretty clear, however, that Percherette was Field's mistress for some time before they were married: as one writer cautiously put it, 'she regarded herself as married to him long before the ceremony actually took place'.[1] That it took place at all was due to the combined efforts of the young lady herself and her allies, Madame Fusil and the Chevalier d'Ysarn. One cannot imagine Field deliberately embarking on such a course of action without an immense amount of prodding and persuasion. In the event, all the preparations were undertaken by Louise and the Chevalier, and Field had nothing to do but to relax and wait for things to happen. Louise Fusil's account of the preliminary arrangements, and of the ceremony itself, are worth quoting in full, for they add much to our appreciation of Field's odd personality, and give a vivid picture of his way of life in Moscow.

'We,' she writes of herself and the Chevalier (they were to be 'mother' and 'father' at the wedding) 'consulted together to arrange the necessary preparations, for we assumed that neither of the principals were capable of this. We wished above all for them to have a suitable home, for Field could not possibly receive his new wife in his own apartment. Not that it lacked a certain luxury of its own, but it bore the stamp of the eccentricity of its owner. A large room surrounded by low divans, with piles of cushions such as one finds in most Russian homes, served Field's lazy indolence only too well, and gave him the air of a Pasha when, wrapped in his fur-trimmed dressing-gown, he smoked his long sandalwood pipe. Near him would be a little table on which were a tray, some carafes of cognac and a spirit lamp. The walls were hung with cigar holders; with all sorts of pipes from every country . . . with little bags of Turkish tobacco . . . with cigars from Havana. All this was great luxury; for there were pipes and cigar-holders of great price; scimitars and daggers, embossed and ornamented with stones; objects in steel and gold from Tula. These gifts, which had been given to him by his admirers, were placed without order about the room. A large round table, covered with music; upturned writing-desks and pens carelessly thrown down; chairs badly arranged; four windows without curtains; and . . . a very beautiful piano —such were the furnishings of this new kind of Pasha. It was thus that we found him when we came to fetch him for the visit of inspection to the new apartment which he was to occupy after his marriage. We had some difficulty in discovering him in the midst of the fog of smoke with which

[1] A. Nikolayev, *John Field* (p. 33.)

he and his friends filled the room. Such an abode would not have been suitable for a little lady like Percherette. When he saw the new apartment he found it much too fine for him, and he was concerned how he could receive his cronies, and where he could keep his dogs. We showed him a room set aside for this purpose, absolutely similar to the one which he regretted losing: after that nothing worried him.

'As we all three lived near one another they dined with me on the day of their marriage, which was to be celebrated in the evening . . . After dinner I went away with Mademoiselle to help her with her toilette. Field sat at the piano and began to play badly out of time in imitation of a young society lady. I warned his friend [Louise had also invited to dinner a young Englishman named Jones, who was to be one of the witnesses at the wedding] not to let him get too absorbed in this occupation, for he was capable of forgetting that he was to be married that evening . . . Returning home to fetch something I found him still in the same place—at the piano. I was seriously annoyed and sent him to dress for the wedding at once.

'Arrived at the church, we saw him beside Monsieur Disarn; he looked like a little boy about to make his first communion. Our excellent priest, the Abbé Surugue . . . made a touching sermon on the harmony of marriage, and on harmonies of all kinds. While this was going on the bridegroom realised that he had forgotten the ring and that he had not brought any money with him. Someone ran to fetch the ring, and M. Disarn supplied the money. The ceremony ended, we joined the newly-wedded pair for supper in their new home. When everybody was prepared to sit down we looked for the husband; he was found standing in the middle of the salon examining all the details—not before it was time! During the dessert Jones began to tell us a very long story which became somewhat boring. Field looked up and said to the Abbé, who sat next to him, "I well remember this story—I told it to Jones on his wedding-day".' Thus ended a very strange wedding.

Detailed as she is about the events of Field's wedding, Louise Fusil failed to record its date correctly. As we have already seen, it took place on May 31st, 1810, but Louise stated that Field was married in September, 1807. She may have been genuinely mistaken—her memoirs were published many years after these events—but they were written when Percherette was still alive (she gave a concert in Moscow in the same year as their publication), and it is possible that Louise wished to do her friend of long ago a good turn by deliberately putting back the date of the marriage to cover the period when she was thought to have been Field's mistress.

We do not know when or where Field and his wife first met; his pupil, Alexander Dubuk, who knew Field only in later years, was under the impression that they met in St. Petersburg, which is not impossible, though their association certainly began in Moscow. Dubuk was mistaken, however, in supposing Percherette to have been a Creole. He evidently confused the West Indies with India, for Adelaide Victoria Percheron was born in Pondicherry and was the daughter of Adrien Louis Percheron, war-commissioner of the French fleet, and therefore a person of some social standing.

Percherette was evidently extremely fascinating. Louise Fusil describes her as 'a tiny little person, perfectly proportioned and extremely graceful . . .' with a lively expression and half-closed eyes which suggested the wit and malice of a 'petit diable bleu', adding that she was possessed of a coquettish magnetism which attracted men towards her. One has the feeling that Louise couldn't quite make up her mind whether she liked Percherette or not. Though she thought her 'a well-brought-up young person, educated and one of the best pupils of her husband', she nevertheless disapproved of her flirtatious manners (she quotes a remark of one of Percherette's 'victims' that 'a hat on a walking-stick would be enough to make her start her little tricks') and deplored her lack of system and economy. She considered her far too much like Field in temperament: 'Two people who resemble each other in so many ways cannot make a happy marriage, for it is necessary to have contrasts: a reasonable woman would have had more control over her husband'. One wonders why Louise was so anxious to promote the marriage.

The newly-married Mrs. Field was evidently not able to bring much organisation into Field's life, which was very unfortunate, for he was greatly in need of it. By 1810 his liking for alcohol, preferably in its more expensive forms, had grown on him to such an extent that for long periods he was never completely sober. Not that it affected the quality of his playing, indeed he often played at his best when slightly drunk; but it added to the disorderliness of his daily life and certainly did nothing to make him any less lazy or absent-minded. Matters came to a climax during the Lent season of 1810, when an enormous audience, which had assembled to hear him play at his annual benefit concert, waited in vain for him to appear. Time passed, and the audience's mood changed from boredom and irritation to anger. Finally the Governor of Moscow, Count Goudovitch, who was among the many important people present, sent the chief of police to find Field and bring him to the hall, whatever his condition might be. He was not at home, but eventually they ran him to earth in a restaurant, surrounded by his drinking cronies. He was bundled unceremoniously into a carriage and rushed to the hall, where the atmosphere was now extremely tense; but as he stumbled to the piano, and, swaying slightly, bowed to the audience, the public's anger evaporated in affectionate laughter and a roar of applause. Nobody could be out of temper for long with dear Field, and in any case it was well known that champagne inspired him to his greatest moments of inspiration. He was lucky in that Count Goudovitch was a mild, kindly man—the Muscovites called him 'Good Papa Goudovitch'—for had the episode occurred a couple of years later he would have had to face the anger of a very different Governor of Moscow, the disagreeable Count Rostopchin, who was quite capable of ordering a flogging for someone who, in his opinion, had treated him without respect. It may well have been this episode which decided his friends that marriage might, perhaps, have a sobering effect on him, for the wedding took place only a couple of months later.

In 1811 Field wrote to Gebhard that he was no longer happy in Moscow and was thinking of returning to St. Petersburg. Perhaps he had been really shaken by the rather shameful affair of the benefit concert, or perhaps the move might have been contemplated because of Percherette's urgings. During Field's absence from St. Petersburg his place had been taken there, to some extent, by the celebrated Prussian pianist, Daniel Steibelt· Steibelt, a man of great ability, but with more than a touch of the charlatan about him, had arrived in St. Petersburg in 1808, and had quickly established an important position for himself in its musical world; he had even taken over the direction of the French Opera on the departure of Boïeldieu in 1810. Field evidently required Gebhard to advise him about the wisdom of his planned return to St. Petersburg in view of Steibelt's popularity there; and Gebhard, who was well acquainted with Steibelt, hit on the idea of an exchange: Steibelt should go to Moscow when Field left it and take over the latter's teaching connection, and perhaps his apartment as well, the new apartment that Louise and d'Ysarn had been at such pains to prepare for him and Percherette. The arrangement seems to have suited all parties and the exchange took place, though whether in 1811 or 1812 is uncertain. There is a little mystery here: why did Steibelt, who had recently secured the directorship of the French Opera in St. Petersburg (an appointment made personally by the Emperor), move to Moscow so very soon afterwards? It is possible that Field went to St. Petersburg to discuss the matter with Steibelt—he was certainly there in March 1811 (as we know from references to him in contemporary letters, one of which mentions a concert at which he played and threw a fit of temperament over the bad orchestral accompaniment), but back again in Moscow early in 1812. He gave two more concerts there, on March 10th and 14th, his last in that city for many years, and at the second of them his wife also played. It was her first public appearance as Madame Field.

The exchange, whenever it took place, proved to be a very fortunate move for Field, but a complete disaster for Steibelt. The Prussian virtuoso had hardly established himself in Moscow before the French army, with Napoleon at its head, was at the gates of the city, and, like thousands of other refugees, poor Steibelt had to abandon everything and go back the way he had come, the flames of Moscow flickering behind him.

In the meantime, Field, as soon as he had returned to the scene of his earliest triumphs in Russia, had been welcomed as rapturously as ever, and Steibelt now found his position in St. Petersburg much less secure than formerly. Despite their traditional rivalry and their habit of adopting quite different cultural heroes, the upper classes of both Moscow and St. Petersburg were as one in their enthusiasm for Field's art. For them he was the ideal pianist, incomparable and unapproachable. And now that he was among them again the Grand Duchess Ekaterina Pavlovna might ask Princess Obolenska to bring 'that nice man, Field' with her to a morning's music-making; the Princess Yousupova might proudly show her friends the copy of that delicious Pastorale in A major which he had just scribbled down for her on the back of another piece of music; and the ladies of St. Petersburg, great and small, might forget for a while their agitations and sorrows (of which they suffered a great many more than usual during that terrible year of 1812) while they listened entranced to his exquisite playing, or earnestly studied, under the guidance of the master himself, his new and beautiful, though often difficult compositions. As for Steibelt —yes, he played very well, and his opera, *Romeo et Juliette*, was really very pretty, but he had never been a Field; merely an agreeable stop-gap while the latter had been away in Moscow.

VI

A Liaison in St. Petersburg

❧

DESPITE HIS reluctance to put pen to paper, Field, by this time, must have completed several of his larger works. Certainly the Second Concerto was in existence (a short extract from its first movement had been published in 1811 in the St. Petersburg journal, *Variétés Lyriques pour les Dames*) as well as the two *Divertissements* for piano with string quartet, and the Rondo in A flat for the same combination. The Third Concerto may also have been composed (there is a possibility that it is an earlier work than the better-known Second Concerto), and perhaps some of the pieces we now know as nocturnes, though Field did not hit upon this title until some years later.

Of the few works which he had published in Moscow the most important were the two *Divertissements*, which had appeared in 1810 and 1811, the first of them tactfully dedicated to the daughter of Governer Goudovitch. After his return to St. Petersburg, the publisher, Dalmas, began to bring out some of Field's other works. Most of these were short pieces, including the first movement of the Fourth Sonata and the *Kamarinskaya* Variations; they appeared in the journals for ladies which were very fashionable at that time and were the usual channels for the dissemination of salon music in Russia.

Dalmas's first Field publication, however, was not taken from the portfolio of new works which the composer had brought with him from Moscow. It was a commission—a bright little patriotic march, one of several such pieces which were hurriedly written for Dalmas by the leading St. Petersburg composers (all foreigners, among them Steibelt) after the defeat of the French in the winter of 1812. Field's *Marche Triomphale en honneur des Victoires du Général Wittgenstein* may have been written even before the French withdrawal, for the victories it celebrates were those of a corps which, while guarding the road to St. Petersburg, had fought some successful actions under the General during July and August. These had greatly cheered the St. Petersburgers at a time when they were much in need of encouragement, and, as a result, the General had come in for a rather disproportionate amount of adulation.

Apart from the composition of this uncharacteristic trifle there is nothing to indicate that Field was directly affected by the world-stirring events of 1812. By good luck he had left Moscow before the *Grande Armée's* invasion of Russia began, and though the atmosphere in St. Petersburg must have been heavily charged with anxiety and uncertainty, the city's remoteness from the path taken by Napoleon allowed its every-day existence to continue almost unchanged.

In his private life, however, there was a great deal of conflict, and for one of his temperament this must have been particularly disagreeable. As Louise Fusil had foreseen, his marriage to Percherette was not turning out well. Field was as lethargic and easy-going as his wife was febrile and emotional, but they were both generally unstable and careless over all practical matters. Perhaps he may not have been much disturbed by Percherette's chaotic housekeeping, but the flirtations and extravagances of them both, which continued unchanged by marriage, inevitably led them into difficulties. There were numerous quarrels (it took a good deal to make Field quarrel), and such affection as there had been between them gradually lessened into indifference, if not dislike.

It was not very long after their arrival in St. Petersburg that Field, tired of exhausting scenes at home, began to look elsewhere for consolation. He found it, without difficulty, in the arms of one of Percherette's compatriots, a Mademoiselle Charpentier, of whom almost nothing is known but her surname. It has been said that she was a *modiste* (there were plenty of Frenchwomen working in the St. Petersburg world of *haute couture* at that time), but recent research has shown that there was a Mlle Charpentier among the members of the French Opera company then in St. Petersburg (one wonders to what extent, if at all, these artists were affected by the state of war between Russia and their country) and it is possible that this was the lady in question. Field's liaison with Charpentier lasted for a long time, which suggests that she was better suited to him than poor Percherette. He continued, however, to live with his legal wife, even though in 1815 Charpentier bore him a son, for whom they chose the name of Leon. Field must have found the double life he was now leading infinitely disturbing; yet he seems to have possessed a lucky ability to withdraw from his problems, for the amount of work he achieved at this time was, for him, unusually large.

There exists a fairly comprehensive record of his concert appearances in the St. Petersburg newspapers of this time, and it is interesting to note that on several occasions he collaborated with his rival, Steibelt, who was now in failing health, and, as we have already seen, rather overshadowed by Field's much greater popularity. Steibelt planned to give a 'come-back' concert in St. Petersburg on April 16th, 1813, and he very sensibly invited Field to take part in it. It was an intelligent move (it reminds one of Backhaus's invitation to Pachmann to share the platform with him at his first London concert after the First World War), and Steibelt showed considerable diplomacy over it. First he composed a new duo for two pianos, and then he commissioned Gebhard to make the initial approaches to Field: the Gebhards were intimate with both pianists, though Steibelt always made himself scarce when Field appeared at their flat. Rather surprisingly Field agreed, stipulating only that he should have his part of the duo in advance of the performance. As the two pianists met for the first time on the day of the concert there can have been no preliminary rehearsal, which seems to have surprised Gebhard much less than the fact that Field was not prepared to sight-read his part—an interesting comment on the rather rough-and-ready public music-making of those days. This concert was to be the first of several such collaborations, and in March, 1815, the two virtuosi gave a joint benefit concert at which Field played a concerto by Steibelt, though it is not recorded whether Steibelt returned the compliment.

The year 1815 was one of great importance for Field. He made more public appearances than usual during the Lent season (at one of them he took part, with three other pianists, in the first performance in Russia of Bach's Concerto, after Vivaldi, for four claviers), and he received, through Count Orlov, an offer of the title 'Court Pianist', an offer which he refused with one of his more successful puns: 'La cour n'est pas fait pour moi, et je ne sais pas lui faire la cour.'[1]

The emotional complications which must have resulted from the birth of his illegitimate son, Leon Charpentier, during this year do not seem to have interfered with his work, for he made good progress with a new concerto, his fifth (the exact date of the fourth is unknown), which he

[1] Field's reply to Count Orlov is quoted in Dubuk's memoirs, in French.

called *l'Incendie par l'Orage*, prompted, no doubt, by Steibelt's 'Storm' Concerto, which had been all the rage for several years.

More important, however, than any of these events was an offer which he received from the famous Leipzig music publishers, Breitkopf & Härtel, to publish all his available compositions and any more that he might write in the future. The text of Field's reply to this offer has fortunately been preserved:

St Petersburg le 18/30 8bre
1815

J'ai recue la lettre que vous m'avez fait l'honneur de m'adrésser Messieurs, en datte du 22 7bre N.S. et serait charme d'entre en liason avec une maison aussi connu et estimée que la votre. Je m'occupe dans ce moment de composer mon cinquieme concert, je pourrai vous l'envoyer vers le mois de mars prochain: J'acquiesce aux conditions que vous me proposès, d'abord pour faire connaissance et puis parce que vous m'assurer que l'édition que vous me livrarez sera belle à tous égards; chose à laqu'elle je tiens beaucoup, et qu'il est difficile d'obtenir ici: car du reste je serait obligé de placer mes examplaires dans un magazin de musique, mes affaires ne me perméttant pas de les vendre moi méme, et on ne me les prendra qu'avec un rebais consideralbe, ce qui n'empéche pas que je ne vous rappelle la condition de n'en point envoyer a St Petersbourg pendant le premiers 18 mois: je vous prie aussi de me mander a peu près le tems que vous mêttrez à graver ce morceau. Quant a mes autres compositions je n'en possêde plus; ayant vendu le tout à un éditeur d'ici: cela m'empéche de vous communiquer ce que vous desirez, mais il vous sera aisé de vous procurer ce qui vous manque, par un de vos correspondans: car tout est gravé: il y a outre mes quatre concerts, un noveau quintetto pour le piano avec accompagnement.

Je vous prirais d'avoir la bonté de m'accuser la reception de ma response et ai l'honneur d'être.

Messieurs
Votre tres humble Serviteur
John Field[1]

It is evident that Field must have been perfectly satisfied with his command of the French language, for this letter cannot possibly have been checked for errors by either Percherette, Charpentier or any of his many French friends in St. Petersburg.

It is interesting to note that he had already sold his first four concertos, and the quintet, to a Russian publisher (almost certainly Dalmas), for the

[1] Most of Field's letters contain numerous errors of spelling and grammar. These inaccuracies have been retained in all the letters quoted.

only trace remaining of these early editions is a single copy of the Third Concerto,[1] in a text by no means identical with Breitkopf's later publication of it. There must at this time have been an extraordinarily large demand for Field's music throughout Europe, for Breitkopf & Härtel issued the First Concerto immediately (it was advertised in the *Allgemeine Musikalische Zeitung* in October, 1815), and brought out the three other available concertos, and the quintet, as well as several solo pieces, simultaneously in the following May.

Field was now thirty-three, and at the height of his powers. His fame had spread far beyond the borders of Russia, and this, surely, would have been the ideal moment for him to appear in the most important European musical centres. In Vienna, Berlin, Prague, Paris and London he would have been welcomed with enthusiasm; he would have made a lot of money and his playing would easily have vanquished that of any rivals, for the era of such young 'Klavier-tigers' as Liszt, Thalberg and their colleagues was still far in the future. His health, too, would have been better able to stand the strain of travelling than it was to be sixteen years later, when he finally left Russia for the first time since 1802. His well-wishers tried hard to persuade him to allow his art to be heard in Western Europe, but he remained adamant: the fatigue of it all would be too much; he preferred the unchanging pattern of his life in St. Petersburg or Moscow, with its round of lessons, concerts and frequent opportunites for the indulgence of his few pleasures—tobacco, champagne and convivial evenings among friends. The complications of his love life must also have made it difficult for him to leave Russia at this time. The birth of Leon was a new tie, for though not able to acknowledge the boy as his own, he spent much of his time with him and his mother. One must suppose that Percherette knew of her husband's liaison with Mlle Charpentier and that she turned a blind eye to it, since she continued to live with Field and to develop her piano playing under his guidance; but without more definite information about their relations we can only guess that during these years they were far from happy together.

In the winter of 1817, Mikhail Ivanovitch Glinka, the future founder of Russian musical nationalism, arrived in St. Petersburg to become a pupil at a newly-opened school for the sons of noblemen. Already, at thirteen, deeply in love with music, Glinka studied the piano outside the school curriculum, and among his teachers was Field. Glinka had only three

[1] Now in the library of the Leningrad Conservatoire.

lessons from Field but they made a lasting impression on him. Field became for him an idol, and in his memoirs, written towards the end of his life, we find one of the most enthusiastic and valuable accounts of Field's playing ever recorded. By that time Glinka had heard many later pianists, including Liszt, but Field always remained for him the *ne plus ultra* of piano playing. Glinka would have continued to study with Field had the latter not decided to visit Moscow once again in the Spring of 1818. We know no details of this visit, but as Glinka was unable to wait for Field (he continued his piano studies with Field's pupil, Charles Mayer) it certainly lasted for some time.

Soon after Field's return to St. Petersburg, relations with Percherette must have improved, if only temporarily, for they not only made a joint concert appearance (their first since 1812) on March 14th, 1819, but by that date Percherette already knew that she was going to have a child, a discovery which probably surprised both of them, after their nine years of childless marriage. Adrien Field (he was named after his maternal grandfather) was born some time in 1819 (the exact date of his birth has not been discovered) and his arrival can only have been an added complication to an already uncomfortable situation. Field had grown deeply attached to the little Leon, who was now aged four and already showing signs of great musical ability; and Leon's mother, whatever her relations with Field may have been by this time, cannot have viewed with any satisfaction the unexpected birth of Percherette's Adrien. The reconciliation with Percherette, on the other hand, was a patched-up affair, unlikely to last long. The whole situation was explosive and had to be resolved by drastic action of one kind or another. Field, characteristically, continued to let matters drift, and endeavoured to expunge from his mind all uncomfortable thoughts by increased indulgence in his favourite dissipations. It was left to Percherette to bring their unsatisfactory marriage to an end, and this she now resolved to do as soon as a favourable opportunity occurred.

It has been said that Percherette left Field shortly after the birth of her child. She is known to have been in Kiev in 1820, without her husband: she gave a concert there, but without having much success. However, the *Moscow News* for April 16th, 1821, contains the announcement of a concert at which they were both to appear: so their final parting evidently took place after that date. According to Dubuk, she left Field while he was still living in St. Petersburg and moved to Smolensk, taking her eighteen-month-old baby with her. In Smolensk she set up as a pianoforte teacher and, in Dubuk's words, 'her lessons were appreciated'. There can be no doubt that she was a very gifted musician, a pianist of sufficient brilliance to appear in concerts with her husband (she was one of his best pupils) and also an excellent teacher. We know from Louise Fusil that Percherette was already earning quite a lot of money from teaching music even before her marriage. In later years she relied heavily on her name; as Madame Field she was thought to have all the secrets of the Master's methods: but she evidently achieved good results, for her pupils sometimes appeared in concerts, even in the two capitals, and were acclaimed by the press. She made an occasional appearance herself, playing for the last time in Moscow in 1842.[1]

During this crucial period in his private life Field somehow managed to produce good work. He made his usual concert appearances in St. Petersburg during the season of 1819 and 1820 (he once played a Fantasia as an interlude between two theatrical performances, a drama and a light opera, at which entertainment Pushkin is known to have been present—the only occasion when they can be proved to have been under the same roof),[2] and completed some new nocturnes and his Sixth Concerto, a rather uneven work, which, however, contains much that is extraordinarily prophetic. He often played in private, and there is a reference to one such performance in a letter dated May 28th, 1820, written by K. Y. Bulgakov to his brother immediately after his return from a party: 'This evening my wife and I dined with Vorontsky. Field was also there, and after dinner, in a half-tipsy condition, he played—amazingly!' By this time Field's dependence on cognac, champagne and other forms of alcohol had greatly increased. They had become both inspiring stimulants to him and a way of escape from the disturbed state of his private life. There can be no doubt that Percherette, with all her faults, had a good deal to endure. To live with Field for several years must have been a considerable strain, and at times she must have been hard put to it to balance the marvellous sound of his playing against the more disagreeable aspects of his personality.

Field's decision to uproot himself from St. Petersburg once more and return to Moscow at the end of 1821 was probably the direct result of the

---

[1] Mrs. Field outlived both her husband and her son. She died at an advanced age in 1869.

[2] See P. Arapov, *Chronicles of the Russian Theatre*, St. Petersburg, 1861, 290.

break-up of his marriage. It is difficult to imagine what other motive he could have had for such a move, for his popularity and financial success in St. Petersburg were as great as ever. In Moscow, where he had formerly been so happy, most of the old glamour was missing. The immense efforts of the Muscovites to rebuild their city after the terrible holocaust of 1812 had left them little time for the arts, particularly music. The Moscow poet, Griboyedov, writing about the changes in his native town, stated sorrowfully: 'Before the war everybody loved music—now nobody cares for it.' Griboyedov was writing in 1818, and perhaps by 1821 matters had improved; but the phoenix city could not, at that time, provide Field with the *dolce vita* he had enjoyed there before the war; nor could it offer him greater rewards or appreciation than he invariably received in St. Petersburg.

A clue to the possible reason behind this puzzling move lies, perhaps, in the fact that Field's natural son, Leon Charpentier, was evidently taken to Moscow at about the same time that his father went there; and since the child was still only six years old, his mother presumably went with him. Whether she and Leon joined Field's household after the departure of Percherette is not known, since she is never mentioned by anyone who knew Field in later years. There may, however, be some significance in the curious fact that during the 1820s Field occupied two flats in Moscow simultaneously: the addresses of both of them are given in a Moscow reference book of 1827, which was published for the benefit of new-comers to the city. Why he should have found it necessary to do this one cannot know, though one can speculate that it probably had something to do with the social taboos which would have prevented Field's numerous lady pupils, with their attendant duennas, from visiting the residence of a teacher, however famous, who was known to have a mistress living with him. It must have been an unwieldy and unsatisfactory arrangement, and it can only have added further confusion to the life of the self-indulgent genius, whose habitual sloth and intemperance were now beginning to undermine seriously his formerly robust constitution.

VII

Moscow: the Unproductive Years, 1823–31

⧉

Aᴛ ᴛʜᴇ time when Field severed his ties with St. Petersburg he had, at the most, three serious rivals among European pianists—Moscheles, Kalkbrenner and Hummel. All three were still constantly undertaking exhausting concert tours, but Hummel had recently been appointed Kapellmeister at Weimar, and the other two were soon to give up their wandering lives and devote themselves to teaching, the one in London and the other in Paris. They were all very conscious of each other's eminence, and they knew and played each other's compositions. Field made no secret of the fact that he preferred such works as the G minor Concerto of Moscheles and the concertos of Hummel to those of any other composers—except, of course, his own.

Moscheles and Kalkbrenner never visited Russia. But Hummel, whose 'Kapellmeister-ship' still allowed him enough time to pursue his career as a virtuoso, appeared in St. Petersburg and Moscow in 1822. Then the most famous of all touring virtuosi, Hummel was naturally very curious about the playing of Field, his legendary rival, of whom he had heard so much.

The two pianists had narrowly missed each other several times during their youth. When Field first arrived in London, in 1793, Hummel had just left for Vienna after a period of study with Clementi; and when Field reached Vienna in 1802, Hummel was in St. Petersburg (on his only visit there before 1822), though he had left before Field and Clementi went to Russia later in the year. Now, at last, the two great pianists were in the same city; but Hummel was disappointed to find that Field had announced no concert during the time of his visit. Hummel was determined not to leave Moscow without hearing his great *confrère*, but someone must have warned him that it would not be easy to persuade Field to play to him, for he went about the matter in a very unorthodox way. Calling at Field's apartment one morning, and luckily finding him at home, Hummel passed himself off as a German business man who loved music so much that he could not bear to leave Moscow without hearing the most famous pianist in Russia. Field was teaching at the time, but when the lesson was over he obligingly sat down at the piano and launched into one of his most brilliant pieces. Hummel was genuinely moved by Field's playing and thanked him sincerely for his kindness. Field then asked his guest, not without a touch of mockery, 'Since you are so fond of music, won't you play something yourself?' After much demurring, and many modest disclaimers of any special ability, Hummel allowed himself to be persuaded . . . and then performed a marvellous improvisation (his particular forte) on themes from the work which Field had just played. Field remained a long time speechless and motionless. Then suddenly he burst out: 'Either you are the Devil, or you are Hummel! Only he could play like that!' Many embraces and much mutual admiration followed, and the two great pianists swore undying friendship.

This anecdote was greatly admired and frequently repeated by the members of Field's circle, and it gathered a good deal of circumstantial detail over the years, several variations of it appearing in print after Field's death. The periodical *Russian Invalid* included it, very much as above, in its issue of September 4th, 1846, and we may as well accept this version as basically correct, and try to believe that Field was genuinely unaware of his visitor's identity, though Hummel's arrival can have been no secret in the Moscow musical world.

An important result of their meeting was Hummel's invitation to Field to assist him at his concert a few days later. They played together in Hummel's own Sonata in A flat, for four hands, and on that occasion Field seems to have been rather less overpowered by Hummel's playing, for he was heard to admonish his great rival quite audibly during the performance with the words, 'ne tapez pas si fort!'

Present at this memorable concert was the celebrated Viennese violinist, Ignaz Schuppanzigh, who is principally remembered today for his close friendship with Beethoven and Schubert, many of whose works he introduced to the public. On his return to Vienna, in 1823, Schuppanzigh visited the deaf Beethoven and wrote down some interesting impressions of Field and his playing in the afflicted composer's conversation book. He began by telling Beethoven how beautifully Field played, stating that the piano had never been treated in such a manner by any other pianist. Then, obviously wishing to please Beethoven, he went on to say that Field's playing reminded him of Beethoven's, that Field was Beethoven's ardent admirer and that to play Beethoven's music was his greatest pleasure. He also mentioned that he had heard Field play Beethoven's C minor Concerto 'in the most beautiful way'. One has to take some of this *cum grano salis*, for Field is known to have been less than enthusiastic about Beethoven's piano music. Schuppanzigh then referred to Field's concert with Hummel, and said, rather ambiguously, that 'the non-connoisseurs, like the connoisseurs, realised the very evident difference between the two pianists', which he presumably meant as a judgement in Field's favour: he also described Field as 'a very good fellow, a real "Falstaff"', whom Beethoven would like very much'.[1] He ended his remarks about Field with references to his notorious carelessness about money matters and his over-indulgence in champagne.

If Schuppanzigh really heard Field play Beethoven's Third Concerto it was probably at a private performance, for there is no record that he ever played any of Beethoven's concertos in public.[2] But if he was luke-warm about Beethoven's piano music, Field was a great admirer of Hummel's compositions and he frequently performed them. Hummel himself was enchanted by Field's way of playing his music, despite the latter's habit of altering the text to suit himself.

The programme of Field's benefit concert, on March 6th, 1822, (Hummel had left Moscow by that date) is of great interest, for it included the first performance of the first movement of his newest concerto, no. 7, in C minor. The rest of the programme included two works by Steibelt (his Duo for two pianos, in which Field was joined by his pupil Rheinhardt, and the 'Bachannale' from his Eighth Concerto, a piece which introduced a male chorus, at that time considered a fascinating novelty) and was completed by another new work by the concert-giver, his Variations in A minor for piano and orchestra on a Russian theme.

[1] 'Falstaff' was one of Beethoven's nicknames for Schuppanzigh.
[2] Field had a low opinion of Beethoven's piano music, which (according to Dubuk) he called 'le torchon Allemand' (German dishcloth). On the other hand, he admired Beethoven's chamber music and his orchestral music, and Dubuk recalls his master's excitement after he had played through, for the first time, the 'Kreutzer' Sonata with Lipinski. Dubuk felt strongly tempted to say 'How about *that* for a German dishcloth?' but he restrained himself.

He also assisted at several other concerts during the season, including one given by his former pupil, the Polish pianist, Maria Szymanowska.[1] With his usual good nature he agreed to play duets with her, but when the glamorous (and evidently rather *décolletée*) lady asked him to turn the pages for her while she played her solos (nobody thought of memorising in those days) he wittily evaded this thankless task by phrasing his refusal in such a way that it sounded like a gallant compliment: 'Non, je vous ferai manquer, parce que je regarderais toujours ces diables d'épaules que vous avez, au lieu de regarder la musique!'

In spite of his frequent indulgence in forms of alcohol and the chronic ailments from which he was now beginning to suffer (even before leaving St. Petersburg he had become a martyr to haemorrhoids and digestive troubles, and had worsened his condition by treating himself with a very powerful drug concocted by a quack doctor named Larue),[2] Field's outward appearance was evidently still very engaging. Alexander Dubuk, who was to become a favourite pupil, and a future biographer, left an account of his first meeting with Field which tells us how he looked in 1823. Dubuk, then a prodigy pianist aged eleven, had given a public performance of Ries's Concerto in E flat, and, at the end of the concert, he was led up to 'an imposing man of about forty, with intelligent and penetrating eyes and a sympathetic smile. His face was clean shaven; he had a thin and somewhat highly-arched nose and fair hair. It was Field. He gently patted my shoulder, and said "I would like to take him along with me." We were all in raptures—Field was then at the height of his fame, one of the best pianists in the world. From that day I started my lessons with him, three times a week.'

Dubuk studied with Field for six years, and was with him constantly during that time. His admiration for Field extended far beyond music: he hero-worshipped the man himself; he observed his habits and character-

---

[1] Maria Szymanowska made a great reputation throughout Europe. She was a composer as well as a pianist, and Field took the trouble to write her a letter of introduction to his own publishers, Breitkopf & Härtel. Her physical attractions appear to have been considerable. Goethe fell in love with her and wrote his beautiful 'Trilogie der Leidenschaft' in her honour. He thought her a **better** pianist than Hummel; 'but those who do', said the precocious schoolboy, Felix Mendelssohn, 'think more of her pretty face than her not pretty playing'. Maria Szymanowska's daughter, Celina, married the great Polish poet, Mickiewicz.

[2] Dubuk was convinced that 'Dr.' Larue's potions were responsible for the deaths of numerous gullible St. Petersburgers.

istics; and, long after Field's death, he faithfully recorded all he could remember about him. Dubuk was among those who thought that there might be some truth in Field's claim to have French blood in him. Rather surprisingly he tells us that Field was 'very lively, and showed nothing of the typical English [*sic*] quiet reserve'. Dubuk also felt that 'Field's intellect, in all its movements and reactions, reminded one far more of someone whose brain had been infiltrated by the free conceptions of Voltaire and Rousseau than of an Englishman.' Like many foreigners, Dubuk seems to have had no idea that an Irishman might think and act differently from an Englishman; or for that matter, that all Englishmen might not be cast in exactly the same mould. But his statements about Field's personality have their interest, since they differ from the more usual pictures of him as a day-dreaming Bohemian who only emerged from his usual alcoholic haze when seated at the keyboard.

We can learn much more from Dubuk: he refers to Field's easy command of spoken French, but he says that his English was less good; and though one wonders how this fact could be known to a Russian it may be true that Field's native tongue had grown stiff with disuse.[1] Dubuk also

[1] John Field does not appear to have had much general education. His epistolary style, whether he wrote in French or English, was crude to a degree; and as for his interest in literature, there is little to be learned from his biographers. An unsigned and rather gossipy article in an obscure Russian journal includes the following statement: 'Field often went to the theatre, the French as well as the German, and his criticisms were always unorthodox and acute. His favourite plays were those of Shakespeare, whose collected works, bound in one volume, were found under his pillow when he was dying.' It is difficult to accept this statement without question. To begin with, if Field attended performances of Shakespeare's plays in Russia he can only have heard them in French or German translations, though he is presumably supposed to have read them in the original. As to his keeping the 'complete works' under his pillow—this can be dismissed as a piece of sentimentalism: foreigners delight in believing that Englishmen (Field was regarded as English, not Irish, by those of his Russian friends who did not think of him as French) must, of necessity, spend their leisure hours reading Shakespeare, whose collected works would make an extremely bulky and uncomfortable pillow for a dying man! The memoirs of Field's friend, the actor Gebhard, who might be supposed to know more about his theatrical tastes than anyone else, are silent on the subject.

The one other mention of Field's literary interests, among all the various writings about him, is more reliable, since it comes from the pen of Dubuk. Dubuk writes, 'He did not have a very profound education; therefore his taste for literature was rather simple. For instance, he liked to read the novels of Paul de Kock.' Now, a liking for Paul de Kock suggests a very different sort of literary taste from that which a worship of Shakespeare might indicate; for, not to put too fine a point on it, de Kock's novels, most of which deal with the seamy side of Parisian life in the early nineteenth century, are distinctly pornographic. As late as 1926 Magnus's Dictionary of European Literature

noted that at this time Field had given up his regular technical practice, contenting himself with a daily run-through of a couple of his own studies. As a result of this change of routine he was able to start teaching much earlier in the morning, and to finish at about 4 p.m. He would then take a droshky and drive to a restaurant, accompanied by his four pet dogs, all with classical names (Herodotus, Socrates, etc.), stopping the cab from time to time, and telling the coachman to drive slowly while he and the dogs snatched a little much-needed exercise. The convivial dinners which followed lasted, as always, into the small hours, and sometimes the first pupil of the next day would arrive before Field had dragged himself out of bed. According to Moscow gossip, he was often awakened in the morning by the sound of a pupil practising in the next room, and it was said that on one occasion he had become so irritated by the mistakes of an invisible pupil that he had wandered in to correct her, clad only in his nightshirt—much to the consternation of the young lady and her attendant governess.

In spite of such behaviour he was always able to pick and choose his pupils. Dubuk states that he visited only four in their own homes, all distinguished amateurs, such as the influential Countess Orlova-Chesmenskaya, who treated him *en prince*. They paid him twenty-five roubles a lesson, and saw to it that he had every possible comfort, including champagne at hand while he was teaching. Pupils who came to his apartment paid less—usually between ten and fifteen roubles a lesson. His average yearly income from teaching was about 10,000 roubles and he charged 500 roubles for a performance at a private soirée, and usually made about 10,000 out of the sale of tickets for his few public concerts. All this added up to a very substantial income, and since his personal needs were few, he should have been able to put by a good deal of money; but somehow he never did. As an example of Field's carelessness about money matters, Dubuk relates how, when rummaging one day among some of his teacher's music, he unearthed a fifty-rouble note which had been 'banked' there and forgotten. 'Field did everything in the grand manner,' says Dubuk, 'but it was mainly his numerous cronies and hangers-on who benefited from his easy extravagance.'

Field made several public appearances in 1823, but before any of them

lists his work with evident distaste, and considers him 'a writer to be avoided'. Field evidently thought otherwise: one sees what Dubuk really meant by his statement that his master's tastes were 'simple'.

took place, another concert was given which probably interested him more than any of his own. Little Leon, now in his eighth year, was following in his father's footsteps and developing into an infant prodigy, and Field had decided that the child should make a public appearance. The concert, advertised in the *Moscow News* for March 23rd, took place in the mansion of Field's friend and pupil, Baron Apraxin. It evidently attracted some attention, for a journalist named Odoyevsky[1] reviewed it in the *Moscow Telegraph*, and praised Leon encouragingly: 'Charpentier is a pupil of Field, and for his age worthy of attention. If the child will continue to study music under Field's guidance then in due course he will attain perfection.' Leon evidently had the makings of a virtuoso pianist, and he would probably have become one had he not developed later a voice and an acting ability which were to make him a distinguished star of the St. Petersburg opera.

The years 1824 to 1831 were the least productive of Field's career. His health was gradually deteriorating, and though he continued to give concerts, always scrupulously returning to his old routine of concentrated technical practice six weeks before the start of each Lent season, he did so less frequently than formerly. His creative gifts seem to have completely failed him for several years, for after the publication of his Sixth Concerto, and the Variations for piano and orchestra on a Russian Theme in 1823, nothing more appeared until 1832. His Seventh Concerto remained unfinished. He had played its first movement at his annual benefit concert in 1822, and again in March, 1824, but he found himself devoid of ideas for the completion of the work. The state of his health must explain, at least in part, both his gradual withdrawal from public view and his silence as a composer.

Although Dubuk refers vaguely to Field's irregular way of life, he passes over in silence his addiction to alcohol; but it was, by 1825, so much common knowledge in Moscow that a visiting Polish musician, Wiktor Kzaynski, noted in his journal that the great pianist was often familiarly referred to as 'Drunken John'. Of course, what would today be regarded as excessive drinking was nothing exceptional in Field's day. Furthermore, the warming power of cognac and vodka were, and still are, a valuable inner protection against the severities of Russian winter weather. Nevertheless, Field undoubtedly drank an abnormally large amount, and it is

[1] This was probably Prince V. F. Odoyevsky, one of the leading Russian writers on music of his generation and the author of two novels on musical subjects.

likely that he now had a more urgent use for alcohol than as a stimulus to creation, or even as a way of keeping warm in cold weather; for it seems probable that he was increasingly in need of it as an anaesthetic. Though his basically strong constitution prolonged his life for another ten years the seeds of his fatal illness (cancer of the rectum) were already sown and he must, from now onwards, have suffered a great deal.

About this time, Percherette moved back to St. Petersburg, where she continued to teach with success, as well as to appear occasionally in concerts. Although she did much to carry on the 'tradition' of Field's style, there is no evidence that they met again, or that she visited Moscow while Field was there. In spite of this, Field never forgot her, and he carried a miniature of her about with him until the end of his life. Not that she, or even Mlle Charpentier, were the last women in his life by any means, though we know nothing specific of the others, unless perhaps they included Agate Goedike, a young musician of outstanding ability whom Field praised extravagantly, saying that she was not only his best pupil (he said that about several others) but that she was the best musician he knew. Agate actually moved into one of Field's two Moscow flats in 1827, and remained there for several months—an arrangement which must have raised a good many eyebrows at the time, though perhaps it was only her rather daring way of ensuring that she had plenty of lessons before she made her début. In later years she had much success, and she, too, did a great deal to perpetuate the essentials of Field's style. It was shortly before Agate's arrival on the scene that Field once more failed to appear at a concert through being too drunk to find his way to the hall. The search party sent out for him on this occasion found him lying in the snow, and rescued him only just in time to save him from being frozen to death. Certainly Agate, who was only nineteen, must have been a courageous as well as an unconventional young woman.

For some years Field had been thinking about the possibility of visiting London once more, though, as always, he found it extremely difficult to come to a decision about the matter. He had several reasons for wishing to go to Western Europe, the state of his health being the most urgent. Medicine in Russia was still in a primitive condition, and though he had the services of a compatriot, Dr. James Quinlan,[1] until the latter's death in 1826, he does not appear to have derived much benefit from his treatment,

[1] Cf. 'James Quinlan, formerly surgeon-general to the Czar of Russia, 1826'. An historical note by J. McAuliffe Curtin, F.R.C.S.I., I.r. *J.Med.Sc.*, pp. 7–15, 1967.

or from that of the various quacks he also consulted. In London or Paris he had a better chance of finding a cure, for the English and French medical schools were, at that time, the most advanced in the world.

Field had another reason for wishing to go to London. His father had died during his years in Russia, but his mother was still alive, and he had a great wish to see her again. He had never lost touch with her, and since his father's death he had sent her an annual pension of 2,000 roubles.[1]

Field evidently discussed the idea of going to London quite freely with his friends for the news of his intention got about, and eventually it reached the Russian correspondent of the *Allgemeine Musikalische Zeitung*, who at once sent off a report to Leipzig. In its issue for January, 1828, the paper announced that 'The famous pianist, John Field, has decided at last to visit his native [*sic*] land—England. He goes first to St. Petersburg, then either by sea straight to London, or, more likely, firstly to Germany . . . next Spring he begins his journey.'

But for one reason or another, the scheme was given up, and another three years passed during which he seems to have been almost entirely inactive. He gave an occasional concert (A. Y. Bulgakov, writing to his brother on October 26th, 1828, mentioned that 'tomorrow night Mozref, a Persian prince, will attend Field's concert in the palace of Prince Dimitri Galitzin, Governor of Moscow'), but he wrote nothing, and presumably lived on the proceeds of such teaching as his health still allowed him to do. That he *was* teaching at this time we know from a short note, rather curt in tone, which he sent to one of his pupils, a Mlle de Stancar, and which has somehow been preserved:

> Mademoiselle, je suis tres fache que M. votre père et vous même soyez malade, vous pouvez venez Mardi à 5 heures, si vous venez à 6 vous trouverez Mlle Chilighiroff, si vous venez à 7 vous vous trouverez avec M. Tal. Mes respect à vos parents, votre devoué John Field.
>
> N'avez vous point de nouvel de Leon?

There is also evidence that Field continued to enjoy one of his favourite relaxations—playing the viola in an amateur string quartet. Field's Sunday chamber music parties are mentioned by several of his earliest

[1] This information is given in an obituary of Field which appeared in the Russian periodical *Khudoshestvyenaya Gazyeta* (Artistic Newspaper) in 1837. The obituary is signed 'T', and it is not known who was the writer. It is, however, remarkably well informed about many details of his last visit to Western Europe and must have been written by someone who knew Field well in his later years.

biographers, and though the names of his quartet-playing colleagues are not recorded they may well have included certain string players who are known to have been among his intimate friends. Among these were the violinists, I. Grassi (a Piedmontese who led the orchestra of Moscow's Bolshoi Theatre for many years) and I. A. Naruishkin, as well as several 'cellists, such as the brilliant amateur, Count M. Y. Vielhorsky, and two Frenchmen, Marcou and Fensil. Though Field is known to have been a capable violinist (his valuable Stainer violin, which he acquired before he left England, was bought by his pupil, Villoing, after his death. It was last heard of in Finland in 1920) he preferred the viola when playing quartets. On at least one occasion (it was in 1829) he even played in an orchestra at a charity concert, a fact recorded in the columns of the Moscow *Ladies Journal*. We catch a glimpse of him in the same year, driving through the streets of Moscow in what seems to have been very inclement weather for the time of year (May): 'Yesterday I met Field. He drove in his great bearskin coat and a hat of Persian fur';[1] but it seems likely that during the following year he was seriously ill, for a rumour of his death was in circulation, and pretty generally believed. Field himself is said to have prompted its contradiction in the Berlin paper *Iris im Gebiete der Tonkunst* which published the following paragraph on April 18th, 1831:

> In December of last year there was spread about a rumour of the death of John Field which was without foundation. The great piano-forte virtuoso still lives, and if he can overcome his depression and apathy ... the rest of Europe may not be obliged to renounce the happiness of hearing ... this extraordinary pianist.

Similar announcements soon appeared in the British and French press, by which time Field's arrangements for his long journey to England were well in hand, which suggests at least the possibility that both the rumour and contradiction of his death may have been a clever piece of advance publicity for his proposed reappearance in Western Europe.

Before leaving Moscow, Field made two farewell appearances, both of them in the role of assisting artist. On the first occasion a Moscow critic wrote: 'In this concert our one and only Field played. What a pity that this distinguished artist so seldom gives us the pleasure of his playing, and long ago ceased to compose ...' The other concert was a benefit for an artist named Charpentier, and it is safe to assume that this was the boy Leon. What Leon played is not recorded, but Field, on this occasion,

[1] From a letter written by A. Y. Bulgakov.

played the Adagio and Rondo from Hummel's A flat Concerto and, in the words of a Moscow critic, he played '. . . inimitably. The fluency, equality and clearness, the strength and brilliance of his touch place Field in the first position among European pianists. We have been able to hear all the best pianists of the present day, and all of them must give place to Field . . .' From such comments as these it is clear that his playing had in no way deteriorated during his years of semi-retirement.

Field was to leave Moscow on April 15th, 1831, and as the state of his health made it imperative for him to have a travelling companion, it was decided that Leon Charpentier should go with him. Leon, though still only sixteen, must by now have shown some signs of the vocal gifts that were to make him famous in later years, and a visit to Western Europe would give him an opportunity to study singing in France or Italy.

The travellers went first to St. Petersburg and remained there for several weeks. Moscow's musical world was still buzzing with rumours about Field, and the latest was that he had reached England only to fall ill again and die almost at once. Someone had heard that the boy, Leon Charpentier, had written the sad news home from London; somebody else thought that perhaps Leon had returned alone to Moscow; nobody seemed quite sure of the facts of the matter. Andrey Bulgakov reported it all in a letter of August 3rd to his brother Konstantin in St. Petersburg, and Konstantin replied: 'So Field has died. I met him here in the summer, walking abstractedly through the town. I pitied him; a great talent—we shall not have such a one again . . .' But once more rumour lied: Field had not died; he had in fact only recently left St. Petersburg, having waited there until he could obtain berths on the new passenger steamer, the *Nikolai I*, which was to inaugurate a regular passage service between St. Petersburg and Lübeck early in the summer. It was a month or so before Moscow knew the truth, as we learn from the gossiping correspondence of the Bulgakov family. On October 1st Andrey Bulgakov wrote to Konstantin about a mutual friend who had just died, and said 'he did not revive, like Field—about which everyone is laughing here; Shchebrin tells me that he is giving lessons quite happily in London to Princess Vorontsova'.

It has sometimes been suggested that during the weeks which he spent in St. Petersburg, *en route* for London, Field was reunited, for the first time since the child's infancy, with his son Adrien, now aged twelve. In the intervening years, Percherette had given Adrien a good grounding in piano playing and had also encouraged him to try his hand at composition. In 1829 the boy had already achieved the honour of publication, and this under the wing of none other than Glinka, who published in that year a 'Lyrical Album', containing a number of his own pieces, as well as some by other composers. Among them was a Rondoletto in E flat by the ten-year-old boy, 'composé et dedié à son père, par Adrien Field': a rather pathetic gesture towards the father of whom he can have had no memory. The theory that Field saw Adrien before leaving for England is based on a misinterpretation of a letter written by him in London on February 17th, 1832, to an unknown French pupil. In this letter Field recommends his son to the pupil in question as a deputy teacher 'during his absence'. As we shall see in a later chapter, Field is not referring here to Adrien, who was only thirteen at the time, but to Leon. Adrien was not to re-enter Field's life until it was too late for them to be more to each other than two unhappy beings, linked only by the ties of blood and by their very different sentiments about the woman who had played so large a part in both their lives.

But in 1831 Field still had the daily companionship of Leon, and it was probably for his benefit that their departure for England was delayed until the sailing of the *Nikolai I*. One can imagine the youth's excitement at the prospect of experiencing his first sea voyage in that most modern of inventions, an ocean-going steamship. The *Nikolai I* was in fact an English-built ship of the very latest design, commanded by an English master, Commander P. Black, R.N., and was fitted up with every consideration for comfort, including 'provisions and wines of the best description . . . at fixed and moderate prices'.[1] The wines, at least, will have been very acceptable to Field, and one can only hope that the Baltic Sea was kind to him, and did not add the miseries of sea-sickness to his chronic physical discomforts.

[1] Cf. Gore's *General Advertiser*, June 30th, 1831.

VIII

The Return to London

How FIELD and his son continued their journey once the *Nikolai I* had docked in Lübeck can only be conjectured, but is likely that they travelled the short distance to Hamburg by road, and re-embarked there as soon as they could obtain passages to England. It has been suggested that they did not go immediately to London (suitable berths might not have been available) but that they sailed round the English coast to Liverpool and completed the last lap of their journey by road. Such evidence as there is to support this theory is not convincing, neither is the idea that Field might have been tempted by the relative proximity of Liverpool and Dublin to revisit his birthplace. He would surely have had enough of sea travel and have been only too anxious to reach London without delay.[1]

John Field's return, after an absence of thirty years, was naturally an event of considerable interest to London's music lovers, but it did not bring him the unqualified admiration to which he had always been accustomed in Russia. For one thing, the tastes of the musical world in London were somewhat different from those of Moscow and St. Petersburg. Since the foundation of the London Philharmonic Society in 1813, the public had become used to a fairly high standard of orchestral performance and, as a result, it had come to recognise the real stature of such great

[1] The exact date of Field's arrival in London is not known. That London's musical world expected him before the end of June is evident from the following notice, which appeared in the *Court Journal* of June 11th, 1831: 'The Directors of the Philharmonic Society purpose giving a dinner at the Clarendon Hotel, during the present month, to Paganini; on which occasion Hummel, Ferdinand Ries and Russian Field, will also be invited; it is intended that the guests shall consist only of members of the Philharmonic body.' In view of Field's delayed departure from St. Petersburg it is unlikely that he arrived in London in time to attend this function.

composers as Haydn, Mozart, Beethoven and, more recently, Weber. True, it mistakenly placed Spohr on an almost equal footing with those masters; but though little of Spohr's music is heard today, its seriousness of purpose and its technical fluency and brilliance go some way to explain the reverence accorded to it in England and Germany when it was new.

At the Royal Italian Opera the works of Rossini, Donizetti, Mercadante and the earlier operas of Bellini were all the rage, and such great stars as Malibran, Lablache, Pasta and Sontag had the town at their feet. Occasionally these glamorous singers were to be heard outside their natural territory, the opera house, as when in 1829 the two leading *prime donne* of the season, Malibran and Sontag, sang excerpts from their operatic repertoires (including a duet from Rossini's *Semiramide*) at the last Philharmonic concert of the season. In general, however, musical London was growing increasingly serious-minded, and it liked to form its own judgements, however great might be the fame which an artist had won elsewhere. For instance, during the 1831 season Field's old friend and rival, the celebrated Hummel, had appeared at one of the Philharmonic concerts (it was his first visit to England since 1793);[1] but though he had been greeted with the respect which was his due, he had not aroused any sensational enthusiasm—not nearly as much as had been created by the very youthful Mendelssohn, whose star had first arisen in England in 1829, and had been glowing ever more brightly since that time. During the season of 1832, Mendelssohn was to introduce his new Piano Concerto in G minor, and several of his other works were also to be heard, among them the first performance of the *Hebrides* Overture. Such events as these aroused a good deal more excited anticipation than the return of Field, who, despite his pianistic reputation among connoisseurs, was still not very well known in England as a composer, though since 1815 his works had become familiar throughout the rest of Europe.

Field's principal link with the London of his youth, his old teacher, Clementi, had said his farewells to the public four years previously, and had then retired to Evesham in Worcestershire, to end his days. His place as the doyen of London's musical world was taken by J. B. Cramer (known to his colleagues as 'Glorious John'), and among other leaders of the profession were Moscheles, Cipriani Potter, George Smart, and one of

[1] At one of his London concerts in 1831, Hummel played his four-hand Sonata in A flat (the same work that he had performed with Field in Moscow in 1822) with Henry Field. See page 10, *n.* 1.

Field's earliest pupils, Charles Neate. By all of these, and many more, Field was made welcome; but his first object on reaching London was not to re-establish himself immediately in the city's musical life, but to find a cure for, or at least an alleviation of, his physical ills.

Unfortunately he was foolish enough to allow a London barber (the traditional association of the barber's trade with quack medicine still flourished) to prescribe for his haemorrhoidal troubles, and the drastic treatment (application of *Lapis infernalis*)[1] naturally only worsened his condition. In view of this, and the rumour of his death which was circulating in Moscow at this time, it seems likely that he fell seriously ill soon after his arrival. Undoubtedly he underwent an operation (it was performed by Astley Cooper, the leading English surgeon of the day), from which he must have taken some time to recover; but recover he did, and the operation seems actually to have given him a certain amount of temporary relief.

Field was now fifty, and no longer the handsome, dignified, fair-haired man described by Dubuk. He had changed a great deal, and of the youthful Field only the blue eyes remained unaltered, though even they probably showed tell-tale signs of his hard drinking. His old mother, on seeing him for the first time, stared at him in amazement and exclaimed that he could not possibly be her son. 'Why, your hair is white,' she burst out, 'while mine is still as black as ever.' Poor Field had to take off his shirt and show her a well-remembered birthmark on his shoulder before she could be convinced that he was her John. He must, however, have possessed considerable recuperative powers, for, once he had recovered from the frightful experience of early nineteenth century surgery, he embarked on what was, for him, an unusually busy life. He was probably forced to do even more than he was equal to by a need to earn money, not only for his medical expenses, but also for the care of his aged mother, who was failing rapidly. There was also the question of Leon's singing lessons, which had yet to be arranged.

It is quite possible that Field did not remain in England continuously from September, 1831, until his final departure for the continent a year later, but that he paid a visit to Paris, taking Leon with him, and while there arranged for the youth's singing studies before returning to England by himself. This supposition is based on the letter, already referred to,

[1] According to 'Mayer's Expository Lexicon of the terms Ancient and Modern in Medical and General Science', *Lapis infernalis* was a term used for caustic potash.

which he wrote to an unknown pupil, recommending his son as a substitute piano teacher 'during my absence'. The full text of this letter is as follows:

Mademoiselle, Je suis parti si vîte que je n'avais pas le temps de vous faire mes adieux et en même temps de vous recommander mon fils jusqu'a mon retour, il ne joue pas mal mais il est très bon maître et connait parfaitement les intentions de ma musique et ne prends pas cher 5 francs et vous ne changerez pas de methode. Je serai de retour dans 12 jours. J'ai l'honneur de vous saluer. J. Field.

17de fevrier 1832

This letter was written in England, but as Field wrote in French and mentioned that the young teacher's fee would be five francs a lesson it is not unreasonable to assume that Leon was now in France. The use of the word francs does much to confirm the correctness of this theory.[1]

Field is known to have been present at a concert given by the Royal Academy of Music in the Hanover Square Rooms on December 21st, 1831, at which Sterndale Bennett made his first public appearance as a pianist in Hummel's Concerto in A flat. On leaving the concert room Field remarked to one of the Academy staff 'that little fellow knows all about it'—a commendation which was reported to Sterndale Bennett and treasured by him all his life. But Field's own first, and most important concert appearance in England did not take place until February 27th, 1832, when he appeared at the opening concert of the Philharmonic Society's season.

Some idea of the seemingly casual way in which such events were organised in Field's day is illustrated by the curiously vague arrangements which were made for his participation in the concert. The idea was first mooted at a meeting of the Philharmonic Society's committee on January 25th, when Charles Neate proposed that Field should be invited to play at the February concert, his proposal being seconded by William Dance and carried unanimously. But the invitation cannot have been conveyed to Field in writing, for on February 11th he accidentally met Sir George Smart, and mentioned that he was not sure if he was expected to play on the 27th or not. Smart immediately reported this to the committee, and on

1 Field states that he will 'return' in twelve days time. He may or may not have carried out this intention. Nothing is known of his movements between February 27th and March 29th, 1832.

Monday, February 13th, William Watts, the society's Honorary Secretary, sent an anxious note round to Field's apartment at Beaufort Buildings, in the Strand:

Dear Sir,

The Directors of the Philharmonic Society request to know whether they may rely on the favour of your performance at the concert of the 27th inst. by a line at your earliest convenience. They trust you will excuse the apparent anxiety upon the subject, Sir George Smart having mentioned his meeting you on Saturday when you expressed yourself in some doubt whether you were expected to play or not on that night.

I remain dear sir,
Yours very truly,
W. Watts.
J. Field. Feb 13th 1832.

The bearer probably waited for an answer, for Field's scrawled reply was despatched the same evening.

J. Field presents his compts. to Mr Watts and begs to state that nothing in his power shall prevent his having the honor of playing at the Philharmonique concert of the 27th inst. If Mr Watts will inform Mr Field the hour the rehearsal takes place he will much oblige.

No. 6 Beaufort Buildings.
Monday Ev. 13 of Feb. 1832.

The recollections of Charles Kensington Salaman, who was present at the rehearsal (in those days the immensely long programmes of the Philharmonic concerts were given on one rehearsal only), describe the scene: 'It was an interesting spectacle to witness his [Field's] cordial reception by the most celebrated musicians of the day whose names now belong to history. His coarse outward appearance gave no indication of his musical genius. He disregarded the habits of social life and was careless in all things . . .'

Field had chosen to play his 4th Concerto in E flat. Though both the work and his playing of it were well received they seemed to many listeners to belong to an older style than that of the day. To some, Field's playing recalled that of his teacher, Clementi; to others it seemed rather like that of Cramer; but all admired its elegance, its ease and its smoothness. The concerto, which was quite new to the audience (it was the first and last work of Field to be played at a Philharmonic concert in London), was praised in a rather negative way: '. . . it was not confused

67

in effect . . . it was not over-loaded with unnecessary ornamentation . . .',
etc., and its most successful movement was undoubtedly the second,
which a contemporary critic described as a 'Pastorale', and which he
thought 'exceedingly delicious', mentioning that it 'excited a universal
encore'. One might easily suppose that the piece in question was the
simple but beautiful *Siciliano* which forms the genuine slow movement
of this concerto; but in fact Field appears to have substituted for the
Siciliano a revised version of his early Pastorale in A major (it had originally been printed in 1811, as part of his *Deuxième Divertissement*); for the
piece was published by Collard later in the year as 'The Much Admired
Pastorale for the piano forte / As played by the author at the / Philharmonic Concert on Monday, 27th, Feby. 1832'. Whether Field played it
unaccompanied or with string quartet can only be guessed, but it was not
unusual for him to put together previously unrelated movements in this
way. What is surprising is his lack of confidence in the success of his G
minor *Siciliano*, since it is one of the most beautiful and touching of his
miniatures.

Early in March, 1832, Clementi died. He was eighty-one, and was in the
fourth year of his retirement at Evesham, Worcestershire. Obituary
notices of the time describe him as having died at a house called 'Elm Lodge',
their writers stating that it was his own property, although perhaps on a
mere assumption. It is curious, however, that Field, who presumably
went down from London to see his old master, told Gebhard later that
he had found Clementi in a lunatic asylum. There is some support for the
idea that Elm Lodge—known locally as 'The Elm'—was not Clementi's
own home, but a place in which he was merely an inmate[1].

At the instigation of the Philharmonic Society, Clementi's body was

[1] The announcement of Clementi's death which appeared in *The Harmonicon* mentioned that he died 'after an illness of short duration, though his mind had for some time
previous been gradually yielding to the attacks of old age'. In 1905, the *Evesham Journal
& Four Shires Advertiser* published a letter written by a Miss Myra Taylor, dated August
1st. Miss Taylor had learned, in the course of a conversation with an old laundress, M. W.,
that she (M. W.) had been living as a young housemaid at 'The Elm' in 1832. Miss
Taylor questioned her about Clementi, and her reply was that she could not remember
the name, but quite well remembered an old Italian suddenly dropping down dead in the
laundry there, and that his body was afterwards taken to London. From what the old
woman said, Miss Taylor gathered that he was staying at the house as a visitor: she did
not think he rented it himself. A cottage formerly stood in the grounds of 'The Elm',
and this was probably the 'Elm Lodge' mentioned in *The Times* of March 13th, 1832,
as Clementi's home.

taken to London, where a public funeral and an interment in Westminster Abbey were arranged for March 29th, 1832. Field was among the many distinguished mourners present (as Clementi's most internationally celebrated pupil he could hardly have been absent), but he must have wished himself elsewhere than at this melancholy ceremony, for his second important concert was to take place the very next day. It was given without orchestra in the Great Concert Room of the King's Theatre, and with the collaboration of various assisting artists, including one of Field's more gifted English pupils, a Miss Jonas, who was entrusted with the revised version of the *Premier Divertissement,* now called for the first time *The Twelve-o'clock Rondo.* This event was immediately followed, on March 31st, by a Haydn Centenary dinner at the Albion Tavern at which nearly a hundred guests were present, all men. The ladies came in after the cloth was removed, and a concert was then given in which Field played Haydn's Variations in F minor, Cramer and Moscheles contributed a sonata each and played a duet, and a specially written ode, set to Haydn's music (selected by Neukomm) was also performed. Certainly a heavy week for Field, who, in poor health and probably without Leon, must, at this time, have been feeling tired and lonely. Doubtless he would have been glad to rejoin his son in Paris immediately, but he had accepted an engagement to give concerts in Manchester during July, and these he could not abandon: he had also to prepare several compositions which were to be brought out by London publishers, some of them mere pot-boilers, based on popular English airs of the day, while others were revised versions of early pieces which had gone down well at his London concerts. The most interesting of these London publications, the Grande Pastorale in E major, was taken from a manuscript which, like the Seventh Concerto, he had carried round with him for a long time, but which he had despaired of being able to finish according to his original intentions. He had planned it as an extended solo with string quartet accompaniment, on the lines of his Quintet in A flat, but he now condensed what he had written of the score and allowed Collard to publish the rather unsatisfactory result as an unaccompanied solo. He dedicated it to the Princess Vorontzova (she was still in London), who must, at this time, have symbolised for him the very different way of life which he had left behind in Russia, perhaps for ever.[1]

[1] At Princess Vorontzova's salon Field may also have met his former patron, Count Orlov, who was then in London on a diplomatic mission.

On May 28th, the twenty-three-year-old Mendelssohn played his own Concerto in G minor at the seventh Philharmonic concert. Its success was so dazzling that he repeated it, by general request, at the following concert on June 18th. The public's memories of Field's Fourth Concerto were sadly dimmed by the brilliance of this new and enchanting music, which, though quite original, could be admired and understood by everybody.

A fortnight after Mendelssohn's arrival in London, he met Field at a dinner given by Moscheles in honour of them both. The party does not appear to have gone particularly well. A memorable evening of music was anticipated by the company invited to meet the celebrated guests, but though, presumably, the host played, he noted in his diary that Field hardly touched the instrument, and that Mendelssohn could not be persuaded to play at all. Mendelssohn's diaries and correspondence make no mention of meeting Field, and we know nothing of Field's impression of Mendelssohn's playing or his music, though he had plenty of opportunities of hearing both while he was in England. Charles Salaman, in his interesting reminiscences, describes a summer afternoon quartet party at Charles Neate's house at which many of the most distinguished foreign musicians then in London were present, among them Field (who ranked as a foreign visitor), Mendelssohn and Moscheles. Mendelssohn was the centre of interest, playing the viola in the quartets (Neate played the 'cello) and rounding off the afternoon's music-making by an unaccompanied performance of his G minor Concerto which won an enthusiastic ovation from all those present. Field merely sat and listened.

Although Moscheles made much of Field while he was in London, inviting him frequently to his house, he did not really like him, and he disapproved strongly of his social behaviour, which he found unpleasantly coarse . . . not at all the sort of thing Mrs. Moscheles was accustomed to in her drawing-room. The Moscheleses seem to have taken particular exception to Field's cynical remarks about Percherette (they evidently knew that Field and his wife had separated), and in general Moscheles felt that 'nothing can afford a more glaring contrast than a Field Nocturne and Field's manners . . .'

Field played once or twice as an assisting artist at concerts in London (early in June he 'assisted' a young musician named Eliason, but the concert received no more than a brief mention in *The Athenaeum*), but his two concerts in Manchester, in July, were his last important appearances in England. He travelled north in the same party with the leading members of Monck Mason's German Opera Company, who were to share the programme with him. What he played in Manchester is not recorded (certainly a concerto, or movements from concertos; that much is discoverable from the reports of the concerts which appeared in the *Manchester Guardian*), but he was evidently in quite good form, for he pleased the audience a great deal more than did the singers, who were rather severely handled by the press. Field's fee of fifty guineas for these concerts does not seem particularly high today, but it was quite generous payment in 1832, and it was certainly the largest fee he received during the whole of his visit to England.

The second of Field's two Manchester concerts took place on July 25th. Six days later his old mother died quite suddenly, and he had the searing experience of finding her dead in bed when he called round to see her at her home in Prince's Street. Grace Field's death occurred in her seventy-eighth year: Field's longed-for reunion with her had lasted for only one year, and now, with her death, his principal reason for remaining in England no longer existed. Probably he had other relations in London—some of his several brothers and sisters with their families; but his ties with them were very slight compared with his feeling for Leon, who, now that Field's mother was dead, was the only being in the world whom he really loved. With unusual celerity he made up his mind to rejoin his son in Paris during the course of the coming winter, and he lost no time in letting the French press know of this intention.

Field's return to the scenes of his youth must have been a disappointment to him. The operation performed by Astley Cooper had made some temporary improvement to his health, but, as he later complained to Gebhard, the great surgeon had advised no dietary regimen (one wonders what he would have said if he had been told to give up drinking and smoking), and by the end of 1832 his physical condition was once again deteriorating. Musically he had enjoyed a certain amount of success, though it had been insignificant by Russian standards; but his earnings from teaching, concerts and publications, even if they kept pace with his personal indulgences and medical expenses, cannot have allowed him to put by much for the future. As he climbed into the London-to-Dover coach, one winter's day in 1832, he can have had few regrets at leaving England, and little reason to modify his rather sour feelings about the English, whose somewhat moderate enthusiasm over his reappearance can only have confirmed his unfavourable opinion of them. In France, surrounded by a people who had always been particularly sympathetic to him, and where he already had many friends and admirers, he hoped for better things.

IX

A Season in Paris

೭ঔ৩৫

Fɪᴇʟᴅ's ᴄᴏɴᴄᴇʀᴛs in Paris took place at a moment when the art of piano playing was turning into new paths of development. Paradoxically, this change of direction was partly due to the influence of the great violinist, Paganini, whose astounding playing had taken Paris by storm in the spring of 1831 and had inspired the young Liszt, among many others, to emulate its fantastic virtuosity. Equally important had been the successful Paris debut, in 1831, of the twenty-one-year-old Chopin, which had set him at once in the forefront of his profession. Chopin, like Liszt, had been stimulated by the art of Paganini, whom he had heard in Warsaw in 1829; but Chopin's early works, despite their striking originality, really owed much more to those of his immediate precursors among the composer-pianists, and above all to Hummel, Moscheles and to Field himself, certain of whose characteristics Chopin absorbed into his style and transmuted by the power of his genius into something wholly personal.

It was such musicians as Liszt and Chopin, with Alkan, Berlioz, Meyerbeer and their colleagues of the sister arts, who were creating in the Paris of the 1830s an artistic climate which greatly favoured the growth of a new and more extreme kind of romanticism, in which the boundaries of taste, emotion and technique were all in the process of being greatly enlarged. To many artists of the older generation this new movement was uncongenial. Some, like Rossini, withdrew from the lists entirely, preferring to rest upon laurels already won; others, such as Cherubini, after closely observing the new developments, firmly rejected them, and held fast to what they felt to be the more important truths and values of tradition. It was a familiar situation, and one which regularly recurs.

Field belonged to the older generation, but until his return to London he can scarcely have been aware of the most recent developments in the musical tastes of Western Europe, and he must have been surprised and pained to find his art considered rather *passé*. And if London found him old-fashioned it was hardly likely that Paris, filled as it was with all the most *avant-garde* spirits of the day, would be thrown into transports of enthusiasm by the quiet poetry of his music and the lack of showmanship in his playing. Nevertheless, his concerts were anticipated with eager curiosity by the Parisian musical world. Chopin himself was agog to hear Field, who had been a legend to him all his life, and to whom he had often been compared. As early as the previous August, in a letter to Ferdinand Hiller, we find him mentioning that Maurice Schlesinger, the publisher and owner of the very influential *Gazette Musicale*, had brought back from London the news that Field was to be expected in Paris during the winter. Very soon *le tout Paris* was reading advance publicity for Field's concerts in the *Gazette's* columns.

Either shortly before he left Russia or during the year he spent in London, Field had finally managed to complete the score of his Seventh Concerto, and it was with this, his latest and last major work, that he was to make his début in Paris. He had played the first movement of the concerto in Moscow ten years before, but for a long time he had been unable to find either the ideas or the energy to compose its finale. Now that the concerto was finished he was rather uncertain about its value, but he knew that Paris expected novelties, and that a first performance would attract a large public to his first concert. In this he judged correctly, for the great *Salle du Conservatoire* was crammed to its fullest capacity, and the audience included so many pianists, piano teachers and composers that there seemed hardly any room for the general public.

The impression made by Field's playing on that Christmas Day of 1832 seems to have been generally very favourable, despite the reservations of some of his younger rivals. The critic of the *Revue de Paris*, who evidently knew what to expect from Field, went to the concert in a slightly sceptical mood, unprepared to be moved by the artist's simplicity and lack of glitter; but he, as well as the majority of the audience, was completely won over. 'In Field's music,' he wrote, 'you find no "noise", no wild thundering—none of the pretensions of a charlatan. So, for his great art, cheap admiration is not enough. It seems strange to attach so much importance to a simple charming melody . . . [we] must hide our enthusiasm for these simple things lest we seem vulgar, and spare our excitement for another kind of music which makes us grind our teeth and makes our hair stand on end [was this sarcasm directed at Paganini and Liszt?] . . .

fortunately . . . this time the public was honest; it enjoyed the music, the great talent and art.' The celebrated critic, Fétis, writing in the *Revue Musicale*, admitted that Field 'lacked the strength of the modern school', but recorded that his elegant style and beautiful *cantabile* were greatly admired, and that 'an enthusiasm impossible to describe, a veritable delirium, was manifested by the audience after the performance of the concerto'. Fétis, in this review, described the Seventh Concerto as 'full of charm', but here he was not being really sincere; he did not really think it a good work. Indeed, on a later occasion he maintained that it was quite unworthy of Field, and only redeemed by his beautiful playing of the solo part. The criticism is justified, for notwithstanding the delightful episode in G major which, though incorporated into the first movement, does duty for a slow movement, and some fine passages in the opening *Allegro moderato*, the concerto as a whole fails to convince. The finale, in waltz rhythm, is particularly weak, though, oddly enough, it was this movement which most charmed Schumann when he reviewed the work in the *Neue Zeitschrift für Musik*, in 1837. According to the *Revue de Paris*, the concerto's success, or at least Field's playing of it, was so great that the 'tremendous applause made the hall tremble in the general excitement of the public. And still more—the Adagio had to be repeated—a very rare happening.' Another critic, Joseph d'Ortigue, who attended all three of Field's Paris concerts, found more to praise in the concerto than his colleagues did. He even admired its orchestration. 'It is', he wrote, 'not less distinguished for the instrumentation than for the novelty of the melody. Scoring has long been considered as a subordinate part in concertos. All attention is held by the principal instrument. However, some great symphonists, who were also celebrated virtuosi, have known how to create a very successful accompaniment part, written with understanding of the various orchestral accents, and the effect of string and wind instruments cleverly managed, in the accompaniment of solos. In this respect the concertos of Beethoven, Paganini and Field must be set together.' Joseph d'Ortigue's astonishing bracketing together of these three names is a reflection on his critical powers: yet one must make some allowance for the effect of novelty.[1] Certainly it must have been surprising to hear, for the first time, the percussion effects in Paganini's concertos, and such

[1] It must not be forgotten that Schumann, when reviewing Chopin's Concerto in F minor, in 1836, wrote, 'His [Chopin's] teachers had been the best—Beethoven, Schubert and Field.'

passages as that to which d'Ortigue calls attention in Field's concerto, where 'one is astonished to hear, in the middle of a pianissimo, a burst of trumpets which produces an unexpected effect; strange, because it is not at all terrifying, but seems, on the contrary, a far-off voice floating in the air'. This critic, unlike those in London, felt that Field could not be compared with any of his rivals, either as to type or method. 'He is not of any recognised system, he is of no school—not that of Dussek, nor that of Clementi, nor that of Steibelt. Field is Field. It is a natural and original talent. All the ordinary mechanical procedures seem to disappear in his style of playing. It is full of carefree and good-humoured wit, and withal a precision and a surprising aplomb, grace and poetry. Field sits quite simply at the piano, as if at his own fireside. He makes no preparatory gestures, as do so many of our artists [this tells us that Liszt was far from being the only pianistic showman about Paris at that time]. In the first bars one is tempted to find his hand heavy, then suddenly the playing becomes agile, delicate, and of incredible cleanness in passages of extreme volubility. He remains little animated—in short he is cool, but this coolness is an essential part of his art.'

All this is enthusiastic praise, but there were some dissentient voices. Chopin, who attended Field's Conservatoire concert, seems to have been disappointed, if we are to believe his friend, Eduard Wolff. Wolff wrote that Chopin found in Field's playing, 'No speed, no elegance', and considered that he was 'incapable of executing difficulties: in a word, feeble'. But this youthfully intolerant criticism may be assumed to be as much the opinion of Wolff as that of Chopin, who left no written account of his impressions of Field. Liszt, not surprisingly, found Field's playing 'sleepy', and 'lacking in vitality', though he appreciated its marvellous fluency and limpidity of tone; while Fétis, who, as we have seen, admired Field's art with more understanding than most critics of the time, nevertheless allowed himself to say that 'perhaps if M. Field were twenty-five we would be more exigent towards him in asking him to add to the qualities which he possesses to such an eminent degree, those which we like to find in other pianists—that is to say, verve and animation'. Verve and animation were, perhaps, never the most remarkable qualities of Field's art (though Glinka thought otherwise, and strongly disagreed with Liszt's opinion), but it was evidently only in comparison with the new style of the younger generation of pianists that Field's playing seemed pale in tone and lacking in excitement.

Field, for his part, was even less appreciative of the art of his younger colleagues than they of his. He attended one of Liszt's recitals, and, after staring in amazement at the young virtuoso's ferocious onslaught on the keyboard, remarked audibly to a neighbour, 'Does he bite?'—a quip which went the round of the Paris salons and greatly displeased Liszt's numerous partisans. Liszt's great rival, Thalberg, did not arrive in Paris until 1835, and Field never heard him play. He knew some of Thalberg's music, however, and dismissed it with the words: 'It takes longer to learn to play such stuff than to write it.'

Field's apparently derogatory remarks about Chopin need rather more careful consideration than they have yet been given. If he was asked his opinion of Chopin's compositions shortly after his arrival in Paris his celebrated reply, 'Chopin? What has he written? Nothing but mazurkas!' is perfectly comprehensible; for in fact the only works which Chopin had published before 1833 were the Variations on *La ci darem la mano*, the Introduction and Polonaise for cello and piano, the Trio Op. 8 (which might not have come Field's way), two rondos—the second of them *à la mazur*—and nine Mazurkas (Op. 6. and Op. 7). Field's other comment on Chopin as a 'sick-room talent' has nothing to do with Chopin's state of health, as has sometimes been suggested (Chopin was perfectly well during the few months of 1833 when Field was in Paris), and must therefore reflect his opinion of Chopin's early music after he had heard rather more of it. Chopin's adoption of Field's invention, the nocturne, and what may have seemed to be his crib of one of Field's own works (the Romance in E flat) in his Nocturne, Op. 9 No. 2, in the same key, may well have irritated the older composer, who in any case will have found the Etudes, Op. 10 and the Concerto, Op. 11, if he ever looked at them, exaggeratedly difficult to play and harmonically very over-wrought. To bracket Field's remark with Berlioz's famous 'sneer', made after Chopin's death, 'he was dying all his life', is absurd: Field himself was dead before Chopin's health showed signs of serious deterioration.

Curiously enough the youngest generation of Parisian musicians, the students of the Conservatoire, usually the most intolerant of all critics, appears to have conceived a greater reverence for Field than anyone else. Four pupils of Zimmerman, a leading teacher at the Conservatoire since 1811, headed by Alphonse Marmontel (later to take Zimmerman's place at the Conservatoire), called on Field at his hotel, armed with a letter of introduction from their teacher. Marmontel, who was sixteen at the time, had created in his imagination a 'fantasy' Field, suggested to him by the charming and poetic works of the Irish master, and liked to think of him not only as the forerunner of Chopin (which in some respects he was) but as similar to him in physiognomy and social elegance. The astonishment and disillusion of the boys when at last they came face to face with Field can be imagined. Marmontel related how they found him 'sitting in an armchair, an enormous pipe in his mouth, and surrounded by bottles of every kind! His head rather large, his cheeks reddened, his features somewhat heavy, giving him a Falstaffian appearace. However, despite his morning tipsiness Field made us welcome, read Zimmerman's letter, and generously offered to play us something; two studies of Cramer and Clementi, executed with rare perfection and an admirable finish allowed us to appreciate the marvellous agility of his fingers, and the delicately exquisite touch of the great virtuoso. When we said our farewells he gave us several tickets [it sounds as if they were not selling very well] for his next concert . . . we left, enchanted by the artist, but with sad impressions of the man.'

Alphonse Marmontel's recollections of Field's playing are particularly precise, as is always the case with the memories of one's youth. He recalled that it possessed quite an individual quality. 'By his expressive touch and extreme delicacy,' he wrote, 'Field obtained sonorities of exquisite colour. His lightness in rapid passages was incomparable; singing phrases took on, under his fingers, a sweet and tender feeling that few virtuosi are able to achieve. Under a rough exterior Field must have possessed great depth of sensibility, for his music is full of charm, of delicacy and of "heart".' Marmontel relates an anecdote about Field's lack of *savoir-faire* in society which makes it clear that in this respect he was still the same disorganised Bohemian as the young man of twenty-five years before, so well described by Louise Fusil. Invited one evening to a soirée at the house of the Duchesse Descazes, he arrived with his dress in disarray, and wearing shoes that were too tight for him. It was an important occasion for Field: the flower of the Faubourg St. Germain filled the salon, and a good impression might have brought him valuable social introductions. Unfortunately the heat in the salon grew so intense that poor Field's feet soon became extremely uncomfortable: so, unconventional as ever, he simply removed his shoes. A moment later the Duchesse was leading him to the piano, where, in spite of giggles and whispers from the more sharp-eyed among the guests, his beautiful playing was warmly applauded. Russian society had long ago accepted Field's vagaries of dress and behaviour, but in the rather stuffy atmosphere of Louis-Philippe's Paris it was necessary for an artist who hoped to find his principal source of income among the élite to have, at least in public, the bearing and distinction of a man of breeding. These attributes Field completely lacked, and it was probably this, more than his unwillingness to compete with the fashionable young virtuosi of the day on their own terms, which prevented him from following up his initial success at the Conservatoire, and led him to terminate his stay in Paris and embark on a long and fatiguing concert tour through Southern Europe in the hope of finding the health and success which still eluded him.

Before leaving, however, Field was heard twice more in public, both times in the large concert room attached to the piano showrooms of Pape, whose instruments he invariably used while he was in Paris. At these concerts he played solo pieces (including a repeat performance, without orchestra, of his Seventh Concerto), and his Quintet in A flat, in which he was joined by a quartet led by the ubiquitous Baillot, who was one of the mainstays of Parisian concert life for half a century. He was also heard in some chamber music by other composers, including a sonata for violin and piano by Dussek, in which his partner was again Baillot. Although he was well received at these concerts, he did not repeat the success he had enjoyed at the Conservatoire, and, in fact, he was somewhat outshone by one of his assisting artists, the flautist, Drouet, whose playing, according to d'Ortigue, 'was accorded a frenetic enthusiasm'.

The only moderate success of these chamber concerts was partly offset by a short sortie to Brussels, where, on February 27th, he was wildly applauded by a large audience in the *Salle du Grand Concert*. In the announcement of this concert which appeared in the newspaper, *Le Belge*, Field was described, quite incorrectly, as 'Maître de Chapelle de l'Empereur de Russie', a post actually held at that time by F. P. Lvov. The *Journal de Belgique* praised his playing with all the now familiar adjectives, and, perhaps as the result of the publicity given to the occasion, he received, shortly afterwards, a 'royal command' from Leopold I to play to the Belgian court on March 11th. This resulted in a useful present of 1,200 francs 'in gratitude for the pleasure his playing had given the royal party'— a more immediately acceptable gift than the rings and enamelled snuffboxes with which royalty, in those days, usually paid their entertainers. As neither George IV of England nor Louis-Philippe invited Field to play to them, this seems to be the only occasion when he appeared at the court of a reigning monarch. It is to be hoped that there were friends at hand to see that, for once, he was properly turned out for the occasion.

Field remained in Paris until the end of May, and it was probably at this time that he turned for medical help to the celebrated French surgeon, Baron Dupuytren. Nothing is known of Dupuytren's advice to Field, but he evidently placed great reliance on the famous doctor, for two years later, when they were both in Italy, he made the journey from Milan to Florence specially so that he might consult him again.

It would be interesting to know whether Field renewed his old friendship with Louise Fusil during his stay in Paris. She had not yet published her memoirs, wherein she writes only of Field as she knew him during his Moscow years with Percherette, though this does not mean that they cannot have met again while he was in France. Poor Louise was at this time mourning the loss of her adopted daughter, a little orphan child whom she had rescued in Vilna during the French retreat from Moscow, and had brought back with her to France. She had trained the child as an actress, and had seen her make a successful debut; but 'la petite orphaline de Vilna' had died in the cholera epidemic which was ravaging Europe at this time, leaving her foster-mother inconsolable. Since 1812, both Field and Louise had suffered much, but they also shared memories of happier days, and it would not have been surprising if they had met to reminisce about the past.

In one respect Field was luckier than Louise Fusil; he still had his beloved Leon for companionship, and Leon's youth and vigour must have been of great value to them both during the difficulties and anxieties which now lay before them.

Before he left Paris, a farewell dinner was given in Field's honour by Fétis.[1] The names of the guests are not recorded, but since Fétis knew everybody of importance they would have included many of the most distinguished musicians in the city at that time. Stimulated by his favourite French champagne (Field once said jocularly that he only decided to leave Russia because the imported French champagne was becoming too expensive), he doubtless enjoyed himself: he had always liked convivial evenings when he could listen, laugh, and not be forced to struggle too often with

[1] The farewell dinner party given in Field's honour before his departure from Paris in 1833 is first mentioned in the obituary article, signed 'T', which is the source of several interesting facts about Field's European tour in 1831–5. See page 59, *n*. 1.

his frustrating stammer; and perhaps he was able momentarily to delude himself that his retreat from Paris was not really the admission of another failure, and to forget for a while that as an artist time was passing him by.

X

A Concert Tour ends in Disaster

❦

THE LIFE of an early-nineteenth-century touring virtuoso, while in some respects no more exhausting than that experienced by his successors of the present day, required him to have a physical stamina strong enough to withstand the taxing strain of what were, by modern standards, very severe travelling conditions. It was also necessary for him to possess the tact of a professional diplomat, considerable organising ability and a ready eye for opportunities of quick advertisement, for the age of the impresario had yet to arrive. Usually an artist travelled alone and, except in rare instances, he did so unheralded by advance publicity. Only the main outlines of a tour could be planned ahead: a few letters would be written, introductions collected (these were often of great importance), and the artist was then ready to set off in search of fame and fortune.

Most artists of that time travelled by the network of public diligences which connected the principal cities of Europe, and on arrival at every destination it was necessary to lose no time in setting about the preparations for a concert—presenting the letters of introduction, obtaining the use of a hall (usually a theatre) and sometimes the services of an orchestra as well, finding an adequate piano and inserting publicity in the local press. Programme details were usually left until the last minute, but printing in those days was done very quickly, often overnight. There could be little rehearsal, if any, and almost the last thing a concert-giver had time for was the quiet, concentrated preparation of his programme. However, instrumentalists were not yet expected to perform from memory, and most virtuosi possessed a small but trusted repertoire on which they could always rely; and as more than one concert was seldom given in the same town, frequent changes of programme were unnecessary. Furthermore, the solo recital was still unknown (it was the invention of Liszt, who first began

82

to give such concerts during the 1840s), and the principal performer made only two or three appearances, flanked by assisting artists, who might be professional colleagues but were sometimes only local amateurs. In the absence of an orchestra, a virtuoso pianist, however celebrated, usually played all the accompaniments, as well as his solos, and apparently lost no prestige by doing so. Pianists still sat with their backs to the audience (again it was Liszt who first presented his profile to the auditorium), and in a theatre, particularly when playing with orchestra, this sometimes meant that they had to sit on the prompter's box, which, in those days, projected a good deal higher above the stage than it does now. This could be a hazardous arrangement, as young Clara Wieck discovered when a rocky prompter's box nearly precipitated her on the floor during the swinging, cross-handed passages of a Scarlatti sonata.

Lighting, heating, the distribution and collection of orchestral parts, the sale of tickets—all such minor matters were also the concern of the concert-giver, and took up much of his time, thought and energy. An artist of established reputation could, however, make a lot of money by touring; for the receipts from his concerts would be net profit, once the expenses of printing and hiring had been paid (the assisting artists usually gave their services without payment),[1] and he generally stayed in a town long enough to give some lessons, and perhaps to make one or two paid appearances at private soirées before moving on. Sometimes, after a very successful benefit concert a second might be announced, but it would still be given at the artist's own risk. Paid engagements at public concerts were extremely rare. To perform for the London Philharmonic Society, in the Paris Conservatoire Concerts or at the Leipzig Gewandhaus was considered reward and advertisement enough in itself, and the fifty pounds paid to Field in Manchester was something quite out of the ordinary.[2] But in 1833 Field's name was so well known in Europe that he could be sure of drawing full houses in most of the large towns on his itinerary, and the venture was not a financial risk for him while he possessed the necessary strength to withstand the strain of travelling and for the inevitable business preliminaries to every concert.

[1] This was not always the case. A violinist named Kiesewetter once claimed ten guineas from Moscheles for assisting him at a concert. Moscheles was disgusted, and wrote in his diary, 'Of course I agreed, but our friendly relations must henceforth be interrupted.'

[2] Seventeen years later, Chopin received sixty pounds for his concert in Manchester, which was, as he wrote to his family, 'not to be missed'.

At first, all went well. Field arrived in Toulouse early in June, apparently none the worse for the long coach journey from Paris, and at once preparations were set in hand for his concert, which was to be given with orchestra. His ingrained dislike of physical exertion, to say nothing of his uncertain health, would have made it hard for him to have done all that was necessary had he not had the constant assistance of Leon, who, young though he was, must have been an invaluable support to his father throughout the tour. Until very recently, it has always been thought that when Field left Paris in 1833 Leon remained behind to continue his vocal training, but in fact he did no such thing. Leon was to be his father's travelling companion throughout the two years of their wanderings in Southern Europe, and to return to Moscow with him in the winter of 1835.

The concert in Toulouse took place in mid-June and was reported in the *Revue Musicale* on June 22nd. The report mentions that Field played a concerto, a rondo and a polonaise (this last undoubtedly the finale from his Third Concerto) and that the whole of the local *haute monde* flocked to Toulouse's *Salle de l'Athenée*[1] to hear the celebrated virtuoso. He was evidently a great success, for the connoisseurs of Toulouse, as accustomed as those of Paris to pianists who thumped the keys and 'made preparatory gestures', found Field's calm delicacy and freedom from extravagance of any kind a most refreshing change.

But Toulouse is after all a relatively unimportant city: and so, after a pleasant month there, the travellers set off again, this time on the comparatively short journey to Marseilles, a place of considerably more consequence on the itinerary of any touring virtuoso.

In Marseilles, Field was heard twice in public, and applauded with an enthusiasm reminiscent of his early successes in St. Petersburg and in the cities of Courland. As usual, the *Revue Musicale*'s local correspondent rushed off accounts of the concerts to Paris (they appeared in the issue for August 24th); but much more interesting is an anonymous writer's impression of Field and his art which came out in the *Semaphore de Marseilles* (actually a shipping journal) shortly after his arrival there. This eulogy, positively dithyrambic in its praise, was such as few artists ever have the satisfaction of reading about themselves. Unmoved as he was by adulation, Field must surely, for once, have felt some satisfaction on reading

[1] The *Salle de l'Athenée* still exists, but it has come down in the world. After various vicissitudes, it is now a cinema (like the Rotunda in Dublin) and rejoices in the name 'Le Rio'.

such purple patches as 'After music everything is of secondary importance to him: his life is incomplete when he is not creating sounds. At other times Field is only a dreamy, isolated being, a soul struggling for the light he lacks as long as the piano, his sixth sense, is silent. His lack of interest in the world he inhabits, in the fellow beings who pass him by, comes from a momentary absence of that sense alone which has the power to awaken, to exalt, and to stimulate others: but when he sits before his piano, then his fingers caress the keys, then his face awakens, his features shine with a sudden inspiration, he lives, and with an exalted, doubly intense life, with the life of those who conceive and create: his eyes shine as if the angel of music had revealed herself to the good Irishman and opened for him the doors of Heaven . . . I like these men for whom art is a sacred thing, a religion whence come their most intimate thoughts, and to whom life is all study and meditation. Such is our delicious pianist. Ah! do not think that the word delicious was chosen carelessly . . . this word I have chosen from fifty others because it seems to me to be the only one to fit the admirable talent of Field . . . there is in his execution so perfect a delicacy of touch, such suavity of colouring, such expression, such clarity of articulation as one rarely finds even in pianists of the first rank.' The writer then continues, 'After having led one through a chain of tender and dreamy modulations the delicious pianist transports you by degrees, and as if by magic, into celestial spheres unknown to the human ear, and where one almost thinks one overhears the sweet murmuring of women's voices, and really imagines the enchanting tones of Mars and Jenny Vertpré, and of Mademoiselle Sontag . . .'

Field's art had often been compared with that of the great singers, such as Sontag, but the unusual idea that it could suggest the dulcet declamation of such celebrated French tragediennes as Mars and Vertpré allows the writer to reach a flowery conclusion in which he (or perhaps she) named Field 'The Racine of the Piano'. For all its various extravagances, this article reflects the immense enthusiasm which Field's playing inspired in France's second city. It also includes an interesting and entertaining pen-portrait of Field as he appeared to the Marseillais, his 'beautiful head, well poised, with a broad brow crowned by strong locks of carelessly floating white hair, the features clearly marked and filled with gentleness and good humour; bright, witty eyes, the dress generally neglected—and you have an approximate idea of Field's appearance. But what, to my taste, makes him interesting, what indicates in him the man of genius, is his unconquerable abstraction, his air of distant preoccupation and sublime vagueness. Invite Field to your soirée, gather together many guests, and you may be sure that the artist will be conscious neither of you nor of the assembled company. If he is polite, it will be the politeness of convention, of habit, or rather of a wish to please; if you talk to him he will reply, but his soul will perhaps be far away, and at the moment when you think he is impressed by your eloquence he will actually be deafer than ever.' Was this a description of Field's behaviour at a particular party? One certainly has the impression that on such social occasions it was as well to get him to the piano and keep him there as long as possible. There can, however, be no doubt of his success in Marseilles, and of the reluctance with which he was allowed to depart at the end of August.

A short journey up the Rhône valley brought Field to Lyons, where he played twice, and received, according to the *Courrier de Lyon*, 'un triple salve d'applaudissements' from full houses. But here he did not linger, preferring to move on immediately to Geneva, where his arrival, announced in the *Journal de Genève*, on September 14th, was described as 'having been awaited with impatience by all music-lovers'.

A fortnight elapsed before the arrangements for his concert in Geneva were completed, but on September 28th the following announcement appeared in the same paper: 'Lundi, 30 Septembre 1833 aura lieu à 7 heures dans la salle du Casino, un concert, vocal et instrumentale, donné par John Field, Pianiste du Russie.' The long programme, given in full, included, as well as a couple of overtures and some songs and clarinet solos (contributions by local assisting artists), Field's Sixth Concerto, the Nocturne[1] and Rondo from his Third Concerto and, as a concluding item, *Pastorale et Rondo intitulé 'Midi'*, *avec accompagnement de quatuor*, this last being yet another version, condensed and rescored, of movements from the two early *Divertissements*. The concert was reviewed in both the leading Genevan papers, the *Journal de Genève* and the *Federal*, and Field's playing was showered with the usual flattering adjectives—delicate, finished, sweet, gracious, suave, etc. Shortly afterwards he appeared as an assisting artist at a concert of the young violinist, Heinrich Ernst, whose acquaintance he had made in Paris earlier in the year. The participation of

[1] The Third Concerto does not contain a nocturne. Field evidently preceded the Rondo movement with a performance of one of his solo nocturnes, though he may have used the version with orchestral accompaniment (still unpublished) of his Fifth Nocturne, in B flat.

such a celebrated assisting artist must have done much to promote the sale of tickets for Ernst's concert, and it is a characteristic example of Field's readiness to help a young artist whose talent he admired.

One does not have the impression that the strain of the tour, considerable though it must have been, had, so far, further undermined Field's health. Not enough, anyway, to affect his playing. Furthermore he seems to have been able, during his stay in Switzerland, to indulge in a certain amount of sightseeing, as we learn from one of his few surviving letters—a short, hurriedly-written note which he addressed to a talented Genevan historian, Jacques-Augustine Galiffe Pictet (also known as James Galiffe):

My Dear Sir

Me and my boy are going to morrow to Mont-blanc, it will take us two days at our return I shall have the pleasure of dining with you and of seeing your Lady, it will be then on Monday I shall have the pleasure of seeing my very good friend.

yours truly
J. Field

Did not you live at Baron Ball?

87

This little note, its faults only too typical of its writer, is clear evidence that Leon was travelling with Field. That it is written, however crudely, in English is curious; but Field may have known Galiffe during his earliest years in London (the Swiss was there in 1798), or later, during a visit which Galiffe paid to St. Petersburg some time between 1805 and 1812, and perhaps they had always been in the habit of communicating in English.[1]

Field may have been well enough for a two-day jaunt to Mont-blanc, but now he had to undertake a journey which, for a man in his condition, must have been much more testing. The shortest route from Geneva to Milan included the unavoidable crossing of the Simplon Pass, and with winter approaching, delay might be dangerous. Mendelssohn, who had crossed the Simplon in 1830, had quite enjoyed the adventure, but he was then a healthy young man of twenty-one, and he travelled in July. In November, when Field was carried up into the Simplon's bitter winds and fearsome icefields, the journey could be a traveller's nightmare, as we know from the vivid account of its hazards and discomforts left us by Charles Dickens, who used the route for his journey from Italy ten years after Field. Dickens's experiences give us some idea of what the effect of the Simplon crossing must have been on a man in Field's physical condition, exhausted as he was by many years of painful illness and by a recent period of great and unwonted activity. He survived the journey without collapsing, but it was from this moment that his health seems to have taken a turn for the worse.

Field's arrival in Milan was mentioned on November 16th, in the somewhat oddly named Milanese journal, *Il Barbiere di Siviglia*. As usual, a fortnight elapsed before he was heard in public, and, perhaps because of his failing health, he did not, on this occasion, shoulder the complete responsibility for a personal benefit concert, but joined forces with another British-born artist, the harpist, Parish-Alvars, who happened to be in Milan at the time. They gave a joint benefit concert, on November 29th, in the great Sala di Ridotto, which is situated on the upper floor of the Scala Theatre. Three days later Field gave his services at a charity concert, held in the same room, in aid of the Pio Istituto Teatrale.

Although some of Field's compositions were much admired by the

---

[1] Like Clementi, J. A. Galiffe was an extraordinarily gifted linguist. His command of English was so complete that his book, *Italy, an account of a tour in that country in 1816–1817* was actually written in that language, and first published in England. He was almost equally fluent in several other languages, including Russian.

Milanese (the Second Nocturne had to be repeated twice), one senses from the press reports that his playing was not having its usual effect on the public. One critic, writing in the same *Barbiere di Siviglia*, listed fairly those qualities which appeared to him to be the best aspects of Field's playing, but then proceeded to compare it very unfavourably with the art of Paganini. Of Paganini's playing he wrote: 'it thrills me through every pore of my skin so that I become almost mad—I weep, and cry, "Hail to Genius". Then I whisper, *sotto voce*, so that none may hear, "Oh you poor Drouet, Romberg, Field; you don't bewitch me, you don't penetrate my soul; you think you can make a sensation with your mechanical dexterity; you believe you are raising an altar of fame for music instead of which you lay her in a magnificent grave". '[1] For Field this was an unusually unfavourable notice, and it cannot be accounted for merely by saying that the special qualities of his art were uncongenial to Italian taste; it suggests, rather, that he was no longer able to play with inspiration, but was struggling through his concerts against the heavy odds of pain and depression.

The day after the concert with Parish-Alvars, Field, whose share of the proceeds may have been a disappointment, seems to have decided to realise such assets as he still had in hand. He sat down and wrote a letter (in his usual careless French) to Breitkopf & Härtel, offering for sale his Seventh Concerto. It is difficult to understand why he had waited so long to do this. One senses, however, that to write at all was a considerable effort. He did not even trouble to spell Härtel's name correctly. The letter, which was long preserved in the archives of the firm, wastes no words:

> *a Messieurs Breitkopf & Hartell*
> *Magazin de Musique a Leipzig,*

Messieurs, Vous avez eu la bonte de prendre mon 6me Concerto que vous avez recu de Mr. Lehnhold—J'espére vous n'avez pas eu à vous repentir du marché, et que vous voudriez accepter mon 7me Concerto sur les mêmes conditions. si vous acceptez alors ayaz la bonté de vous arranger Mons. Meissonier Magazin de musique à Paris vous pouvez m'envoyer un 20 Exemplaire à reduire de la somme en question c.a.d. mille francs

> J'ai l'honneur de saluer
> J. Field.

[1] Drouet, the brilliant French flautist (he had collaborated with Field in both Moscow and Paris), and Romberg, the celebrated 'cellist, had both appeared in Milan earlier in the season.

The offer was, of course, accepted and one hopes that the money reached Field before he and Leon left Milan. They were going to need every sou of it in the difficult months that lay ahead.

The concerts in Milan were Field's last appearances in Italy; for though he moved on to Florence[1] it was not to play, but to consult, once more, the celebrated French physician, Dr. Dupuytren, who, though ill himself (he was recuperating in Italy after suffering a stroke while giving a lecture in Paris), did what little he still could to help the sick pianist. But Dupuytren left Florence only a week or so later, and Field then struggled on to Southern Italy, travelling by sea from Genoa to Naples. Once arrived in that famous city, however, he became so ill that he could no longer play, or even teach, and any thought he might have about giving concerts there had to be abandoned. That Leon was still with his father is confirmed by an entry in a Neapolitan police register entitled 'General Movements of Foreigners in the Capital'. In this we read that 'John Field, inglese, gentiluomo, arrivato il 27 Marzo in Genova, e stato obbligato a dar garanzia; dimora per diporto; domiciliato in strada Medina 72, con un figlio': which tells us not only the exact date of the travellers' arrival, but that, whatever may have been Field's private intentions, they were 'officially' in Naples for a holiday, and not for professional reasons.

In the political climate of the time Field could rely, as a 'gentiluomo inglese', on being given every assistance during his stay in Naples, and he was, unfortunately, all too soon in dire need of help. The very thought of what the poor man must have suffered during the next eighteen months makes the imagination flinch. Unable to earn any money, in constant pain, anxious about the difficult situation of his young son and knowing hardly anyone who might help him in his desperate straits, he was reduced as never before. His complaint demanded the best and most urgent medical attention, but though Naples was not without forward-looking medical practitioners (Dr. Dupuytren had lectured to them during his Italian tour) it was, even so, no place in which to fall seriously ill. Ten years later, Dickens, familiar as he was with the sight of the misery and squalor endured by the poor of France, Italy and his own country, was startled and appalled when confronted by the mixture of beauty, filth, starvation and luxury which was Naples. In Field's time conditions there must have been at least as bad as Dickens was to find them, and very soon he was to

---

[1] Not Venice, as is stated in more than one Field memoir.

experience something even worse: the daily horrors of life in a public Neapolitan hospital.

Field's own account of this sad time in his life, recorded later by his friends in Russia, contains only the bare facts that he lay in hospital for nine months and underwent numerous operations, but this is more than enough to give an idea of what he endured: it also raises the question of how he can have found money to pay for so much medical attention.

In 1834 Naples was still a capital city, with a British *chargé d'affaires* in residence, but British though Field still was, it was to his friends in distant Russia that the desperate man turned at last for financial help. When the news of Field's plight reached Moscow in July, 1835, his old friend and pupil, Count Vielhorsky, immediately set about the organisation of a concert to raise money for his assistance.[1] The money, once collected, was to be conveyed to Field by a member of the Russian embassy staff, named Matushevitch, who was being posted to Naples, but if it ever arrived it is probable that help had already come to Field from another quarter.

It may have been through the Russian embassy in Naples, where Field's difficulties would have been frequently discussed, that news of his tragic downfall became known to a party of Russian tourists who arrived in the city early in 1835. These Russians were a family named Rakhmanov, leading members of Moscow society. Count Rakhmanov was himself an Imperial Privy Councillor, and his wife, born a Princess Galitzina, was closely related to some of the most important and influential aristocrats in Russia. According to the police files already mentioned, the Princess arrived in Naples, accompanied by her two sons and her servants (her husband is not mentioned, though he appears to have rejoined the party during its journey from Italy to Vienna later in the year). Princess Galitzina-Rakhmanova was much shocked by Field's pitiable condition, and, learning that his one desire was to return to Moscow, where he still hoped to support himself by teaching, she compassionately offered to convey him and Leon back to Russia. As befitted such great aristocrats, the Rakhmanovs travelled with an immense retinue (their progress through Italy was reported in the local press of the principal towns on their route), and there could be no difficulty about finding places for Field and his son in one of their enormous Berlin travelling coaches.

[1] Letter of K. Y. Bulgakov to his brother, July 27th, 1835.

It may have been the prospect of an escape from his dreadful predicament which produced in Field's health at this time a slight but surprising improvement. The Princess realised, however, that he was by no means ready for a long and exhausting journey. So, delaying her own departure, she took Field to the island of Ischia for a period of recuperation. Ischia's thermal springs were then, as they still are, regarded as a panacea for almost every known disease and disablement. Perhaps the island's waters did prove beneficial to Field, but it is as likely that its scenic beauty and wonderful air, so refreshing after the torrid atmosphere of Naples, did even more to calm his spirit and strengthen his weakened limbs in preparation for the long journey before him.

The party travelled surprisingly fast and reached Vienna in time for Field to make three important concert appearances there during the first half of August. It seems evident that instructions for the organisation of these concerts must have been sent in advance of the arrival of Field and his hosts, for the first concert took place only a day or so after they had reached Vienna. The rich and influential Rakhmanovs were probably responsible for this (it would have been beyond Field's powers at any time), and it must have been a great satisfaction to them that the celebrated artist whom they had befriended in his hour of greatest need achieved a real triumph at his first Viennese concert on August 8th. He played his Sixth Concerto and the Nocturne[1] and Rondo from the Third Concerto, much the same programme as that which had proved so successful in Geneva; but it is hard to believe that, after so much mental and physical suffering, his playing can have remained unimpaired. It is true that the critic of the *Wiener Zeitschrift für Kunst, Literatur und Mode* wrote in the most enthusiastic terms of Field's playing and of his music,[2] but only a few months later, on his return to Moscow, Field's most ardent admirers, among them his worshipping disciple, Alexander Dubuk, were almost as shocked by the deterioration in his playing as by the sad change in his outward appearance.

At his second concert, three days later, the fact that Field was suffering was quite evident to the public, and the same critic noted 'the discomfort of the artist, due to his bodily pain . . . he seemed to be out of sorts, and

[1] See page 86, *n.* I.

[2] Field's compositions were then very popular throughout Europe. Mendelssohn, during a visit to Munich in 1835, was surprised and rather disgusted to find the music of Hummel, Field and Rossini more admired than that of Beethoven.

... as if impatient, whereby part of the otherwise certain effect of his playing was lost'. Though tactfully put, it is obvious that all was by no means well. However, at the third and last concert, on August 13th, he seems to have been in better form. The programme included the recently printed Seventh Concerto, a rondo, and a 'new' nocturne. This last was probably either the Eleventh, in E flat, or the Thirteenth, in D minor: it is, however, possible that it was the Fourteenth, in C major, since this work (among the finest of Field's compositions, and apparently the outcome of the first stirrings of his muse since he had left Paris in 1833) was actually composed during the first weeks of his stay in Vienna. It is one of the few works of Field which can be dated with fair accuracy, for the manuscript became the property of Aloys Fuchs, a Viennese singer and an enthusiastic collector of autographs who struck up an acquaintance with Field during his visit.[1] Fuchs noted on the manuscript that Field had composed the nocturne 'im Gasthof "bei den drei Kronen auf der Wieden" im Monat August 1835'.

Field stayed in Vienna for several weeks, and one deduces that, on arrival, he put up at the Gasthof mentioned by Fuchs. He did not remain there throughout his whole visit, however, for he eventually accepted an invitation from Czerny to be his guest for about two weeks (his Russian saviours, on whose plans his return to Moscow depended, appear to have been in no special hurry to continue the journey). Field must have been rather a worrying guest to have in the house. The presence of a man in the grip of a mortal illness, and whose personal habits were very trying, would have been strongly felt even in less well-organized households than that of the efficient and super-methodical Czerny. Whether Czerny had reason to regret his kindness one cannot know, for Field's account of his sojourn in Czerny's house was limited to a description of his host's method of composing, the spectacle of which he found highly diverting.

There probably never was a more industrious composer than Czerny (his opus numbers topped the two thousand mark), but we learn from Field that he did not cover all that mountain of music paper unaided. At the time of Field's visit, Czerny's works, transcriptions, technical studies and original works of all descriptions, were in immense demand, and in order to keep pace with the constant flow of his publishers' orders he had to set up a kind of composing 'factory' in his house. Czerny used to sit in

[1] One of the few autograph letters of Field still extant is a note addressed to Aloys Fuchs.

a big round room, working at the same table at which his guests also sat. When he finished writing he would go to a large cupboard and rummage among its many drawers, which were filled with samples of cadenzas and passage-work of all kinds. When he found what he wanted he sent it into the adjoining room, which was a kind of office in which several assistants, good musicians who understood his methods, were busily fitting the various passages into Czerny's latest 'composition', transposing and modulating them as required. Only in this way did he achieve his fantastically large output, and it is not surprising that, with such a method of 'composing', almost the whole of it proved to be ephemeral. Field looked on at this peculiar but profitable activity with amusement, and succinctly summed up his host as a 'living inkpot'.

Field liked Vienna, and later told Gebhard that he wished he could have remained there. But his return to Moscow was now a settled thing, and though he probably did not realise how little time remained to him, he must have felt that in Moscow he would be safer than anywhere else; that there he could rely on his many faithful friends, and on the support of his numerous and adoring pupils. When, therefore, his benefactors left Vienna in the early autumn, Field and Leon travelled with them.

We have no record of their route, or whether, once the Rakhmanovs had arrived at their estates in the Ukraine (according to Dubuk they parted from Field in Kiev) father and son were able to complete their journey to Moscow in one of the Rakhmanov's coaches and attended by some of their servants: but it is unlikely that, having cared for the ailing artist since the early summer, they would have allowed him to fend for himself during the last few hundred versts. Certainly on arrival he would have been welcomed by all his old friends and pupils, among them Dubuk, Charles Mayer, Alexander Gurilyev, as well as the Count Vielhorsky and many of the other aristocratic dilettantes who had always been among his greatest admirers.

XI

Death in Moscow

SHORTLY AFTER their return to Moscow, Field and his son were obliged, at last, to part. Young Leon Charpentier, presumably having developed his 'big, strong and sympathetic voice' during his period of training in Paris, and perhaps also during his year of enforced waiting in Naples (another famous training ground for singers), left Moscow and went to St. Petersburg to begin his long and successful career as an opera singer under the name of Leonov.[1] Field must have felt his loss very deeply, but perhaps he may have found a certain interest and consolation in the addition to his circle, after Leon's departure, of his other son, Adrien Field, now a youth of seventeen. Adrien had been quite well trained as a pianist by his mother, but his great ambition was to study under the guidance of his celebrated father, and, learning that Field had returned to Moscow, he had gone there specially for this purpose. What were Percherette's views about the matter one can only guess; it was a curious situation, and behind it one senses a sad story of frustrations and family tensions. For Adrien, the child of a genius and a woman of great talent, was not destined to be a famous pianist. He had ability and perhaps, given more time, Field might have made something of him; but now it was too late. The father welcomed his son, hoping, perhaps, that he might fill the empty place left in

---

[1] Cf. Cheshikhin's *History of Russian Opera*. Apparently Leonov's acting ability was almost nil at the start of his stage career. Later (the end of the 1850s) he became 'a delightful actor, but already voiceless . . . suitable only for comic roles'. During the visit of Berlioz to Russia in 1847, Leonov sang the title role in the first Moscow performance of *La Damnation de Faust*, delivering the part in what Berlioz described as 'French (Baltic Style)'. Though Berlioz says nothing about his voice, it may already have deteriorated badly, for Adolphe Adam, who visited St. Petersburg some years earlier, stated that Leonov was 'absolutely without a voice'. He is said to have been a good pianist, an agreeable companion and very like his father in appearance.

his life by the loss of Leon, and the boy remained with him until the end; but after Field's death Adrien drifted hopelessly, took to drink (he seems to have had his father's weaknesses without his great gifts) and ended his life as a *tapeur*—a humble dance pianist, earning a meagre living in taverns and public ballrooms. The date of Adrien Field's death is unrecorded, but he was still alive in 1851, for in that year he sold to the St. Petersburg publisher, Bernard, one of Field's manuscripts, a previously unknown *Andante* in E flat, which he had treasured for fourteen years and which may well have been Field's last work. The mystery of what became of Field's other relics, including the bulk of his manuscripts, is probably explained by the fact that Adrien was his legal heir and therefore the most likely person to have taken possession of what remained. It included very little money, for though Field died solvent he left only about 10,000 roubles out of the vast sums which he had earned in his earlier years.[1]

Field had now little more than a year to live. Ill as he was, he still tried to carry on a normal life. He received his pupils, dined in restaurants as of old, and sometimes, when the 'Green Winter', as the Muscovites call their summer, allowed it, he even ventured into the streets, walking slowly and with the aid of a stick. His stick used sometimes to fall from his weakened grasp, obliging him to wait until a passer-by picked it up for him, for the act of stooping now caused him too much pain.[2]

During this last year of Field's life, his artistic career gradually came to a standstill, but in the first months of 1836 he was still able to work a little. The wonderful Nocturne in C major, which he had composed in Vienna, had to be prepared for publication, and he wished to provide it with two companion pieces, and to dedicate all three, not, as one might have expected, to that Princess Rakhmanova, *née* Galitzina, who had cared for him throughout the long and trying journey from Naples to Moscow, but to her near relative, the Princess Galitzina, *née* Suvorova. Though the shorter nocturnes, in F and C, with which he completed the set, lack the inspiration of the Fourteenth Nocturne, the Princess had every reason to feel touched and charmed by such a poetically beautiful tribute.

For some reason Field did not apply to Breitkopf & Härtel for the

[1] Gebhard, 'John Field: a Biographical Sketch', *Severnaya Pchela*.

[2] Field's bodily weakness at the end of his life, and in particular his tendency to drop his walking-stick, is first mentioned in an article, published shortly after his death, in the Russian periodical *Variety*. Here it is made quite clear that this occurred in his 'old age' (he died at the age of fifty-four!), but later writers, notably Liszt, have seized upon it as an illustration of Field's 'notorious laziness'.

A view of the Kremlin from the Parade Square, 1823, engraved by Edward Finden after a drawing by Lavrov

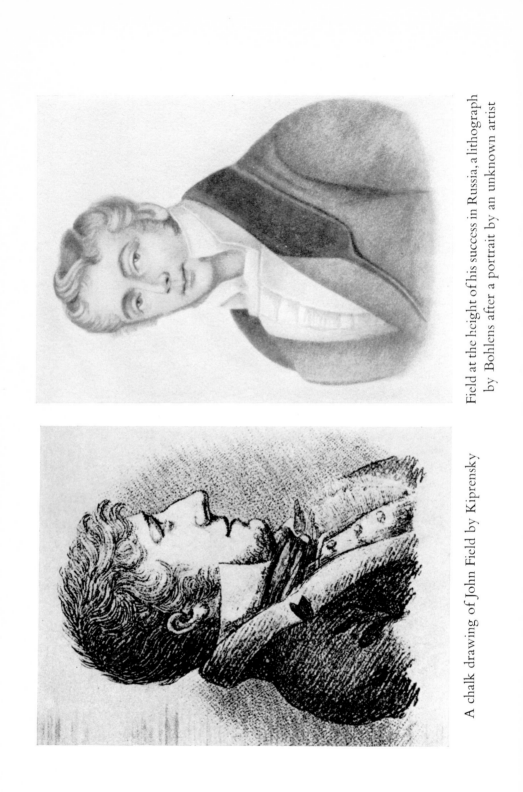

Field at the height of his success in Russia, a lithograph by Bohlens after a portrait by an unknown artist

A chalk drawing of John Field by Kiprensky

publication of these nocturnes: perhaps it was to save himself the trouble of writing letters, or perhaps to get a more immediate financial return that he had them printed by a Moscow publisher, named Lehnhold (he is mentioned in one of Field's letters to Breitkopf), who arranged for their almost simultaneous publication throughout Europe. They were the last of Field's works to be published in his lifetime, though possibly not the last music he composed.

Throughout 1836, Field's illness became steadily more aggravated until he was no longer able to sit in a chair without being placed on a specially made rubber cushion. Even so, he continued to make occasional public appearances, though only as an assisting artist at the benefit concerts of other musicians. His last performance seems to have taken place in March, when he played at a soirée arranged by his former pupil, Charles Mayer. The *Moscow Gazette* reviewed this concert, and, after praising Mayer (who played, among other things, some Polonaises for piano duet with his young son) the critic went on to say that Field 'sang' on his piano the Quintet of Dussek. It was with this chamber music performance that Field's pianistic career drew to its close, and the reviewer's choice of the word 'sang', rather than 'played', allows us to believe that, despite the deterioration in his playing, which had so saddened Dubuk, it had not entirely lost what had always been its most important characteristic—the quality which, from his earliest days, had earned him the title of the 'Singer among Pianists'.[1]

Despite the gravity of his illness Field's death was actually the result of an attack of pneumonia, following a chill caught during the severe weather of December, 1836. For two weeks he fought for life but with his once strong constitution so severely undermined it was a battle he could only lose. Eventually those who watched by his bedside, among whom were some of the most high-born ladies of Moscow society, realising that the end was near, asked him if he would like to have the ministrations of a priest. Field smilingly replied that he did not belong to any congregation, but his friends continued to worry about the matter, and finally, without his knowledge, they persuaded an English clergyman to visit him—not

[1] A. Nikolayev states that at the end of 1836 Field made a supreme effort and gave another public concert in Moscow, at which, 'as if to underline the fact that he now ceded his place to new creative beauties, Field, at the end of the evening, played several compositions by Chopin'. However, no references to such a concert in the Russian press of the time have come to light. Chopin's music, of which Field can have known extremely little, was not sympathetic to his taste, and it is very unlikely that he considered Chopin to be, in any way, his successor.

without some demur on the part of the cleric who was naturally dubious about attending someone who did not profess to being a Christian. Dubuk, who was present at the interview, could not help smiling through his secret tears as he listened to the following exchange:

'Are you a Prostestant?'—'No.'

'So perhaps you are a Catholic?'—'No.'

'Then probably you are a Calvinist?'—'Not exactly that. I am not a Calvinist, but a *Claveciniste*.'

With this quip, a delicate play upon words, if not quite one of his favourite puns, the dying Field, with gentle humour, but also with an underlying seriousness of intention, declared that art, music and the piano were his only 'true religion'. It was, in a way, a confession of faith.

His old friend and future biographer, Gebhard, was with him in his last hour, and as he bent over the dying man to wipe his forehead he heard Field whisper, 'Thank you—but don't kiss me: it is the sweat of death. I'm dying, and it's for the best.'

John Field died on January 23rd, 1837. The funeral took place four days later. The coffin was carried from the chapel of the Reformed Church to the Vedensky Cemetery, which lies on the outskirts of Moscow. It was followed by a great crowd of people—pupils, friends, fellow-artists and the innumerable music lovers who had admired his art for so many years. The whole of Moscow's musical world was greatly saddened by his death, and plans were very quickly formed for the erection of a worthy monument to his memory. The first intention was that money should be raised by a great oratorio performance, for which all the leading musicians in Moscow volunteered their services; but eventually a public subscription list was opened and very soon a substantial sum had been collected. In 1838 a simple but impressive monument, made of a very fine, dark green stone, inset with gold lettering, was erected over the grave. The inscription (in somewhat faulty English) reads:

John Field
Born in Ireland
in 1782
Dead in Moscow
in 1837.

On the back of the stone is added,

> *Erected*
> *To His Memory*
> *By*
> *Mis grateful Friends*
> *and*
> *Scholars.*

By a fortunate chance the subscription list has been preserved, though it may not be quite complete. It is an extremely interesting document, containing as it does some of the greatest names in Russian history, including that of Denis Davidov, one of the most honoured heroes of the 1812 campaign, as well as others, such as Galitzin, Orlov, Gagarin, Bulgakov, and Tolstoy which are equally well known. It is probable that the full list was originally even longer than the fifty-eight names included in the two pages preserved in the State Historical Museum in Moscow (they subscribed 1,467 roubles between them), and that other, missing pages would have revealed the names of less socially exalted contributors—the musicians, friends and artistic confreres of all kinds who must also have subscribed willingly to this final tribute to a great and much loved artist. Not that monuments of marble and gold were needed to remind Russian music lovers of what they owed to the Irish-born musician who had lived among them for the greater part of his life. Field's memory was kept green in Russia long after it had become faded elsewhere, and the traditions of his pianistic style were handed down by his many pupils throughout the nineteenth and even into the twentieth century. These traditions are still alive today and in the pages which follow an attempt will be made to assess their nature and to evaluate Field's true legacy to the arts of piano-playing and composition.

XII

Field as Pianist and Teacher

❧

In 1831, Friedrich Wieck, anxious to recommend his prodigy daughter, the future Clara Schumann, to the influential Spohr, claimed, 'I have trained her, as far as music is concerned, in the magnificent school of Field, to which the so-called Viennese school always seems to me to be entirely subordinate.' Shortly afterwards, in a letter to Friedrich Kalkbrenner, then a leader of the Paris musical world, Wieck again stated, 'I am well acquainted with Field's method and have trained my daughter and my [other] pupils by this principle alone.'

Kalkbrenner himself, on hearing Chopin play for the first time, remarked that his touch reminded him of Field's, and enquired whether Chopin had studied with the Irish master. It was by no means the first time that Chopin had been compared to Field. When passing through Dresden, in 1830, he had played to August Klengel, who had at once noticed the similarity between them, and even Chopin's own teacher, Józef Elsner (according to Chopin's sister, Louise) considered him to have Field's style of playing. Klengel was in a position to make such a comparison, for he had lived in Russia for several years and had heard Field play many times. But Wieck and Elsner had no first-hand knowledge of Field's playing or teaching, and though Kalkbrenner, as a youth of eighteen just emerging from the Conservatoire, might have encountered the twenty-year-old Field during the latter's brief visit to Paris in 1802 (there is no evidence that he did), he had no opportunity to hear him as a mature artist until some time after his first meeting with Chopin. Chopin was evidently flattered by the frequent comparison of his playing with Field's, for in a letter to his friend, Titus Woyciechowski, he reported Kalkbrenner's remarks with obvious satisfaction; and in another letter, written in 1833, he boasted that all the most advanced pupils in Paris now came to him for lessons and set his name next to Field's.

It is evident that by 1830 Field had become a legend, and that his superiority among pianists was so generally recognized that Elsner, Wieck, Kalkbrenner and Chopin all regarded him as a leader of his profession, though none of them had actually heard him play. He had acquired his great fame throughout Europe without having troubled to leave the two Russian capitals in which he was idolised. The publication of his concertos and nocturnes by Breitkopf & Härtel, which began about 1815, supported his already brilliant reputation as a pianist: these works quickly became an essential part of the repertoire.

The art of Field represented a new pianistic ideal, and it was an inspiration to such men as Wieck, who strove to raise piano playing to even greater heights than it had already reached. Possibly the very fact that to hear Field remained an unattainable dream for most musicians added to the glamour which surrounded him and so increased his influence. Some pianists did make the arduous journey to Russia in the hope of lessons with Field (at one time so many of them crowded into St. Petersburg that its musical world facetiously renamed the city 'Pianopolis'), but to most he remained a slightly mysterious figure, surrounded by anecdote and rumour. Even Hummel, his most formidable rival, generously contributed to the Field legend by maintaining that his compositions were heard at their best when played by Field.

It is clear that such a reputation must have been well earned, even though allowances must be made for the tendency of travellers' tales to become exaggerated. That Field was a pianist of unique quality becomes evident as one studies the many detailed descriptions of his playing left by his pupils and friends, by critics and colleagues, and by such great musicians as Spohr, Hummel and Glinka, all of whom heard him in his prime. Here it is necessary to remember that when Field finally made up his mind to reappear in the principal cities of Europe, after an absence of thirty years, his playing, like his health, may have begun to decline and so perhaps did not always measure up to the expectations of his audiences. He should not be judged on his last, sad years, when illness and intemperance had dulled his art, but on the records of those who heard him during the first three decades of the nineteenth century.

Field was recognised as a pianist of outstanding ability at the beginning of his career (the *Morning Post* for February 9th, 1799, describes him as one of the best performers in the kingdom), but there is little evidence that the strikingly individual qualities of his mature style developed as quickly as his technical brilliance. Indeed, one of the earliest accounts of his playing (to be found in Parke's *Musical Memories*) describes the seventeen-year-old composer's performance of his own First Concerto as 'more remarkable for rapidity than expression'. Parke's judgement is suspect, since he found nothing more in Mozart's Requiem, which received its first English performance at the same concert, than 'infinite science and dullness'. Nevertheless, one searches other contemporary records in vain for hints that the boy's playing was as poetic as it was brilliant.

Clementi, who knew what was in his pupil, describes him, in a letter written to Pleyel in 1801, as 'a very promising genius'; and when, a few months later, the Parisian connoisseurs heard Field, the extremely favourable impression he made on them was as much the result of his musicianly playing of fugues by Bach and Handel as of his technical virtuosity. But the first musician who seems to have fully appreciated the most important quality of Field's playing (at all events the first to leave a written account of it which draws attention to other aspects than its brilliance) was Louis Spohr.

In his autobiography Spohr mentions not only the young pianist's technical fluency, but also . . . 'the dreamy perfection of his execution. As soon as his touching performance began one forgot everything and became all ear.' Here, at last, one begins to sense that the individual voice of the romantic poet of the keyboard, 'The Singer among Pianists', was beginning to emerge from the wonderfully accomplished pupil who had been trained by the greatest teacher of the day. From this time onwards all accounts of Field's playing eulogise its poetry, and the beautiful singing quality of his tone even more than his superb technical facility.

The most interesting impressions of Field at the height of his powers were those left by Alexander Dubuk. Although Dubuk despaired of being able to find words to describe the beauty of Field's playing he succeeded, nevertheless, in giving a very striking impression of it. 'As a musician he was unique,' wrote Dubuk. 'I have heard many good pianists of my century [Dubuk's long life allowed him to hear even the youthful Rakhmaninov and Scriabin during their years as students of his own pupil, Nikolai Zverev] but none of them played with such deep understanding, such emotion, and in such a wonderfully accomplished way as Field . . . Much as I liked some of Field's compositions the chief beauty lay in his playing [of them]—his touch on the keys—the way his melodies sang— the easy, heavenly "floating" of his scales and passages—the nobility of the interpretation: all this—the typically "Field-ish" way to play—no words can describe.' Another who heard him play frequently, his friend Gebhard, sketches Field at the keyboard: 'Perfect assurance—gracefulness—a wonderful touch—utmost exactness and clarity—the interplay of light and shade—everywhere artistic feeling . . . in short, the best and highest in art is concentrated in this musician.' Glinka wrote of him in similarly enthusiatic terms: 'Although I did not hear him very often, even now I well remember his vigorous, yet sensitive and precise playing. It seemed to me that he did not actually strike the keys, but that his fingers simply fell, as if they were raindrops, scattering like pearls on velvet. Neither I nor any sincere lover of the art of music can agree with Liszt, who once said in my presence that Field played languidly; no, Field's playing was often bold, erratic and varied, but he did not disfigure art like a charlatan . . . as do most fashionable pianists.' We have already touched on the lack of sympathy between the ageing Field and the youthful Liszt;[1] Glinka was, of course, a faithful partisan, but the affection and admiration in which he held Field were shared by most cultured Russian music lovers, as the following extract from a periodical of the 1830s makes clear: 'Russia has the right to be proud of the fact that the famous founder of the newest method of piano teaching, the best musician who ever lived—in a word, Field . . . has been for thirty years her citizen. It is difficult to describe his music [like Dubuk, the writer immediately tried to do so]; one has to hear him if one is to be persuaded that no other pianist is comparable to Field. Such limpidity, such tenderness, such astonishingly expressive playing—nobody can play such scales . . . so evenly, and with such perfectly graded crescendos and diminuendos. He possesses some kind of magic ability to touch the keyboard in a special way: under his fingers it is no longer the usual piano with a limited sound—it reminds you rather of the singing voice with all its nuances.'

Other great pianists have been praised for this precious singing quality, but none more frequently or more fervently than Field. And he must surely be the only one who has been held up as a model for singers themselves. Even in his last years, when his art had lost some of its bloom, a writer in the *Manchester Guardian*, reviewing a concert given in that city on July 28th, 1832, suggested that 'Some of the vocalists, we think, would have benefited by attending to Mr Field's piano playing, who [*sic*] united distinction and delicacy of expression and facility of execution.'

[1] See pages 76–77.

This was directed against the singers who shared the programme with Field, the stars of a German Opera company then playing in London, among whom was the celebrated Wilhelmine Schroeder-Devrient, one of the supremely great artists of her epoch. She came in for some sharp criticism in the later part of the *Manchester Guardian's* report.

From these and other similar 'ear-witness' accounts of Field's playing one can, after sifting away some of the hyperbole, grasp what were the essential characteristics of his art. Its technical perfection, though never an end in itself, was a very important aspect of it, and this he owed to the rigorous training of Clementi. Towards the end of his career Field was regarded as the upholder of a great classical tradition of piano playing. This tradition, which he shared with Cramer, and had received from Clementi and Dussek, was, above all else, one of restraint. Everything must be made to seem easy, however difficult it might really be. Field's appearance while playing was described by a writer in *The Harmonicon*, in 1833, in these words: 'To look at his hands, which scarcely seem to move, to contemplate the calmness of his countenance while playing, one would be tempted to suppose he was performing nothing but the easiest music in the world; while the fact is that the greatest, the most complicated difficulties are no difficulties at all to him.' Another observer wrote: 'It was curious to watch how his most interested listener was himself. Perfectly calm, he seemed to see nothing of his surroundings —he cared least of all for the attention of his audience . . . because he tried to avoid all hasty movements Field used to practise every day special exercises which are now forgotten. He practised with a coin on the back of his hand and never dropped it.'

In his earlier years Field practised many hours a day, but later he considerably reduced his practice routine, except in the weeks before a concert. The 'special exercises' were then limited to the daily performance of either his 'Grand Scale Study through all the keys' or his *Nouvel Exercise*, which, like the scale study, modulates through all keys and is based on scale figures. These two pieces are designed for the promotion of finger independence and agility. Balancing a coin on the back of the hand is an old trick for ensuring a quiet style; it was part of Clementi's training, and it remained in use for many years, outlasting the fashion for such mechanical aids as Logier's Chiroplast. Dubuk, who studied Field in performance more closely than anyone else, made interesting observations on the physical aspect of his playing. 'He possessed all the qualities a great pianist should have,' he wrote. 'He was beautifully built, with beautiful broad hands. His wrist looked as if it had been cast in bronze—there was no movement in it. Only his fingers moved and played . . .'

Dubuk also stated that the perfection of Field's muscular control was such that he needed to use only the smallest possible finger action to produce a wide range of tone. He regarded the key as an extension of the finger, and what he most disliked was a percussive attack on the keyboard itself. His usual method of correction for pupils who erred in this respect was to depress a group of keys with the flat of his hand and then oblige the pupil to hit those keys with force. The inevitable dull thud was, in itself, sufficient illustration of his point. In achieving his rounded, un-forced, singing tone and marvellous agility Field was very dependent on the character of the pianos of his time. It cannot be too strongly em-phasised that early-nineteenth-century pianos differed almost as much from those of today as from the harpsichords and clavichords which they gradually replaced. Their pure, transparent tone and, above all, their relatively easy action made the pianist's task something quite different from what it was to become after the changes which were forced on piano makers by the next generation of virtuosi—Liszt, Thalberg and their followers.

Field used Clementi's pianos in his youth, and sometimes those of Broadwood, but in later years his particular favourites were the instru-ments made by Tischner—a Prussian who emigrated to Russia at the beginning of the nineteenth century and opened a successful piano factory, which, however, went into liquidation on his death in 1830. Tischner's grand pianos are now very rare, but the best surviving instruments are still ideally suited to Field's style of playing. Their sweet, silvery tone and immediate response to infinitely small gradations of touch are exactly what Field's music demands. Furthermore they are elegant in appearance and beautifully finished.

It has sometimes been stated that Field preferred to play on a square piano rather than on a grand. There is no proof of this other than the fact that he used a square piano, made by Pape, for his Paris concerts of 1833. Two of these concerts actually took place in Pape's own concert room, which suggests some kind of business arrangement between them. What is not generally realised is that such instruments as Pape's 'table grands' bore absolutely no resemblance to the tinkling spinet which is suggested nowadays by the term 'square piano'. They were magnificently solid instruments, imposing and handsome in appearance, with actions constructed on a system of down-striking hammers which produced a tone full and rich enough to compete with the orchestral accompaniment of a concerto. It is unlikely that Field would have jeopardised the success of the vitally important first performance of his Seventh Concerto in the great *Salle du Conservatoire* (an occasion of breathtaking interest to the Parisian musical world) by playing on an inadequate instrument. The effect of Field's playing on Pape's piano at that concert was remarkable. The *Revue de Paris* contained an account of it which mentioned that 'at first one had the impression that Field wished to impress the public as a virtuoso who was able to play on a piano too small for the huge hall; he chose a square piano. But under his fingers it gave forth a rare fullness. These square pianos have been constructed on the perfect system of Pape. The hammers fall on top of the strings and this increases the sound . . . all honour to Pape, who by his improvements has rendered service to the musician.'

Many of Field's pupils, when describing his technical methods, laid great stress on his original manner of fingering. In the article by V. Vissendorf, written with the help of one of Field's pupils (the author describes him as 'an honoured musician, to whom my readers will be as grateful as I am') we read that 'Field's fingering is entirely different from German fingering: it is something special, something perfect, which gives the music an unusual beauty.' It is obvious that for Field fingering was of primary importance. Dubuk mentions that 'he took great care and trouble over the fingering, so that often there was hardly any time left for playing during the lessons'. Field's manuscripts are now very rare, but those that remain show that, even in preliminary sketches, the fingering was immediately written beside the notes. Fortunately Field's fingering methods are extremely well documented. Many copies of his concertos, edited by the master for the benefit of his pupils, still exist. They are liberally fingered: even ornaments and trills are written out in full, with fingering for every note. Dubuk, feeling that a great deal could be learned from these relics, published a collection of eighty-eight fingered passages taken from Field's works, mostly the concertos. They contain much that is unorthodox, and a study of them shows that many of Chopin's fingering methods (long regarded as without precedent and extremely iconoclastic) were anticipated by Field. For example, passages in which a rich, bell-like sonority is required may be played by the same finger throughout:

Ex. 1 (7th Concerto)

Ex. 2

This type of fingering may also be used for light, staccato effects:

Ex. 3 (4th Concerto; Rondo)

Quick repetitions may also be played by the same finger:

Ex. 4 (7th Concerto)

It will be noted that Field has no objection to the use of the thumb on black keys. He sometimes deliberately places the hand near the centre, or towards the back of the keyboard when more 'traditional' alternatives would have been possible:

Ex. 5 (2nd Concerto)

Occasionally there are curiosities of fingering such as the following scale passages:

Ex. 6 (5th Concerto)

Ex. 7

For most pianists these would seem to be unnecessarily difficult, but Field probably obtained from them a more brilliant effect than from more orthodox fingering.

It is surprising that a favourite pupil of Clementi (whose playing of double notes was the envy of all his colleagues, including Mozart) should apparently have had no special facility in this type of passage, since Clementi's training must have included every branch of piano technique. Rapid passages in thirds are extremely rare in Field's music, and scales in sixths and octaves non-existent. That their avoidance was not entirely due to a dislike of such passages on artistic grounds is suggested by the changes which Field was in the habit of making when playing the music of other composers. Such a passage as

Ex. 8

taken from Hummel's A minor Concerto, he played in this way:

Ex. 9

Dubuk's collection of fingered passages includes only one in double notes; a four-bar exercise in double thirds. This may well be one of those exercises which Field is said to have practised daily during his earlier years. There exists also an exercise in double thirds, still unpublished, which he wrote out for a pupil, Madame Caspari. This exercise, eighty-two bars in length, is based on a figure similar to the *Nouvel Exercice*, and, like that study, it modulates through all keys.

In 1822, Field published an *Exercice Nouveau* in C major designed for the development of trills with the third and fourth fingers. Schumann, reviewing a later edition of the piece, wondered whether it could really be by Field: 'We do not know how old this exercise is—as a matter of fact we would not even vouch for its authenticity, since it is only its thoroughly simple and lucid design which seems to imply that it is written by a great master; but it strikes us as being primarily an exercise in trills, which were not the strongest aspect of Field's virtuosity.' This is an interesting comment. Here again we have a confident assertion about Field's playing by one who never heard him. Wieck, Schumann's teacher, was probably his main source of information about Field (though, as we have seen, Wieck himself must have learned what he knew of Field's playing from others). Our own knowledge of Field's trill technique can only be based on the passages which he wrote out and fingered for his pupils. The following—an extract from the Third Concerto—indicates that his trills were not particularly rapid and were played with frequent changes of finger:

Ex. 10

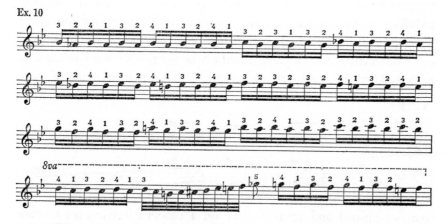

It will have been observed that all the examples so far quoted are for the right hand only. It is a fact that in Field's music the left hand is seldom submitted to any very testing difficulties. Its role is usually to support the right hand with accompaniment figures, or to follow its lead in flights of thirds, sixths or octaves. There are a few exceptional passages, such as the final section of the *Fantasie sur une Polonaise favorite*, where both hands are required to perform extended intervals of considerable difficulty, and the Rondo from the Fourth Concerto, in which long and tiring passages in broken octaves are fingered by Field in this way:

Ex. 11

Such passages are, however, unusual and, for the most part, Field requires no more of the left hand than the provision of an effective background for the right hand's cantabile and bravura.

Field's music depends more than that of any earlier composer on the special tone colour produced by the almost constant use of what we now call the sustaining pedal. The left pedal he used very sparingly (according to Dubuk, he never used it for achieving a pianissimo, but only to produce a special timbre), but his use of the sustaining pedal was continuous. In his few extant manuscripts the pedalling is usually marked in full, but in the early editions of his works indications of pedalling are sparse, and often so carelessly printed that one can regard them only as a very rough guide to the composer's intentions. As one studies Field's pedalling it becomes clear that it is not possible to reproduce exactly on the pianos of today all the pedal effects available on those of his time; the subsequent developments in the art of piano building have been too numerous and too fundamental. Such a passage as the following, from the *Fantasia on a theme by Martini*, though perhaps acceptable on a Clementi piano of 1807,

Ex. 12

sounds confused and unsatisfactory on a modern instrument. Certain romantically beautiful effects were lost once the strings of the piano had been thickened, the wooden frame replaced by metal and the brilliance and tonal range increased in response to the demands of later virtuosi. Thus the codas of many of Field's nocturnes, designed to be played with the pedal depressed throughout, are heard nowadays with unavoidable pedal changes where none were intended. The end of the beautiful Fourth Nocturne is a case in point; on Field's pianos it was possible to keep the pedal unchanged throughout the resolution of the final cadence, since by the time the last chord was played little more than the bass of the previous harmony remained clearly audible:

Ex. 13

The opening of the *Siciliano* in G minor from the Fourth Concerto (solo version) is a striking example of the beautiful effect obtained when the pedal is held throughout a succession of changing harmonies. Played on an early-nineteenth-century grand this passage sounds entirely convincing, but, like many similar passages in Field's works, it cannot be played in exactly the same way on a modern piano without sounding too blurred to be wholly agreeable:

Ex. 14

However, after due allowance has been made for the more limited sonority of early-nineteenth-century pianos, it seems probable that Field sometimes positively preferred a slight haze of pedalled tone to the 'clean' harmonies for which the well-trained modern pianist strives. His pedal markings in the manuscript of his Fifth Nocturne ('Serenade' version) clearly illustrate how important it was to him that the sound of the implied tonic pedal should not be lost, regardless of phrasing and changes of harmony:

Ex. 15

On the rare occasions when Field wished to ensure that the sustaining pedal should *not* be used he clearly marked the passage *con sordini*, as was customary in his day; but such indications are very few.

Until fashion brings about a vogue for newly-constructed reproductions, accurate in every detail, of the best early-nineteenth-century pianos (an unlikely development in taste, perhaps, though not an impossible one in view of the revival of the harpsichord which has taken place during the past fifty years), pianists wishing to interpret Field's music or, for that matter, any music composed before about 1840, are faced by problems to which no satisfactory solutions exist at present. It must at least be helpful, however, to realise that there are such difficulties; to know that the quality of sound with which Field charmed his listeners has been lost, and that the perfection of his finger technique was closely associated with the types of piano action in use during his time: it is also essential to have an understanding of the pedalling problems already mentioned. Such knowledge among pianists interpreting the music of the past must have its value: it could even provoke a reconsideration of accepted methods of piano construction, an art which has become somewhat stereotyped and unadventurous since the later part of the nineteenth century.

Of Field's ability to impart to his pupils the secrets of his technique and style we know a little from the accounts of his teaching left by some of them. Unlike many of his contemporaries, Field published no 'School' of piano playing, and of his celebrated 'method', of which so much was talked in his day, but of which so few, outside of Russia, had any direct experience, little remains. As a pedagogue he probably had considerable limitations. Even Dubuk, one of his most enthusiastic disciples, looking back from the vantage point of his own distinguished career as a teacher, wrote of him in these words: 'On the pure facts of Field's teaching I would find a number of failures: for instance, he rarely explained the structure of a composition—you had to study it, and get into the depths of it by yourself. One's efforts were fully repaid, however, by his playing: when I studied a composition he would play it to me, and that did more than any explanation could have done.' But Dubuk went on to point out that his master's method of teaching by illustration was suitable only for those pupils who already had a good musical training, and one suspects that though he attended to the work of pupils who interested him, a great deal (perhaps the greater part) of Field's teaching was no more to him than wearisome drudgery.

Like most fashionable teachers of his day, Field depended very largely on the patronage of the wealthy. He accepted pupils more often for their ability to pay his high fees than for their talent, and he does not appear to have been over-conscientious about the lessons of the dullards among them. A story is told of the mother of one such pupil opening the door of her drawing-room and revealing Field dancing with her daughter, instead of teaching her the piano. In reply to her expostulations he said, 'Well Madame, you absolutely insist that I teach your daughter—I assure

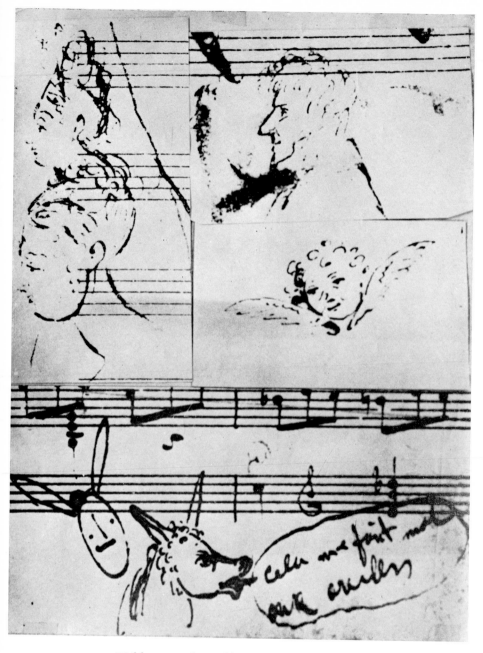

Field amuses himself during boring lessons

A lithograph of the composer by Engelbach

Part of a sketch for the rondo of the Fifth Concerto

you it makes far more sense for me to teach her to dance than to play!'
One cannot but feel a certain sympathy for poor Field in these circumstances, though a really good teacher can be judged by the progress of his
less talented pupils rather than his more brilliant ones. Certainly Field's
indifference to an obtuse pupil could be carried too far: sometimes he was
even caught dozing during a boring lesson. Moscheles, much scandalised,
left an account of how Field 'bragged of going to sleep whilst giving
lessons to the ladies of St. Petersburg, adding that they would often rouse
him and enquire why they were paying him twenty roubles an hour
merely for him to sleep', an anecdote which suggests that Field was by no
means ashamed of his somnolence. Yet such behaviour does not appear to
have diminished the number of his rich and aristocratic pupils. Among
them, of course, were some who were genuinely gifted: Countess Orlova,
for instance, is said to have been among his best pupils, and, like Chopin's
favourite aristocratic pupil, Princess Marcelline Czartoryska, to have
played in a style which faithfully reflected that of her master. To such
gifted players he gave his full attention: we have already seen that he
could be scrupulous about fingering, extremely critical of the use of force
in tone production, and prepared, on occasion, laboriously to write out
technical exercises. But the number of serious students trained by him is
smaller than one might have supposed in view of his long and illustrious
career. It includes, however, some important names, among them Dubuk
and Villoing, from whom stems the great tradition of Russian piano
playing which has continued unbroken to the present day. It also includes
such celebrated virtuosi of the time as Anton Kontski, Charles Mayer,
Maria Szymanowska and I. Reinhardt, and such important figures in early
Russian musical history as Verstovsky, Gurilyev, Alabyev and Glinka. With
pupils like these Field was quite prepared to reduce his high fees; even, if
necessary, to teach them for nothing: that he was genuinely interested in
their progress and able to inspire them to develop their gifts is proved by
the wide range of his influence. Towards the end of his life a writer in a
Russian periodical claimed: 'Russia may boast that she has the best school
of piano teachers. We possess a number of teachers, pupils of Field, who
pass on his method to others, and in this way it has spread over the whole
of Russia.'

The material used by Field for the training of his better pupils reads
oddly today. Apart from Bach's '48', and the *Gradus ad Parnassum* of
Clementi, it seems to have been selected almost entirely from the works of

the fashionable virtuosi of the time—Hummel, Kalkbrenner, Moscheles, Cramer and their like and, of course, from Field's own compositions. It was natural enough that one who taught more by illustration than by explanation should make use of his own repertoire, but the neglect of Haydn, Mozart and Beethoven is noteworthy. Much as he admired their chamber and orchestral works Field had little use for the piano music of these masters. Even Weber, a contemporary whose music might well have won his sympathy, he appreciated principally as a composer of opera. In this we are, once again, reminded of Chopin, whose interest in his great contemporaries, Mendelssohn, Schumann and Berlioz, was grudging, and whose love of Bach and Mozart was not extended to the works of Beethoven.

One is left with the impression that Field was not a teacher by vocation, but that his own marvellous playing and engaging personality obviated most of his pedagogic deficiencies, though they cannot have entirely offset the unfortunate effect of his fatigue and boredom when enduring the struggles of unmusical amateurs. The pupils who studied with Field during his thirty years in Russia included some very talented pianists, but his great international reputation owed less to these, less even to the romantic charm and originality of his compositions than to his genius as a performer. As a pianist he was incomparable—an innovator who, in his constant search for ever greater perfection, revealed beauties of sound unheard before his time, and who, in the words of one of his most celebrated pupils, the Polish pianist, Anton Kontski, 'achieved the impossible'.

Dubuk concluded his memories of Field with the lament: 'It is the tragedy of all great pianists that their art died with them.' Today, thanks to scientific progress, this is no longer completely true. Unfortunately science moved too slowly for the great artists of Field's time to be recorded for posterity, but so vivid are the descriptions of his art left to us by those who heard him that we almost persuade ourselves that its sound cannot be quite lost, and that, like Wieck and Schumann, we possess an intimate knowledge of his playing without ever having had the joy of hearing it.

XIII

Nocturnes

༻❦༺

THE SERIES of delicate and poetic piano pieces for which, in an inspired moment, Field found a perfect title in the word nocturne have become, since the fading of his great fame as a pianist, his principal claim to remembrance.

The word nocturne was not entirely new to music. During the eighteenth century its Italian or German equivalents had headed the scores of numerous vocal and instrumental works intended for performance at night. But the *Notturni* and *Nachtmusiken* of that period have little in common with the wordless love-songs which Field called nocturnes. His invention was something more important than a mere title; it was the crystallisation of an idiom through which a new aspect of the romantic movement could be channelled into the mainstream of music.

Something of the dreamily poetic mood which permeates Field's nocturnes had occasionally been caught by earlier composers. We hear it in certain of Mozart's slow movements—though expressed in quite different terms—and there are superficial resemblances to Field's manner in the work of some of his more immediate predecessors. But all these are no more than the faint foreshadowings of things to come. To Field alone must be given the credit for having created in his nocturnes a new style of piano writing which was to have far-reaching effects on the music of the future.

It took him some time to find the ideal name for these lyrical miniatures. At first he intended to call them romances, and the earliest of them accord very closely with the type of vocal romances which were popular in the Russian salons of his day. 'Serenade' and 'Pastoral' were words which also attracted him, and it was not until 1814 that he published the first three of his works which bear the title 'Nocturne'. Even after this publication he seems to have wavered, for the following year saw the appearance in print of three romances, one of them being identical with the First Nocturne, while another seems to be, most confusingly, an *earlier* version of the Second Nocturne. The third pieces of the two sets are entirely different works.

The First Nocturne, in Field's favourite key of E flat major, already epitomises the principal characteristics of his best work.[1] In this piece we find a type of melodic line which suggests the *bel canto* of an Italian singer, and an accompaniment in undulating triplets which demands a highly developed pedalling technique:

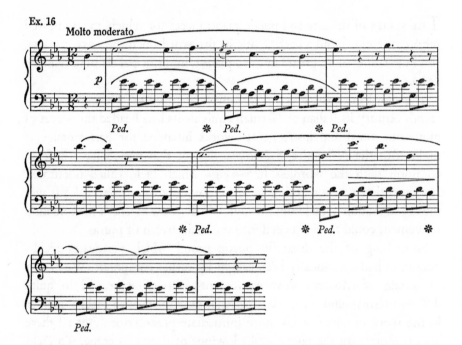

Ex. 16

The preference for decoration rather than development, the lack of contrast and modulation, and the extremely simple formal scheme of the piece are all typical of Field's mature style. Each of the nocturne's three sections ends with a full close in the tonic key, followed by a short codetta:

[1] Some admirers of the Bolshoi Ballet's production of *The Fountains of Bakhchisarai* may have noticed that several of the leading themes in Asafyev's otherwise extremely banal score are variants of the opening bars of Field's First Nocturne. The melody is used as a kind of *Leitmotif* for the heroine, Maria, though it never appears in its original form but always in some disguise.

these codettas are very suggestive of the instrumental ritornellos of a vocal romance of the period, a resemblance which is emphasised by Field's application of the word *scherzando* to the first of them:

The decorations added to the principal theme on its restatement are exactly what the music needs to intensify its poetic effect without altering its mood:

Though nothing could be less complicated than this nocturne, it bears, for all its apparent naivety, the hallmark of a perfect work of art in its exact matching of form with content.[1]

---

[1] Examples 16, 17 and 18 are taken from the original version of this nocturne, of which the first known publication dates from 1814. In a revised version which Field published in London, in 1832, the passages quoted in Examples 17 and 18 were considerably modified.

Field wrote few pieces in minor keys. With one exception (the Tenth Nocturne) they express gentle resignation rather than tragedy or despair.

In his Second Nocturne, in C minor, Field sings in sad, love-lorn tones, but otherwise the piece closely resembles its predecessor. It has the same lyrical melodic line, the same type of accompaniment and the same simple design. The Romance in C minor—the earlier form of the piece—though based on the same material, includes elaborate and beautiful decoration which was afterwards discarded. The elimination of such **a** passage as:

Ex. 19

must have cost Field a pang of regret, but the nocturne is undoubtedly an improvement on the romance: it is less repetitious, it contains more harmonic tension and it reaches a stronger climax.

Field's second thoughts about the ending of the piece are of considerable interest. The earlier version ends in this way:

Ex. 20

but in its revised form the emotional feeling of this passage is intensified by the addition of a beautiful, arching arabesque, all the more effective because of the simplicity of the preceding pages. Field also adds a wistful, almost impressionistic coda, containing one of his favourite pedal effects—a haze of shifting harmonies above a sustained tonic:

Ex. 21

[*Continued overleaf*

Ex. 21—*contd.*

The Third Nocturne, in A flat major, is a delightful, though rarely-heard work. It deserves to be better known.

The texture of the piece is different from that of the preceding nocturnes, much of it being in four or more parts. The charming effect produced by a long-held pedal point is nowhere more striking than in this nocturne, in which the murmuring semitones surrounding a dominant pedal in the tenor and alto voices create a drowsy, honeyed atmosphere, more suggestive of an afternoon reverie in sun-dappled glades than the mysterious sounds of a summer night:

Ex. 22   (Un poco allegretto)

The main theme, not particularly memorable in itself, and lying within the range of an octave, contains no interval wider than a fourth . . . it could be the pensive humming of an abstracted day-dreamer. The great charm and distinction of the music lie elsewhere—in the delicately-organised part-writing, and in certain dissonances, whose gentle clashing

Ex. 23

suggests the invisible but faintly audible activities of a plundering honey-bee.

An adventurous modulation to what is really B major, though Field uses an E major key signature (Ex. 23) and another sudden turn to F minor are short-lived interruptions of the prevailing mood, but with them comes a slight increase in the amount of murmurous activity, the gentle semiquaver movement of the opening bars being replaced by a triplet figuration which is maintained until the coda, where, with one of his beautiful pedal effects, Field brings this admirable little work to a perfect conclusion:

Ex. 24

The Fourth Nocturne, in A major, sometimes considered to be the finest of them all, is the first to be written in a clear ternary form. The principal melody, an inspired piece of *bel canto*, consists of four perfectly-balanced phrases set above a very simple accompaniment. This accompaniment will repay close scrutiny, for every note of it is chosen with the utmost care, and nothing could be changed or omitted without damage to the whole:

Ex. 25 Poco adagio

What seems at first to be merely a reaffirmation of the theme's final cadence flowers into a codetta of remarkable originality and romantic beauty:

Ex. 26

The middle section starts with what appears to be a return of the opening melody, but in the minor mode. However, this proves to be merely a short modulatory link to an entirely new theme, beginning in C major:

Ex. 27

The animated accompaniment figure, its triplet semiquavers surging and throbbing in ever-increasing agitation, soon dominates the music and brings it to a grandiose climax in C sharp major. The transition from this climax to the reprise is as imaginative as the rest of the piece, and the restatement of the first theme is filled with charming variation of detail.

In some respects this beautiful nocturne is not the most characteristic of Field's creations: its ternary shape, the passion of its middle section and its powerful climax are all unusual features in his work. But its great and deserved popularity is fully justified, and one cannot quarrel with Liszt's fanciful and witty association of the name of its dedicatee, Madame de Rosenkampf, with the heady perfume, the glowing richness of colour and the highly-charged romantic feeling of such fragrant music.

Slighter than its predecessor, the Fifth Nocturne is probably the best known of them all, perhaps because it seems to be the easiest to play. It reverts to the style of the First Nocturne: a gentle melody floating above a placid accompaniment in triplet quavers. Nothing could be simpler— until one tries to play those triplets with unbroken legato and with pure, transparent harmonies.

Perfect performances of this piece are rare, and it must be admitted that the pedalling problems which it sets a pianist of today are not easy to solve, since, as we have seen, they are the result of important differences between the pianos of Field's time and those of our own. The beautiful codas, for instance, can sound unsatisfactorily blurred if pedalled exactly according to the composer's directions. Each performer must search for the best solution to this difficulty.

Though most of Field's manuscripts have disappeared, several copies of this work in his hand exist. One of them is of particular interest, since it contains many variants from the final version (printed in 1816), and is headed 'Serenade', which may have been its original title.[1] It is interesting to compare some of the differences between the two versions. In the familiar nocturne the second statement of the principal melody is very simple, almost without adornment:

Ex. 28

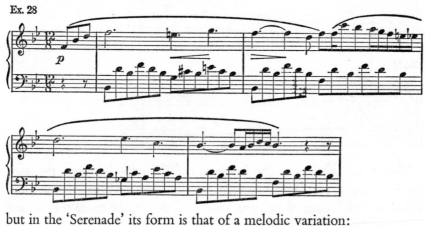

but in the 'Serenade' its form is that of a melodic variation:

Ex. 29

---

[1] Though this version of the piece was printed in 1863 by Senff, of Leipzig, it has never superseded the well-known version of 1816. It was, however, used as the basis of a tasteless concert transcription by I. Friedman, which was published by Universal in 1928, and it was also known to Hamilton Harty, who used it for his 'John Field Suite' for orchestra.

It is also worth noting how the closing phrases of the melody in the 'Serenade' are (Ex. 30) compressed to one bar in the nocturne (Ex. 31).

Ex. 30

Ex. 31

There are other, equally important differences between the two versions, and it must be a matter of opinion which of these is the more effective. Field's own choice was, characteristically, the more concise and direct of the two.

Field intended to provide this nocturne (or rather the 'Serenade' version of it) with an orchestral accompaniment, perhaps for use with his Third Concerto, which has no slow movement. The unpublished score is still in existence. It appears to be complete, except for the first eleven bars, though it is possible that Field intended these to remain unaccompanied.

The Sixth Nocturne in F, as fresh and charming as any of its companions, does actually exist both as a solo and, transposed in E and lightly accompanied by woodwind, horns and strings, as the slow movement of the Sixth Concerto. Apart from the transposition, the two versions are identical. But a manuscript copy of the nocturne, recently discovered, shows the work in an earlier stage of development—as usual, longer and more ornate than it later became. This manuscript illustrates Field's use of the alto clef to avoid leger lines:

Ex. 32

Examples of this sensible practice often occur, not only in his manuscripts, but even in early editions of his published works. As a 'Sunday' viola-player Field was, naturally, very much at home with the alto clef, but he felt it necessary to provide an explanation of its use for his pupils, and on most of the manuscripts in which he used it he also wrote down a two-octave scale in the alto clef, and set beside it the same scale written in the bass and treble clefs.

The first six nocturnes, despite differences of texture and form, are all expressions of the same basic idea: a *cantilena* for the right hand accompanied by left-hand figurations which depend for their effect on subtle pedalling.

The Seventh Nocturne is in quite a different style. It is the first in which the left hand is given the principal melodic interest; and the influence of vocal music is much less evident. The left hand plays a melody in unbroken quaver movement, very simply harmonised and frequently supported by a tonic pedal:

Ex. 33

Above this melody Field places a dominant pedal in the form of a broken octave (Ex. 34), and after nine repetitions these chiming, bell-like notes become a gently-curving ornament:

There is no other material in this fairly lengthy piece, yet the work is far from dull. In restricting himself to such a limited means of expression, Field deliberately set himself a difficult problem which he overcame with complete success. It finds an interesting parallel in the work of certain impressionist painters who rendered special effects of light with the use of a palette limited to only two or three colours. The hypnotic repetitions of Field's Seventh Nocturne, when played with absolute calm and the utmost refinement of tone, can, in their entirely different way, be as magical in effect as Whistler's subtle masterpieces in blue and silver, or in black and gold: it is not without significance that many of the great American painter's finest canvases are also entitled nocturnes.

Of all Field's many examples of the charming effects to be obtained from pedal points held through passages of shifting harmony, none is more delightful than the opening pages of an unknown and unnumbered Nocturne in B flat which was published in an obscure Russian journal, of which only one copy remains. Liszt did not know of the work when he was collecting material for his edition, and it has never been reprinted. The date of its composition is unknown, but such evidence as there is suggests that it was written between 1816 and 1821.

Field's harmonic resource is very striking in this nocturne, as is the skill which prevents his constant repetitions of the dominant from becoming wearisome. The following beautiful passage, which must have seemed daringly original to the St. Petersburg society audiences of his day, still strikes us as being very advanced for its time:

Ex. 36

(Andantino)

All future editions of Field's Nocturnes should include this wonderful composition.

The Eighth Nocturne, in A major, was not originally composed for piano solo and Field never intended it to be a nocturne. Despite its relative popularity it is not, in the form in which it is usually heard, an entirely satisfactory work. Its origin as the first movement of a *Divertissement* for piano and strings is discussed elsewhere, and we need only be concerned here with the versions for piano solo, the first of which Field published, in 1815, as the third of three romances. This consists of the first forty-one bars of the piano part from the original chamber work, followed by what is largely repetition. In this form the piece was frequently republished throughout Field's life, usually with the title 'Romance', but occasionally as a pastoral (its title in the original *Divertissement* of 1811).

Over the years Field returned to this piece, attempting to improve its unsatisfactory form and weak ending; and in 1832, during his last visit to London, he was persuaded by Collard to publish what must be regarded as his latest version of it. This includes important embellishments to the earlier sections of the piece, such as those in the following extract, which may be compared with the more familiar version included in collected editions of the nocturnes:

Ex. 37

Field also wrote an entirely new ending which is certainly more convincingly conclusive than the earlier version.[1]

Since Liszt's inclusion of it in the second edition of his collection, this pastoral or romance has been known as a nocturne, though its position among the other nocturnes has sometimes varied. In modern editions it is generally placed eighth among them but neither the title nor the numbering is of the composer's own choosing.

In 1816 Breitkopf & Härtel published a Romance in E flat which, like the Pastoral (or Romance) in A major, was later to be renamed a nocturne. In this case the change of title occurred during Field's lifetime, for in 1835

[1] Though published as a piano solo by Collard, this version of the Pastoral in A major is identical with the piano part of The Pastoral with string quartet accompaniment, published by Ricordi in 1834. It would seem, therefore, that to the end Field regarded this work as complete only when accompanied by strings.

the Leipzig publisher, Hofmeister, brought out an edition of it, together with the Romance in A major, as one of *Deux Nocturnes ou Romances.* In most collected editions it appears as the Ninth Nocturne.

Attention has often been called to the likeness between this piece and Chopin's celebrated Nocturne in E flat, Op. 9 No. 2. Such resemblance as there is lies more, perhaps, in their accompaniments than in their melodies; for though Chopin plumbs no greater depths of feeling than those sounded by Field, his melody has a more sinuous elegance than Field's limpid Romance. The quasi-valse style of the left-hand part (Ex. 38), is very rare

Ex. 38   Andantino

in Field's work, but in Chopin's it was to recur—notably in his great Ballade in F minor.

That Field could write intense and concentrated music is evident in the Tenth Nocturne—a short Adagio in E minor. Though first published by Breitkopf & Härtel in 1822, it belongs to an earlier date; for a copy of it, in a Russian edition, has come to light. This is ten bars longer than the familiar version, and very different in detail. The copy itself is of exceptional interest, since it once belonged to the composer, and contains fingering and alterations to the text in his own hand. The fingering reveals much about Field's methods of tone production. The thumb is used with unusual frequency, and there is a passage for the right hand which is given to the fourth finger only:

Ex. 39

Liszt, in his edition, fingered this passage in quite a different way, his aim being to ensure an unbroken line. Field concentrates on equalising and deepening the sonority of each note by repeating identical movements of the hand and arm.

The triplet accompaniment supporting the melody in this nocturne is of the utmost simplicity, yet it is exactly right for the tragic feeling contained in the melodic line. A more elaborate texture would have diminished the pathetic effect of the desolate theme. Particularly striking are the gasping repetitions of a single note in bars 14 to 16 (as of a voice momentarily choked by weeping) (Ex. 40), and the sudden scale which rushes upwards

Ex. 40

(Adagio)

a few bars later, like a cry of despair:

Ex. 41

That Field knew and admired Beethoven's Sonata in C sharp minor is suggested not only by what appears to be an echo of its *Allegretto* movement in his Quintet in A flat, but by such passages as the following, on which the celebrated *Adagio* of the same sonata seems to have left its mark:

Ex. 42

Between 1823 and 1832 Field published nothing, but this does not necessarily mean that he was quite inactive as a composer throughout those years. The completion of his last concerto, and the composition of some of his later nocturnes, may belong to this period.

In 1833 the Eleventh Nocturne, in E flat, was published by Schlesinger. This work is more broadly planned than any of its predecessors, and though it bears a superficial resemblance to some of them, it relies less on decorative variation, and contains more thematic development than any of the earlier nocturnes.

For the first time Field does not begin with an immediate presentation of his main theme, but with five bars which prepare for its entry by establishing the dominant as a pedal for the whole of its first section:

Ex. 43

Only in the final phrase of the long melody does the expected resolution relieve the tension created by this insistence on B flat. The poetic *cantilena*, sailing serenely above the left hand's murmuring triplets, is immediately followed by an impassioned outburst in C minor: it is as if a sudden storm cloud had thrown its shadow over a moonlit landscape. This brief darkening of mood occurs twice, but is always followed by a return to the closing phrase of the first section; it is as if

'the emergent moon, freed from obscuring clouds, reveals again its silver radiance.'

The coda, which is unusually long, includes a brief excursion into B major (Ex. 44), and also a certain amount of new melodic material;

Ex. 44

but these elements in no way disturb the rapt calm of the music which concludes this neglected masterpiece.

We have seen that Field often became dissatisfied with his works, and revised them, sometimes more than once, even after publication. The Eleventh Nocturne was no exception. Its first edition, brought out by Schlesinger, in 1833, differs in several important details from Mori & Lavenu's reissue of it in 1836. But with the later version of the piece Field must have been perfectly content: though among the least known of his nocturnes, it is one of the peaks of his achievement.

There is still some doubt about the origin of the Twelfth Nocturne, in G major. It was published as a nocturne in 1834, but it had already appeared as an interlude in the first movement of Field's Seventh Concerto. The composer performed this movement in Moscow as early as 1822, but we do not know whether the work was differently constructed at that time. It is possible (though unlikely) that the nocturne was composed later and the concerto movement altered to admit its inclusion.

The principal interest of the piece, apart from its charming melody, lies in the harp-like accompaniment, which is the only instance in Field's music of a formula which was to become over-popular with later pianist-composers:

Ex. 45

It is not necessary to linger over this work, or over the Thirteenth Nocturne, in D minor—the last of Field's pieces in minor keys. Its melancholy does not go very deep and is lightened by a delicate, transparent middle section in D major (Ex. 46), which sounds suspiciously

Ex. 46

like an echo from one of Field's Sunday afternoon quartet parties:

Ex. 47 Haydn: Quartet Op. 76, No. 6 (Finale)

[*Continued overleaf*

135

Ex. 47—*contd.*

It is music of an agreeable, domestic charm, but with little of the romantic lyricism we associate with Field's works in the nocturne genre.

One cannot pass as lightly over the Fourteenth Nocturne, in C major, the longest of them all, and one which contains some of Field's most interesting and poetic music.

This is the nocturne which Field composed in Vienna while on his way back to Russia in 1835, after his disastrous illness in Naples. It is his last important work.[1] Its form is, for Field, unusually complex, and it begins, unprecedentedly, with an independent introduction which plays a part in the later development of the work:

Ex. 48

Molto moderato

This introduction is followed by a long melody with a gentle, serenade-like accompaniment, very Schubertian in effect:

Ex. 49

[1] With the possible exception of the Andante in E flat. See page 255.

With dramatic abruptness, this rapturous song is interrupted by loud repeated chords and wild, cadenza-like runs:

Ex. 50

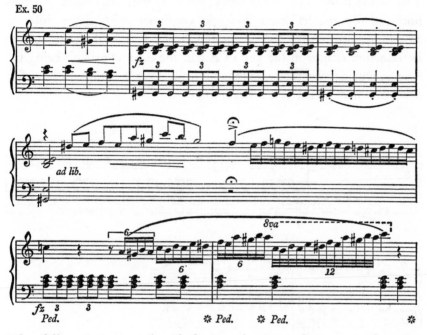

What follows is connected with the introduction, where repeated quaver chords had supported a short motif which is now used for development—a very unusual procedure in Field's work. Eventually an episode in G major occurs in which a new theme, mostly in thirds and sixths, is heard above a swaying left-hand arpeggio:

Ex. 51

[*Continued overleaf*

Ex. *51—contd.*

This theme is the core of the work, yet it appears only once. After its final cadence the left-hand arpeggio continues, with slight shifts of harmony, until it settles on a repeated G, whereupon the music of the introduction returns in the key of A flat, the connecting link being the note G, which is absorbed into the dominant seventh of the new key. The effect is as unexpected as it is beautiful:

Ex. 52

Of this nocturne, two copies in Field's hand survive. One of them shows the work in a preliminary stage of its composition, and includes, among many minor differences, a theme in G major, which was Field's first idea for the central episode, but which was later suppressed:

Ex. 53

Nocturnes

[Continued overleaf

Ex. 53—*contd.*

Though Field's decision to discard this theme was obviously the right one, it is a pity that he did not use it in some later work, for it is potentially more valuable than anything to be found in his last two nocturnes published in 1836, a year before his death.

The Fifteenth Nocturne is a disappointing work. Though it dates from the end of his career, the theme with which it begins was certainly conceived very much earlier, for it appears in a manuscript sketch of the rondo from the Sixth Concerto (a work first published in 1817). This manuscript begins with a bright but rather trivial little motif in C major:

Ex. 54

Field soon replaced this idea by an elaboration of it which became the rondo theme of his concerto. The relationship between the two themes is perfectly clear:

Ex. 55

Some twenty years later, however, he returned to his original sketch and transformed it into the principal theme of the Fifteenth Nocturne:

Ex. 56

The middle section of the piece also proves to be a re-working of old material, for it is a pale echo of the codetta theme from the Fourth Nocturne:[1]

Ex. 57

It seems likely that it was only Field's wish to pay a magnificent compliment to the Princess Galitzina (one of his most important patrons, and the wife of the then Governor of Moscow) which led him to add this not altogether satisfactory piece, and its successor in F major, to the great Fourteenth Nocturne. All three bear the Princess's name as the dedicatee.

The principal interest of the final nocturne is that it is the only one to be first published with a string quartet accompaniment. The work in its

[1] The third and fourth bars of this theme are taken from the early *Grande Walze* for piano duet, also in A major.

quintet form is discussed elsewhere. Here we are concerned with the version for piano alone, which, in fact, is identical with the piano part of the quintet. It is not an important addition to the cycle of Field's Nocturnes; it seems rather unsure of its *raison d'être*, being neither essentially pianistic throughout nor genuinely suited to the chamber music medium. Apart from the Fourteenth Nocturne it is the only one to begin with an independent introduction—a passage of no special significance, which sounds rather better when played by strings than as a piano solo. This is followed by a melody, very Italianate in character, which might be a romance sung by a heroine from some Bellini opera:

Ex. 58

But even this pleasant idea contains reminiscences of Field's earlier compositions; the concluding phrase, for instance (Ex. 59), is to be found

Ex. 59

a tone higher, but otherwise exactly the same, note for note, in the *Fantaisie sur une Polonaise favorite*, first published in 1816.

Two pieces in E major are usually included in collected editions of the nocturnes, though neither of them was so named by Field. The first was published during his visit to England in 1832. Its correct title is *Grande Pastorale*. It is a long and elaborate piece which was originally conceived for piano with string quartet, a medium which Field had already used several times. It has all the appearance of a compressed full score. This version of the work is more fully discussed in the chapter devoted to Field's quintets: here we are to examine the revised version of it which Field made towards the end of his life, and which was first printed in 1851 from a manuscript in the possession of his pupil, I. Rheinhardt.

In this version, which became widely known after its inclusion in Liszt's collected edition, all those passages which were conceived for the strings alone are omitted, and the work begins with what was to have been the first entry of the piano in the original quintet:

Ex. 60   Andante con moto

There are alterations of detail in almost every bar and many cuts, reducing the work to reasonable proportions and making it consistently pianistic. It is worth noting that almost the only two melodies by Field which feature the rhythmic figure known as the 'Scotch Snap' are the early Pastoral in A major (Nocturne no. 8) and the work under discussion, which is also a pastoral. It is evident that for him this figure possessed an essentially bucolic character.[1]

For the inclusion in most collected editions of the Rondo in E major, known as *Le Midi*, there is little justification. This rondo first appeared in 1810 as the *Premier Divertissement*, and in this form it had a string quartet accompaniment.[2] It immediately became popular, and was reprinted many

[1] The figure does occur in some of Field's very early works (1st Concerto, 2nd Sonata, etc.) and occasionally as a decorative element in concerto passage-work. Curiously enough, it is hardly used at all in his one avowedly 'Scottish' piece, the *Rondo Ecossais*.

[2] See chapter on works for piano with string quartet.

times under various titles, and subjected to more than one revision; but never during all these vicissitudes was it dubbed a nocturne until the French publisher, Schlesinger, brought it out in 1833 as *Midi—Nocturne Characteristique*, stating, quite falsely, that it had been 'composé à Paris'. This gave Liszt an excuse to include it in his 1869 edition of Field's Nocturnes, where its lively Polka-like rhythm and its cheerful, open-air character make it seem quite out of place. Liszt does seem to have had some qualms about it, for in his oft-quoted preface he attempts to account for the piece's sunny gaiety, and its sobriquet, *Le Midi*, by an ingenious reference to the white nights of St. Petersburg! Future editions of Field's Nocturnes should exclude it.

The inclusions of the Pastorals in A major and E major and the Romance in E flat in collected editions of the nocturnes may be allowed, since these pieces accord reasonably well with the general style of the authentic nocturnes. There are also two pieces which were printed as nocturnes in Field's lifetime but which were not included in Liszt's edition. One of them, the remarkable unnumbered nocturne in B flat, has already been discussed. The other, a short piece in C major, published in London in 1832 as *The Troubadour, Notturno for Piano Forte*, is an unimportant trifle. Its sub-title, *Notturno*, may well have been added by the publisher, as in the case of Schlesinger's edition of *Le Midi*.

Field's first seven nocturnes, as well as the tenth, eleventh, fourteenth, and the unnumbered nocturne in B flat, are all works of great distinction, and they form a valuable part of the piano's literature. Some of the others suffer from defects of form, and in some of them the flame of inspiration burns fitfully, but the majority do not deserve the neglect into which they have fallen. These pieces now need the advocacy of an interpreter of genius. Busoni planned a Field revival which he did not live to bring about, and since his time the greatest pianists have ignored Field. He awaits the attention of a master of pianistic *bel canto*, and until such an artist allows us to hear Field's best music in performances worthy of it, it will probably remain underestimated.

XIV

Concertos

By THE time John Field was ready to make his debut, the virtuoso concerto had already cast its spell over the music-loving public, and concertos, in the modern sense of the word (that is, works in which a soloist can dazzle by technical skill and powers of expression, with an orchestral accompaniment to highlight his performance), had already become an essential part of almost all concert programmes. Indeed, the establishment of the public concert as a popular entertainment coincided significantly with the emergence of the concerto as one of, if not the most successful of major instrumental forms.

During the later years of the eighteenth century the art of music, no longer the prerogative of the ruling classes, had created for itself an immense new audience which, in its turn, was beginning, inevitably, to demand larger venues in which public concerts could be given. The rise of the concerto is so intimately linked with this social widening of interest in music that it is difficult to distinguish cause from effect; to know whether the form itself or its ever-increasing audience of admirers was the more vitalising factor in the growth of public concert-giving. Certainly by the beginning of the nineteenth century the concerto had gained so great a hold on the affections of music lovers in England that it was preferred to all other types of instrumental music, even by amateur performers, a fact noted by Jane Austen in her earlier novels, in whose pages musical young ladies inflict 'long' (*Pride and Prejudice*) and 'very magnificent' (*Sense and Sensibility*) concertos on their less musical but long-suffering friends.

This is not the place for a detailed account of the process by which the dignified, down-to-earth larva of the *Concerto Grosso* was metamorphosed into the brilliant, though often sadly ephemeral, butterfly of the virtuoso concerto: nor is it necessary to mention here all those composers whose experiments contributed to the form's development. It will be enough to name only those whose work played a part in the formation of Field's own concerto style.

They include, naturally, his mentors, Giordani and Clementi. Giordani's pert and buoyant little concertos, several of them in two movements only and perfectly suited to performance by a child virtuoso, obviously left their mark on Field, who long retained a liking for the two-movement form, using it for all his sonatas, some of his chamber music and the third of his seven concertos. Clementi's well-made, though rather formalistic, concertos were studied by his pupil as a matter of course (Clementi's creative genius is not much in evidence in these works), but the composer whose concertos most attracted Field was Dussek.

Dussek's concertos, particularly the ninth, in G minor, are very advanced for their time, and contain surprisingly prophetic anticipations of Field's style in their poetically decorated *cantabiles* and wavy accompaniment figures. Dussek was one of the leading figures in the London musical world during Field's most impressionable years, and the young artist must have learned much from the older musician's playing, as well as from his compositions.

Another composer whose concertos undoubtedly left their mark on Field was Steibelt. Field was fifteen when Steibelt, then aged thirty-one, and newly arrived in London, scored a great success with his Second Concerto, and an even greater one with his third. The latter, which was specially composed for London, contains a rondo in which a naïve representation of a storm so much took the fancy of the public that it became the rage, not merely of London, but throughout Europe. This rather ridiculous popularity it retained for many years, and in 1815, when Field and Steibelt were in direct competition with one another in St. Petersburg, the continued success of the latter's 'Storm' concerto led Field to cap it with his own Fifth Concerto, *l'Incendie par l'Orage*.

But in 1798, when Steibelt's concerto was first heard, it was a different aspect of its success which seems to have impressed the younger composer —the use of a Scottish air as the basis of its slow movement.

Precedents for introducing popular airs into virtuoso concertos (usually as subjects for variations) had been established long before, notably by J. C. Bach, whose concertos, more than those of any other composer, had launched the form on its successful career; and at the time of Steibelt's arrival in England, the public's appetite for 'Scottish' songs (perhaps partly inspired by the celebrated 'Ossian' forgeries of Macpherson, and constantly fed by innumerable publications, such as those of the Edinburgh publisher, George Thomson, and his rival, James Johnson) was such that an extremely opportunist composer (and Steibelt was certainly that) would naturally make one of them a first choice for the principal theme of his slow movement. Not that he was the first composer to introduce an *Air Ecossais* into a concerto: earlier in the very same year (1797) the seventeen-year-old composer, George Griffin, one of John Field's most dangerous rivals, made his London debut in a concerto of his own composition with a movement in it based on 'The Blue Bells of Scotland'. Griffin's success, as well as the celebrated Steibelt's example, may have had something to do with Field's decision to use for the centrepiece of his own First Concerto another popular 'Scottish' air, though it was not really a folk song, but a composition by the contemporary English composer, James Hook.

Field's First Concerto, in E flat, was first performed on February 7th, 1799, at the King's Theatre, London. Its composer was then seventeen.

Ex. 61

The work scored an immediate success and was repeated several times during the next two years. It was not printed, however, until many years later, and we do not know how often, or to what extent, it was revised before publication. That it certainly was revised is proved by the existence of a manuscript copy of the concerto, written in the hand of a copyist, but with the rondo movement liberally fingered and edited by the composer himself.[1] This manuscript differs in many details from the published version, and proves that Field revised the concerto at least once.

The introductory orchestral tutti is surprisingly assured for so young a composer, though its thematic material is rather anonymous. The martial opening theme recalls the 'galant' style of many of Viotti's concertos (Ex. 61), and it is relevant that Viotti was another prominent figure in London during Field's youth.[2]

The orchestra used is large for such light-footed music: it includes strings, flute, and two each of oboes, bassoons, horns and trumpets, plus timpani. The use of trumpets and drums is natural enough in view of the military rhythms of the first movement, though they are given little of significance to play. The smoothly flowing second subject is as well suited for the violins that announce it (Ex. 62), as for the later, pianistic

Ex. 62

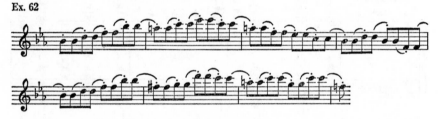

version of it, in broken octaves. Broken octaves are, in fact, a technical feature of the solo part and are used with poetic effect in the development section:

Ex. 63

---

[1] Now in the State Library, Leningrad.
[2] Viotti was the leader of the King's Theatre orchestra from 1795 to 1798.

Some critics, notably A. Nikolayev, have found, even in this early work, prophetic hints of Chopin's style in such passages as the following:

Ex. 64

Ped.

[*Continued overleaf*

Ex. 64—*contd.*

It is my opinion that in this and similar passages there is the strong influence of Dussek, who was the young composer's idol at the time of the composition of the First Concerto.

According to Dubuk, Field used sometimes to play this Allegro as an unaccompanied solo piece, omitting the tuttis completely, and reducing the coda to a mere four bars. The result was probably more effective than might have been supposed, for the opening orchestral theme plays no part, either in the piano's contribution to the double exposition or in the development section. As in all Field's concertos, there is no provision for an improvised cadenza.[1]

James Hook's pretty song, ' 'Twas within a mile of Edinboro' Town', is presented very simply at the outset of the slow movement, the piano part being doubled at first by strings, though flute and horns are added later:

Ex. 65

---

[1] But the Fifth Concerto contains a written out, and accompanied, *cadenza in tempo.*

The two variations which follow are highly decorative, but the ornamental arabesques (var. 1) are so delicate, and the broken-chord figurations (var. 2) so discreet that the calm of the opening remains undisturbed. The first variation is accompanied by strings alone; the second variation by the gradual addition of strings (pizzicato), horns and finally flute and oboes; and there is a short coda in which the pianist takes a valedictory glance at the theme before ending with a gentle right-hand run over a left-hand tremolo. This movement can be regarded as the first of Field's pieces in what was to become his nocturne style, its effect being achieved by the deliberate avoidance of contrasts, whether of key, dynamics or tempo. As such it is of some historical importance.

The rondo makes considerable use of the keyboard's highest register, and requires the player to possess a voluble right-hand technique. Its naïve theme, based on a 'cuckoo' motif, has nothing specially 'Scottish' about it—nothing to justify the four-bar introduction which imitates the droning fifths of a bagpipe (see Ex. 66).

Though this drone effect continues after the entry of the piano, and is taken up again by the orchestra whenever the main theme is restated, the manuscript copy tells us that the introductory bars, like the only other touch of local colour in the piece, the 'Scotch Snaps' in bars 113 and 114, were an afterthought. Neither of these passages appears in the text of the manuscript, though the later version of bars 113 and 114 is to be found scribbled into a spare corner of its final page. Field's attempt to add a little

Ex. 66

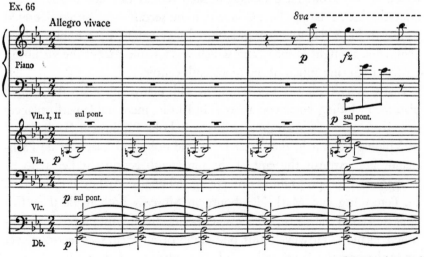

[*Continued overleaf*

Ex. 66—*contd.*

Scottish flavouring to his rondo, *after* its completion (and thus to relate it to the preceding *Air Ecossais*), suggests the possibility that the concerto was originally planned in the two-movement form adopted for his next important work, the Three Sonatas, Op. 1, and that the middle movement was perhaps added as a direct result of the successful 'Scottish' movements in Griffin's and Steibelt's concertos.

It is a far cry from Field's engaging and remarkably accomplished but none-the-less immature First Concerto to his second—the once-celebrated Concerto in A flat which was admired and taught by Chopin, which Schumann thought 'divine', and which was a staple part of the virtuoso's repertoire during much of the nineteenth century.

Clara Wieck played the work, as did many other great German pianists, including Hans von Bülow. In Russia, memorable performances of it were given by such great artists as Nikolai Rubinstein (as the pupil of Villoing he was in the direct Field tradition) and Vladimir de Pachmann; but towards the end of the nineteenth century it began to be relegated to the programmes of young debutants. Arthur Friedheim in St. Petersburg and Mark Hambourg in Moscow both made their first appearances in the work, but now it was less frequently played by established virtuosi. However, this one alone of all Field's concertos never quite disappeared from sight, and new editions of it continued to be brought out by Breitkopf & Härtel, its original German publishers, until well into the 1930s.[1]

A first glance at the concerto reveals at once that it is an immense advance on its predecessor, but how many years elapsed between the composition of the two works it is impossible to determine. For his important début in St. Petersburg, in March, 1804, Field chose to play his own First Concerto, which implies that he had not yet written a second. It is possible that the concerto mentioned by Clementi in the letter written to his partner, Collard, in 1806, is this Concerto, but it is more likely that it was the first, or even the third, which is dedicated to him. The publication of the first four concertos almost simultaneously, by Breitkopf & Härtel, in 1816, only adds to the difficulty of attempting to date the composition, or even of deciding the correct order of Field's second and third concertos. There is evidence, however, that the Second Concerto was in existence by 1811, at the latest; for in that year a fifty-seven-bar extract from its first movement was published in the St. Petersburg journal, *Variétés Lyriques pour les Dames*. Furthermore, the Moscow publisher, Elbert, brought out a version of the slow movement, complete with accompanying parts for two violins, two violas, 'cello and bass in the same year. This publication, entitled *Serenade*, was dedicated (by the publisher) to Marie de Bachmetiev, *née* Lvov, though the complete concerto was eventually dedicated by Field to his pupil, Irene Poltoratska. This *Serenade* differs in many details from the version published by Breitkopf & Härtel in 1816: it seems probable, therefore, that the concerto had been composed, but was still being revised when Field moved from Moscow to St. Petersburg in 1812.

The opening of the Second Concerto immediately shows the change which had taken place in Field's style since the concerto of 1799. In place of the sprightly martial rhythms of the earlier work all is now soft,

Ex. 67

[*Continued overleaf*

---

[1] It is also the only one of Field's concertos to have been issued in an edition for two pianos.

Ex. 67—*contd.*

expressive and lyrical. Strings announce the main theme, joined at bar 9 by a solo clarinet (clarinets replace oboes in this work) (see Ex. 67).

There is a vigorous and effectively scored bridge passage leading to the livelier rhythm of the second subject, which, however, soon gives place to a return of the lyrical opening theme, allowing the tutti to end much as it began.

All this is very promising, but it hardly prepares one for the new sound-world which opens with the first entry of the piano. The orchestra's initial theme is transformed by the kind of piano writing which, for want of another word, we may as well call romantic:

Ex. 68

Throughout the movement there is endless invention of ornamental figuration, and a constant awareness of the beautiful sonorities to be obtained by skilful pedalling; but nothing is more striking than the B

Ex.69

[*continued overleaf*

Ex. 69—*contd.*

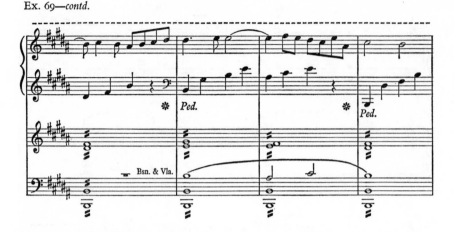

major episode in the development section. Here the soloist introduces an entirely new melody, its pure line quite unornamented, over an accompaniment of pedalled arpeggios and tremolo strings. This tremolo accompaniment was something quite new, in 1811, outside the opera house: it was not forgotten by Chopin when he was writing his F minor Concerto in 1829 (see Ex. 69).

The little *Poco Adagio* is the first of Field's slow movements on original material, unless one excepts the *Pastorale* of the *Deuxième Divertissement*. It is as much a nocturne as any of Field's pieces of that genre, though it has never been included in any collected edition of them. It has, however, been published separately as a romance, which title suits it equally well. Probably it was the quasi-guitar, pizzicato second violin part of its accompaniment which prompted Field (or perhaps his publisher) to issue it with the title 'Serenade', in 1811, though he also used that word for one of the several versions of his Fifth Nocturne. In fact three versions of the *Poco Adagio* exist: the 'Serenade'; the slow movement as it appears in the concerto; and a manuscript version, now in America, which contains several important differences from either of the others. But they all share the hypnotic mood of improvisatory musing, resulting from the music's reluctance to leave the tonic pedal to which so much of it adheres, and owing much, also, to its beautifully-shaped *fioraiture*. It expresses a timid, almost childlike sensibility to which the Italian adjective *innocente*, sometimes used by Haydn, might well have been applied. That word, however, was reserved by Field for his rondo, to whose principal theme, announced by the soloist, it is equally appropriate:

Ex.70

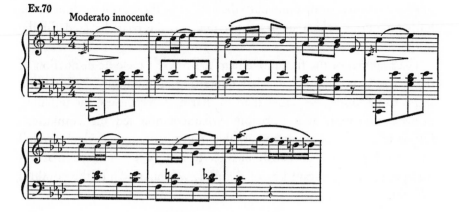

The rondo is undoubtedly too long, but it contains much of great interest: secondary themes of charming grace; brilliant and elegant passage-work; and (something very unusual in Field's work) a lengthy fugato, based on one of the subsidiary themes, which lends credence to a statement by one of Field's Russian biographers that he underwent, about this time, a course of contrapuntal studies with the great theoretician, J. H. Miller, who was, for many years, an important figure in Russian musical circles, and who numbered Glinka among his pupils. It is difficult to believe that Field ever possessed the mental discipline necessary for a prolonged study of counterpoint, but this concerto makes clear that he had acquired enough practical knowledge of the art to write an effective fugato.

As a whole, the Second Concerto, like all Field's longer works, suffers from his imperfect grasp of form; but its charming and often beautiful material, its admirable piano writing and its peculiarly romantic atmosphere easily account for the former popularity which, after some neglect in recent years, it is now beginning to regain.

The Third Concerto, in E flat major, reverts to the two-movement form which was a favourite with Field in his earlier years, and in which, as we have seen, his First Concerto may also have been originally conceived. Both movements are extremely long and brilliant, and, consequently, the concerto is not well balanced. It needs more contrast. In later years, Field often preceded his performances of the rondo movement, in polonaise rhythm, with one of his nocturnes; and there exists an unpublished score of an orchestral accompaniment to the longest of the several versions of the Fifth Nocturne, which suggests that this was the piece he used for the purpose.

The material of the first movement has not the melodic distinction of the A flat Concerto, and it is less interesting harmonically. Its intention seems to be to impress rather than to charm. Nevertheless, the unfailing pianistic invention and capricious ornamentation led the composer's fingers to light upon many remarkable *trouvailles*, some of which foretell later developments. It is hardly possible to believe, for instance, that this passage, in the significant key of F minor, was unknown to the youthful Chopin.

Ex.71

But in spite of such interesting moments, the movement has far too many *longueurs*; and unfortunately the rondo which follows it has them too.

The rondo begins with some rather primitive 'till-ready' chords from the lower woodwind and strings, designed to usher in this tune:

Ex. 72

It is necessary to forget all about the future developments of the polonaise if one is to understand something of the enthusiasm of contemporary Russian audiences for the dignified, brilliant, but somewhat over-loaded piece which Field developed from these not very promising beginnings. In the early nineteenth century, the polonaise in Russia was an essential part of the ritual of the court and high society, and it is this aspect of it, and not its national associations, which Field has expressed in his music, and which made the piece a resounding success with the aristocratic audiences which applauded him. Field's own magical performances of it undoubtedly had much to do with the movement's popularity, as we learn from the memoirs of the Polish musician, Wiktor Kazynski, in which Field's playing of it is described in these words: 'When on the Tyszner [*sic*] piano which he preferred to those made by Clementi and Brod-wood [*sic*] Field played the beautiful *Moderato* in the rondo of his Third Concerto, it seemed as though he slid his wet finger over the glasses of his Scottish [*sic*] Aeolian harp, and drove straight to the heart . . . the listeners wept—for probably none but Field alone could sing so beautifully on this ungrateful and unmelodious instrument.' One suspects that Kazynski was probably a string player. After reading this impression of Field's playing one turns with interest to the passage in question, only to find a series of soft arpeggios and broken-chord figurations of little moment supported by a simple orchestral background, and one sighs for the lost sound of that mysterious art which, even with such unpromising material, could move an audience to tears. Curiously enough, it was this very passage which Field was at pains to eliminate when adapting the polonaise for unaccompanied performance.

It has been suggested that Field's Third Concerto is possibly his second in order of composition, and with this theory I am inclined to agree. The use of the two-movement form, the relatively unsophisticated texture of some of the piano writing (particularly in the rondo), and the narrower harmonic range all support the idea that it is an earlier work than the

Ex. 73

Concerto in A flat. It may well be, therefore, that the concerto which Clementi saw during his visit to St. Petersburg of 1806 was the work under discussion. Its dedication to him proves nothing, it is true, but it could be interpreted as the outcome of the temporary reunion of master and pupil after the first parting of their ways in 1802.

The Fourth Concerto, again in E flat, returns to the poetic world of the Second. The introductory tutti begins in the same soft, singing style as the opening of that work (see Ex. 73), though martial rhythms are used here, too, for the linking material to the suave second subject:

Ex. 74

The soloist's grandiose chordal entry is not really as characteristic of his part as the lyrical, sometimes even passionate *cantabiles* and profuse, but always essentially melodic passage-work of which it mainly consists, and of which the following is typical:

Ex. 75

Ex. 76

The orchestration of this movement is effective but mostly predictable: there is, however, one strange passage in which the entire string orchestra is required to play *sul ponticello*, while the soloist's right hand reflects the violin line in a higher octave (see Ex. 76).

The glistening sound produced by this scoring indicates an interest in exotic orchestral colouring which is rare in the concert music of Field's time. But perhaps nothing in the concerto is more delightful than the nocturne-like episode, beginning in C minor, which opens the development section:

Ex. 77

[Continued overleaf

Ex. 77—*contd.*

Field prepared an edition of this concerto, for playing without accompaniment, which was published in Paris in 1824, but of course he could not recreate the beautiful effect of the violin parts in this passage when the work is played with orchestra.

The slow movement is one of Field's most delightful inspirations. The composer described it as a *Siciliano*, but it is somewhat slower than most typical examples of that dance rhythm. Of the utmost simplicity, it alternates short phrases for plucked strings with the separated phrases of a touching *cantilena* for the soloist (Ex. 78). At one moment the soft voice

Ex. 78

of a viola is heard below the sound of pizzicato violins and piano *in altissimo*, but otherwise the strings reserve their bows for the consoling major tonality of the little coda. So perfect is this miniature that Field's successful transcription of it for piano alone (it is much more than an arrangement) is the more remarkable.

The soft chord at the end of the Siciliano should melt straight into the pianissimo opening of the rondo, which, like that of the First Concerto, is presented above a drone bass. In this case, however, the tonic-dominant

Ex. 79

pedal has a very different function, for Field has surprises in store: after gently lulling us with its insistence on E flat major, the theme suddenly slips nimbly in and out of G major; a delightful piece of musical sleight-of-hand which Field wittily varies on subsequent returns of the theme, in one case diverting the music into the more remote key of C flat

Ex. 80

[*Continued overleaf*

Ex. 80—*contd.*

major (Ex. 80), and in another to the even wilder regions of E double flat (it does not seem to have occurred to him to make a temporary alteration to the key signature):

Ex. 81

But these are only a few among the many felicities of this delightful piece, which includes some lively orchestration (the final statement of the rondo theme by wind instruments against a background of piano figuration is particularly effective), brilliant piano writing, some of it unusually testing for the left hand, and a vein of humour which was an important facet of Field's musical personality, and which he himself once described as 'Arlequinage'.

That Field knew this concerto to be among his best works is indicated by the choice of it for his reappearance in London, in 1832, though on that occasion he appears to have substituted another piece for the exquisite *Siciliano* movement.

Field's Fifth Concerto is not the great work it was once thought to be, but it is a remarkably interesting one. This is the concerto in which he outdistanced Steibelt by introducing into his first movement a more brilliant and exciting (and, it must be admitted, a much louder) musical impression of a storm than that which the Prussian composer included in his Third Concerto. The title, *l'Incendie par l'Orage*, indicates that Field was trying to suggest not merely a storm but some kind of catastrophe resulting from it; though whether this was merely a fire caused by lightning or a symbol of some larger event (the burning of Moscow?) one can only guess.

The opening tutti reveals a close relationship between the first subject, announced by the strings after an initial call to attention (Ex. 82), and the

Ex. 82

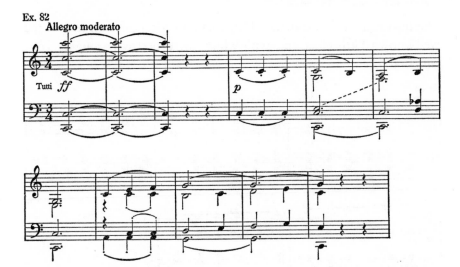

second main theme, allotted to the woodwind:

Ex. 83

The violin motif, *à la* Rossini, which links these themes, has an important part to play in all the later orchestral passages:

Ex. 84

The tutti ends with a codetta which is almost identical with that of the well-known Fifth Nocturne, with which the concerto is roughly contemporary:

Ex. 85

The solo part of the movement is brilliant and difficult, and it contains a number of technical *tours de force* which are not to be found elsewhere in Field's work. They include rapid passages in thirds for both hands, and much right-hand figuration in which thirds also play an important part,

Ex. 86

as well as a scale in the form of six-three chords, played by alternate hands, which remains a difficult feat to this day:

Ex. 87

There is also a written-out *cadenza in tempo*, accompanied by pizzicato strings, in most of which the left hand remains crossed over the right. Despite the example of Beethoven's Fifth Concerto, published in 1811, an accompanied cadenza was still a very great innovation in Field's day, and for many years after it. It was to be a long time before another composer ventured to include one in a concerto for any instrument.

The orchestration of this concerto (its scoring is for the same forces as the second and fourth concertos, with the addition of a bass trombone and some extra percussion) contains no unusual colour effects until the 'storm' episode occurs; but here the use of percussion is quite extraordinary for its time, and, in one respect, it remains unique to this day. For this must be the only piano concerto which includes an orchestral part for a *second* piano. The pianos of Field's day were not capable of producing enough tone to dominate a full orchestra, playing forte, without their keyboards being given the kind of treatment he abominated. Even Steibelt, though probably less sensitive to refinements of tone than Field, had met the same difficulty in his own 'Storm' concerto, and had suggested that it might be overcome by the doubling of the solo part on a second piano. This probably gave Field the idea of writing an independent second piano part for *his* 'storm', and thus making musical history. But Field's concerto has further surprising touches of instrumentation; for its principal climax is marked by a resounding crash on the tam-tam; while a little later, after the storm has begun to subside, an extremely long pedal (45 bars) is given out by a bell, tuned to the note B. Both these effects probably originated in the pit of the opera house: certainly it was the first time they had made their appearance in a concerto.[1]

Like the 'storm' movement in Beethoven's *Pastoral* Symphony, Field's is followed by a 'Hymn of Thanksgiving': for such is the character of the next piece—a short *Adagio* in C major, which is not so much a slow

[1] Paganini's Violin Concerto in B minor, in which a bell is used for the celebrated 'clochette' rondo, is a later work than Field's Fifth Concerto.

movement proper as an introduction to the vivacious rondo which follows it. The theme of this *Adagio:*

is closely related to the principal theme of the rondo itself:

This is a further indication of its purely introductory function. An interesting feature of the *Adagio* is that it is entirely orchestral except for a moment when, as if unable to contain the high spirits he is waiting to unleash in the rondo, the pianist interrupts the orchestra's hymn-like strains with a momentary anticipation of the rondo theme, and then, as if abashed, stops short in mid-passage to allow the orchestra to conclude its sedate theme.

The finale, in two-four time, is of more concise proportions than the rondos of Field's earlier concertos, and it contains, in addition to his usual light-fingered virtuosity, a charming pastoral episode in six-eight, in

Ex. 90

which the bucolic pipings of flute and clarinet give place to elegant piano decorations above a long tonic pedal:

Ex. 91

[*Continued overleaf*

Ex. 91—*contd.*

It is in this delightful *Allegretto* that Field included a passing reference to *La Danse des Ours*, a little piano duet piece which he had published in 1811.

Unfortunately, the concluding *Allegro* section is the weakest part of the movement, a fact of which Field was aware, for at some later date he wrote on a printed copy of this page, 'cela ne valut rien'. However, though he never revised the score of the concerto movement, he produced, towards the end of his career, a solo arrangement of it which, among other changes, includes a greatly improved version of its final section.

The whole of the Fifth Concerto is in unrelieved C major, which is its principal weakness. But despite this, and other imperfections, its engagingly naïve charm is more than enough to compensate for its shortcomings. It could be an entertaining and unusual addition to the repertoires of adventurous virtuosi.

The Sixth Concerto, again in C major, opens as a grandiose, flag-waving military march:

Ex. 92

It is scored for strings and woodwind, with horns, trumpets, bass trombone and timpani.

The long introductory tutti is effectively orchestrated and contains several distinctive themes, but much additional material is reserved for the soloist, and even for the orchestra in later tutti sections. This interesting *ostinato* for violins, for instance, which occurs twice as a link between two flights of pianistic virtuosity, is remarkably dissonant and forward-looking:

Ex. 93

Compare bar nine with the following from Debussy's *Petite Suite* of 1889:

Ex. 94

The first entry of the soloist, an intrusion of only eight bars well before the real end of the orchestral exposition, is also very unorthodox, as are many later details of this interesting work. But perhaps the most intriguing part of the movement occurs in the central episode, a *Meno Mosso* in B flat. At this point an entirely new theme appears in the left hand of the solo part, with an accompaniment of right hand triplets and soft chords for strings, horn and woodwind. The second part of this theme, in D minor, is strongly suggestive of, though not quite identical with, a certain famous melody by Schubert:

Ex. 95

Field's concerto was first performed in St. Petersburg during the Lent season of 1819. Schubert's *Der Wanderer* was published later in the same year. There can be no question of one composer having influenced the other.

For a slow movement Field returned to his Sixth Nocturne, published some five years before the concerto. This he transposed from F to E and

Ex. 96

provided with the lightest of accompaniments for strings, woodwind and horns. The accompaniment is ingenious; for though the temptation to add new counterpoints is never succumbed to, the texture is interestingly varied throughout. The delicate intermingling of solo clarinet and oboe in the following passage is typical (see Ex. 96).

However, a few discreet omissions by the soloist of doubled melodic phrases are advisable.

The rondo is the slightest and lightest in all Field's concertos. It is based on an unusual theme in which, except for the sixth bar, Field seems to be using a quasi-oriental mode:

Ex. 97

The piece includes much florid and attractive passage-work but no contrasting episodes of melodic distinction. There is a moment near the end of the coda when the prevailing mood of easy inconsequence gives

Ex. 98

A table piano by Pape. Field used an instrument of this type for his Paris concerts (1832–33)

A grand piano by Tischner. Field is known to have preferred this make above all others

A page from an unpublished exercise showing Field's use of the alto clef

place to a few bars of a mournful Russian air (it sounds like a variant of the air *Go home my dear little cow*), desolately intoned by clarinet and bassoon, (Ex. 98), but this is over before one has time to wonder at its intrusion into such a frivolous piece of musical confectionery.

It is known that the first movement of Field's Seventh Concerto was performed by its composer in Moscow in 1822. The completed work was not published until 1834, owing to his long indecision about its finale. The first complete performance took place in Paris, on December 25th, 1832.

It is Field's only concerto in a minor key, and its first movement has some claim to be the most interesting, if not the most successful, of his extended pieces.

Two soft timpani rolls introduce a serious, even pathetic, theme on clarinets and bassoons with pizzicato cellos and basses:

Ex. 99

This is clearly derived from a little album leaf that Field had composed not long before for his pupil, Maria Szymanowska:

Ex. 100

[Continued overleaf

Ex. 100—*contd.*

An energetic violin figure which follows is of considerable importance in the work's subsequent development (Ex. 101), though the structural

Ex. 101

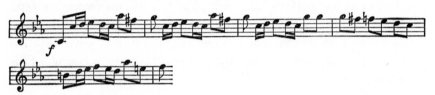

principles of sonata form are in fact largely abandoned during most of this movement, the usual development section being replaced by two independent episodes, one in G and the other in A, which are complete in themselves, though they merge into the outbursts of pianistic bravura which frame them. The beautiful G major interlude was subsequently published as Nocturne no. 12, and it soon became one of Field's best known melodies (see Ex. 45). The A major interlude is in a different style. It retains the basic tempo of the movement (*Allegro moderato*), and features a pulsatingly syncopated piano part, enriched by strings, woodwind and horns:

Ex. 102

The movement ends with a recapitulation consisting of the first subject, played forte by the full orchestra, followed immediately by the second main subject as a piano solo, and then a brilliant coda, which, however, ends with a final hint of the first subject in the restrained woodwind scoring of the opening.

The experiment of introducing a slow interlude, rhythmically unrelated to the rest of the work, into the first movement of a concerto was certainly a remarkable innovation in 1822, and was not without its influence on Schumann, who, in 1835, wrote an enthusiastic review of the concerto for the *Neue Zeitschrift für Musik*. Schumann's own Fantasie in A minor for piano and orchestra, composed six years later, contains just such an interlude, though his greater creative genius led him to relate it closely to the rest of the work.[1]

The extremely episodic character of Field's movement is both its most original feature and its principal weakness. Despite many incidental beauties, it fails as a whole, and it is easy to understand the composer's difficulty in adding to it the rondo which he felt to be *de rigueur* for a concerto, but which was really redundant here. Schumann, strangely enough, was particularly enthusiastic about this rondo, which, as he pointed out, is really a prolonged waltz. It was probably this very fact which attracted him, fascinated as he was by the Viennese waltz rhythm which pervades so much of his early music, and in which the finale of his own piano concerto was to be composed.

The principal melody of Field's rondo could be, and perhaps once was, one of the many little ballroom dances which he jotted down from time to time throughout his career (see Ex. 103).

But though the thematic material is nowhere very distinguished, the whirling passage-work is as inventive and effective as ever; and there is rather more give-and-take between the orchestra and the soloist than in Field's previous concerto rondos. As in the first movement, the onward impetus is twice interrupted: once by a cryptic little passage for strings,

[1] Eventually to become the first movement of his Concerto, Op. 54.

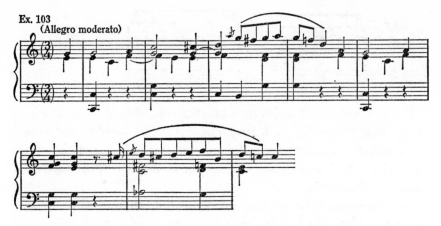

placed, as if in parenthesis, between pauses (Ex. 104), and later by a short
Adagio, immediately preceding the coda, and containing the little three-

note trumpet fanfare which, at the first performance, so strangely impressed the leading Parisian music critic, Joseph-Louis d'Ortigue, who likened it to 'a far-off voice floating upon the air'.

The Seventh Concerto was an immediate success with the Parisian public—so much so that Field was induced to repeat it at one of his recitals in Pape's salon, in February, 1833, though on that occasion he played it unaccompanied, a procedure which seems very strange to us now but which was quite usual in his day.[1] It is not, however, one of his best concertos, and, despite the affection in which it used to be held by Charles Hallé, and other pianists of his generation, it gradually fell into the desuetude which it merits rather more than several of Field's earlier essays in concerto form.

[1] A year earlier (1831) Chopin had introduced himself to the Parisian public with an unaccompanied performance of his Concerto in F minor. One would like to know how he overcame the problem of combining the *recitativo* in octaves, in the *Adagio*, with its accompaniment for strings *tremolando*. It is difficult to accept the solution offered by Edouard Ganche in his edition of Chopin's Concertos (O.U.P., London, 1932) which he claims, though without substantiation, to be the work of Chopin himself.

XV

Works for Piano with String Quartet

❧

FIELD'S CHAMBER music is so rarely played that even its very existence is as unknown to most musicians as it is to the general public.

But it is not surprising that he wrote such music, for the majority of his concerts did not take place in large public halls, but in the elegant salons of the Russian nobility. It was for such occasions, when it was sometimes necessary for him to play with accompaniment in surroundings which precluded the use of a full orchestra, that he composed those of his works in which the piano is joined by a string quartet.

While it would be too much to claim that Field's quintet pieces are an important contribution to the chamber music literature, they contain much that is both interesting and beautiful. In some, the quartet provides only a discreet accompaniment, but in others, and above all in the *Andante con espressione* in A flat, the only one which Field dignified with the title 'Quintet', the interest is much more evenly divided between the two mediums.

Music that is designed to display the virtuosity of one member of an ensemble at the expense of the others is not always easy to classify as chamber music in the modern sense of the term. Nevertheless, such works as Haydn's Piano Trios, and those of Mozart's chamber music works in which a single *concertante* instrument focuses the listener's attention, provide a respectable chamber music ancestry for works of this type. It was not unusual, in the early years of the nineteenth century, for the string or wind parts of pianoforte chamber music to be regarded as accompaniments by public and performers alike: thus it could seem quite natural for a young pupil of Beethoven to refer to his Trio, Op. 1 No. 3, as the 'Sonata in C minor, with violin and 'cello accompaniment', even though she had studied the work under the guidance of the master himself. And at a much later date it was still possible for so serious-minded an artist as Clara Schumann to look upon herself as a soloist (she was apt to complain about her 'accompanists') when she performed such a work as Beethoven's 'Archduke' Trio.

Mendelssohn, who seems to have shared Clara Schumann's point of view, was perhaps the last great composer to have consistently treated the piano as a *concertante* instrument in his chamber music. But there have been many composers since his time who have remained interested in the solutions of the problems that are raised by setting a soloist in the midst of a small chamber music group. Chausson's *Concert* for violin, piano and string quartet, and Ravel's *Introduction and Allegro* for harp, with flute, clarinet and string quartet, are later examples of such hybrid compositions.

However, Field, in his quintets, was not much worried by the problems of texture and balance. His intention was, quite simply, to write light, and lightly accompanied solo pieces for his own use. And if, in some of them, the string quartet began to assume an unexpected importance, even, occasionally, to carry the main burden of the music without any piano part at all, one feels this may have been as much a matter of accident as of design.

The reader should not assume that Field's choice of the normal classical string quartet as an accompanying medium was inevitable. A quintet for piano with two violins, viola and 'cello was, at that time, unusual. It is true that Boccherini had written several works of this type, but these had long since been forgotten, and quintets by later composers, such as Hummel, Cramer, Dussek and Steibelt, invariably used a single violin, viola, 'cello and double bass with the piano; exactly that combination of instruments for which Schubert was to write so felicitously in his *Trout* Quintet (a work which, whatever its other admirable qualities, is by no means the unprecedented innovation in instrumentation it is often thought to be). Apart from Boccherini, Prince Louis Ferdinand, the beloved pupil of Dussek, appears to have been the only composer to have anticipated Field in the use of the more normal quartet as a support for the piano, and it is worth speculating how it came about that Field should have invariably used what was, in his time, an exceptional combination.

Quartet-playing was a favourite relaxation of Field's. In his youth he had studied the violin but, like Mozart and Mendelssohn, when playing quartets, he preferred the viola. His Sunday quartet parties may have suggested to him the suitability of a string quartet as an accompaniment for the piano; but it is even more likely that the custom of his day, whereby solo performers rehearsed their concertos with the string section-leaders of an orchestra in private before the final orchestral rehearsal on the day of the concert, first put the idea into his head. This practice, which was still in force in Chopin's time, only fell into disuse when the technique of conducting had developed sufficiently for it to be no longer necessary. One can easily imagine that such rehearsals (they must often have become semi-private concerts) could have been the origin of the works under discussion. It is only surprising that other composers had not already hit on the same idea, and that, despite Field's lead, it took so long for the piano quintet as we now know it to be become an established chamber music medium.[1]

That Field composed his first piece for piano with string quartet quite early in his career we know from a letter of Clementi's, dated 1806, in which he refers to a 'Quintetto' by Field as being already in existence. The work in question was probably one of the two *Divertissements*, which were published about 1810–11 by the Moscow publisher, Charles Elbert. These works, often wrongly catalogued as having accompaniments for *flute* and strings, are the earliest of Field's quintet pieces. They differ greatly from one another. The first, in E major, is a single movement in rondo form, which, when shorn of its accompaniment, was later to become one of the composer's most popular solo pieces. It shows Field's use of the strings at its least inventive. Here the piano has everything to play, from the first bar to the last, while the strings add nothing but a soft cushion of sustained tone here, a touch of sprightly pizzicato there and an occasional added rhythmic motif at points of climax. As an accompaniment it differs in no way from the kind of support given by the orchestra to a solo passage in any typical concerto of the period, and it lies so much in the middle and lower registers of the stringed instruments that it can be played without the use of the A strings of the viola and 'cello or the E strings of the violins. Field soon found that he could dispense with the strings entirely, and he must have included in many a concert the unaccompanied version of the rondo, to which he later gave the title *Le Midi*.[2]

*   *   *   *

[1] Schumann's famous Quintet, Op. 44, composed in 1842, is the first work to give the five instruments parts of equal, or almost equal, importance, and to blend, as well as to contrast, the timbres of the strings and piano.

[2] This title can be applied only to the solo version, which ends with the note E ringing twelve times through a haze of soft, pedalled tone. In the original *Divertissement* the clock strikes only nine!

The *Deuxième Divertissement*, in A major, is a very great advance on its predecessor. A work in two movements, it opens with an extended *Andante Pastorale* in which the strings are, from the first, an integral part of the texture:

Ex. 105

[*Continued overleaf*

Ex. 105—*contd.*

The immediate success of this charming idea induced Field to make a
shortened version of the Pastorale for piano solo, but it proved to be a
much more difficult undertaking than had been the simple elimination of
the accompaniment to the *Premier Divertissement*. Though he worked at it
more than once in later years, he never succeeded in making a convincing
solo version of the opening melody: in fact he could think of nothing
better than to leave the piano part as it stood for the first eight bars and
make a few slight adjustments to the succeeding phrases. The truth was

that, for the first time, Field had begun to write something very like genuine chamber music, in which the notes and the medium cannot be separated without some damage to the original conception. Not that the whole piece is scored in this way. The second theme, which follows immediately, like a solo after a tutti in the slow movement of a concerto, reverts to something like the manner of the *Premier Divertissement*, its delicate and ornamental piano writing being supported by the lightest of accompaniments. But even here there are moments of charming

Ex. 106

interplay, such as in Example 106, and a variation of the same passage in which, for once, the piano subsides into an accompanying role:

Ex. 107

Like many of Field's more extended pieces, this pastorale is in a kind of free variation form. The variation of the principal theme which immediately follows still keeps the pianist in the background. It is as if the first violinist, having at last got the bit between his teeth, is so unwilling to relinquish it that Field feels obliged to give him his head. Even his more lowly colleagues are allowed some measure of independence:

Ex. 108

The elaborate variation of the second theme which then follows is replete with ornamental scales and arpeggios for the piano, but even here the melodic outline remains with the first violin, and the movement concludes with a short coda in which the quartet echoes the opening of the work while the piano intersperses delicate arpeggios and arabesques between each phrase.

The second movement, a lively rondo, with more than an echo of

Haydn about it, is less interesting texturally than the pastorale, but it does not give the impression (as does the *Premier Divertissement*) that Field began by composing a pianoforte solo to which he later added an accompaniment. It contains lengthy passages in which all the essentials are doubled in the piano and string parts, and even brief moments, such as the following, when it seems as if Field had, once more, become uneasy about the servile status of his first violinist in relation to the pianist— though he shows less concern for the feelings of the other players:

Ex. 109   (Allegro moderato)

This rondo, like nearly all Field's concerted pieces, was later published as a solo; but it failed to achieve much popularity, and even its composer eventually lost interest in it. Nevertheless, it has considerable vitality and, in its proper context, it is still well worth an occasional hearing.

Field's next publication for piano and strings, a long and brilliant Rondo in A flat, undoubtedly began life as an unaccompanied piece.

Among the manuscripts which formerly belonged to Prince Yousupov, and which are now in the State Library in Leningrad, there is an incomplete copy, in Field's hand, of an early, unpublished version of the work. Only the first and last pages of this manuscript still exist, but they show that in its original conception the rondo differed very much from its later, published versions. The manuscript pages are not dated but they were certainly composed before 1811, for by that year the work had been completely rewritten, and a short extract from it published in the St. Petersburg journal, *Variétés Lyriques pour les Dames*, where it appeared as a 'Walze, tirée d'un Rondo de J. Field, arrangée par lui même'. The 'Walze' (which forms the coda of the rondo), when compared with the primitive version of it in the Leningrad manuscript, illustrates the very considerable extent of the revision.

About 1812 or 1813 Field published the rondo complete for the first time, rewritten once again, and now provided with a string quartet accompaniment; but even this was not to be its final version, because a few years later it was republished, without accompaniment, and with numerous cuts and alterations.

The version with strings is the only one which begins with a short introduction, marked *Andantino*:

Ex. 110

          [*Continued overleaf*

Ex. 110—*contd.*

This introduction recurs just before the coda—the so-called 'Walze'. For the rest, the work is a brilliant show-piece for the piano with a not ineffective, but ultimately dispensable accompaniment. In many respects it is a retrogression from the *Deuxième Divertissement*, but it does what it sets out to do effectively enough.

Though the exact date of the composition of Field's next and most important work for piano and strings is not known, he refers to it in a letter to Breitkopf & Härtel, dated 30th October, 1815, as 'un nouveau quintetto'. It may therefore be assumed that it dates from 1814 or 1815.

There is no question here of a mere accompanied pianoforte solo. The piano is silent during 185 of the work's 338 bars. Nevertheless, the pianist's part is always *concertante* in style, whereas the quartet writing is extremely simple. There is little attempt to blend the timbre of the piano with the strings; rather are they used as two separate tone masses which contrast with and complement one another. The concerto principle undoubtedly still influenced Field in this quintet, even though his intention was, for once, to compose a piece of genuine chamber music; but his conception of the work as a single movement, and a slow movement at that, was certainly an innovation.

By the time that the quintet was composed, Field had already invented the nocturne, and had even published the earliest of his pieces bearing that title. The opening of the quintet, which is marked *Andante con espressione*, is decidedly 'nocturnal' in style, its mood and pace being

Two views of John Field's tombstone in the Vedensky Cemetery, Moscow

The original subscription list of the contributors to the cost of the composer's tombstone

somewhat reminiscent of the Third Nocturne, also in A flat, which dates
from the same period:

Ex. 111

The entry of the piano, 38 bars later, with what at first appears to be an
ornamental, melodic variation on the gentle theme announced by the
strings, proves to be but the starting point of a long stream of lyrical
melody in which even the decorative arabesques are an integral part:

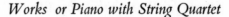

Ex. 112

Field's melodic invention flowers easily and naturally from the very first bars of the work and continues through several pages of score until the music of the opening recurs. At this point the strings play a condensed version of the main theme, with slight but telling changes of harmony.

Then follows much ornate passage-work for the piano, backed by a light accompaniment. This, like the piano's first entry, seems at first to be only a decorative variation of the main theme:

Ex. 113

It is, however, no such thing, for it pursues its own path and makes no attempt to follow the original course of the melody. In this section of the work, which is very characteristic of Field's concerto style, the pianist ripples along, demonstrating his mastery of the *jeu perlé*, but never moving far from the 'home' key until he comes to a rather abrupt halt and subsides into silence, whereupon the quartet begins another extended development and eventual restatement of the main theme, this time more or less complete, though with many subtle changes of detail. The next entry of the piano with yet another 'false' variation (still in the tonic key) was, perhaps, a mistake; and the tripping motif on which it is based needs extremely careful playing if it is not to sound dangerously trivial:

Ex. 114

The music builds up to a solid climax, with a pause on a sustained dominant seventh and a decorative flourish on the piano, at which point the strings take command until the end of the long and beautiful coda, which, like the opening of the work, makes characteristic use of a tonic pedal.

Field's Quintet in A flat is a beautiful, but by no means a flawless work. While it cannot be denied that the string writing lacks invention, its very monotony of style and its avoidance of all extreme registers contribute, in some strange way, to the piece's attractive atmosphere—a mood of entranced calm, which remains equally unruffled by the gentle song of the first violin and the more florid eloquence of the piano. But a more serious

Ex. 115

weakness is the work's lack of key variety. So much of it remains anchored to the tonic key that the final 'variation' (Ex. 114) seems redundant. It is true that there are certain moments when new motifs and even new keys are introduced. The passage illustrated in Ex. 115, which occurs early in the piece, might, despite its obvious derivation from the first theme, have become a secondary subject of some importance; and there is an interesting moment during its subsequent development when one suspects that Field knew and admired the second movement of Beethoven's Sonata in C sharp minor, Op. 27 No. 2:[1]

Ex. 116

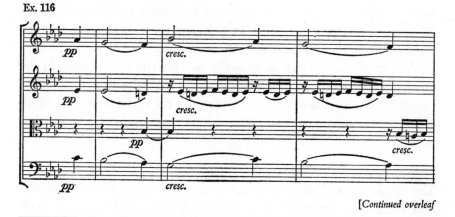

[*Continued overleaf*

[1] The Nocturne in E minor also suggests that Field admired Beethoven's C sharp minor Sonata. See page 132.

Ex. 116—*contd.*

But all these are no more than passing episodes which are hardly referred to again but for a faint echo near the end of the coda.

The quintet is really a monothematic work in which everything stems from the opening melody—a theme of narrow range and few rhythmic cells, winding its way with almost morbid constancy about the tonic, yet bearing within it the seed from which flowers music that, despite flaws, is as charming as it is unique. It deserves a place beside the best of Field's nocturnes.[1]

The last of Field's published works was also his last composition for piano and string quartet. It appeared in 1836 as *16me Nocturne, pour le Piano-Forte avec Accompt. de deux violons, alto et basse ad libitum.*

Liszt's inclusion of it in his collected edition of Field's Nocturnes is perfectly legitimate, since the string parts were never more than optional. The piano part is quite complete in itself, and it is difficult to understand Field's motive in providing it with an accompaniment which merely doubles the harmony and occasionally the melodic line as well. In the unlikely event of this nocturne's being played as a quintet today, it would probably be advisable for the pianist to omit the first sixteen bars of his part and to use his discretion about one or two possible omissions elsewhere.

Though the tale of Field's published works for piano and string quartet is now complete, mention must be made of another work which, though

[1] Even in Field's lifetime his celebrated pupil, Maria Szymanowska, sometimes billed this work in her programmes as a nocturne, presumably with her master's approval.

Ex. 117

originally planned as a quintet, was published only in a piano reduction. This is the *Grande Pastorale* in E major, which Field published in London during his visit of 1832.

The composer's reasons for abandoning his first intention are unknown, but they are to be regretted, for the compression of the full score into the confines of a piano solo is not very convincingly done. Had the work been published as first conceived, it would have taken its place beside the Quintet in A flat as a genuine piece of chamber music, and would probably have surpassed that work in the interest of its quartet writing.

Ex. 118

Field was still influenced by the concerto principle when planning the piece: the first edition actually marks the long introduction, obviously meant for the quartet alone, with the word tutti, and clearly indicates the first entry of the piano with the word solo. But there is a welcome tendency, already noticeable in the thirty-four bar introduction, to aerate the string parts by the use of rests (Ex. 117),[1] and also a new freedom of part-writing in such passages as shown in Ex. 118.

To reconstruct the work as a quintet is not a very difficult undertaking and requires only a minimum of additions to and adjustments of Field's text.

The composer soon became aware of his mistake in publishing the pastorale in piano score, and towards the end of his life he completely rewrote it, eliminating the whole of the introduction, and some other passages which are too obviously unpianistic, and making wholesale alterations to what remained. This revision, which was not published until 1851, should be used whenever the work is played as a piano solo, since it represents Field's final thoughts about the music. But the first published version contains many additional beauties which, belonging essentially to the chamber music medium, can only be properly effective if played by the ensemble for which they were originally conceived.

[1] Illustrations 117 and 118 are taken from the writer's own reconstruction of the *Grande Pastorale* as a quintet.

XVI

Sonatas

⁓ﾟ⌘ﾟ⁓

In 1801, John Field, then nineteen years of age, published a set of three piano sonatas, dedicated to his master, Clementi, as his Op. 1.

He was already known as the composer of several ephemeral pieces based on popular airs of the day, and of a piano concerto which had made some stir in London's musical world, but the appearance of this set of sonatas, with an opus number attached to it, was evidently designed to mark his official début as a serious composer.

To begin with, a substantial publication of this kind suggests an intention of embarking on a more ambitious career than the one which Field was actually to pursue. That he failed to follow up his first opus with others of the same type was largely due to his early and phenomenal successes as a performer in Russia. Little more than a year after the publication of his Opus 1, Field had become the fashion in St. Petersburg society, and from this time onward he seems to have had no thought of composing anything not expressly designed to further his pianistic career. If he continued to write concertos it was because he sometimes needed new material for his public concerts, while in the salons of the nobility, where he was most frequently to be heard, he was expected to play not substantial sonatas, but the elegant rondos, the brilliant variations and the dreamy nocturnes which best displayed the most admired aspects of his playing.

The Three Sonatas, Op. 1, are all in two-movement form; that is, they lack slow movements. Field is known to have once remarked that 'the man who writes Adagios for the piano is a fool'. It is a remark which should not be taken too literally (in later life Field himself occasionally made use of the word *Adagio*, though he continued to prefer such terms as *Andante* or *Moderato*), for it can only refer to very slow music which lacks moving figuration to enliven its texture. It does suggest, however, that in his early years Field was uncertain how best to compensate for the weak sustaining power of the pianos of his time. The theory held in some quarters that he did not bother to write slow movements for his sonatas because he was in the habit of inserting one of his nocturnes into these works when performing them will not hold water. Apart from the fact that there is no evidence that he did so, his sonatas all date from several years before the composition of his first nocturnes; furthermore, two-movement sonatas were not at all unusual at the end of the eighteenth century. There can be no more justification for the insertion of a Field nocturne into one of his sonatas (as has been done) than there would be for adding music from elsewhere to a two-movement sonata by Haydn or Beethoven.[1]

The late Eric Blom considered that the first movements of Field's sonatas were modelled on the style of Clementi and the rondos on that of Dussek. With this opinion I am unable to agree. On the contrary, the influence of Dussek seems to me to be more clearly evident in the first movements than in the rondos, and nowhere more so than in the first movement of the Sonata in E flat which is the first of the set. Here the opening theme seems to be a reflection of the *cantabile* style of Dussek, whose music the young Field is known to have greatly admired:

Ex. 119

This theme contains quite a wide variety of rhythmic figures, but Field makes little attempt to develop their potentialities. The music is agreeable

[1] That Field undoubtedly preceded some performances of the rondo movement of his Third Concerto with one of his nocturnes (probably no. 5) has no bearing on the fact that his sonatas are all genuine two-movement works.

and fluent, and if it lacks something of science there is compensation in its satisfying unity of style.

The rondo is even less pretentious than the first movement, but it is, in its way, equally successful. Though its air of elegant frivolity and the youthful high spirits of its principal theme must have seemed fashionably up-to-date at the time of its composition, they now endow it with a period charm which a wide audience still finds endearing. Usually heard out of its proper context, it has become one of the best known of Field's pieces outside the nocturne genre, mainly due to Hamilton Harty's inclusion of it in his 'John Field Suite' for orchestra.

It contains several features which were unusual in its day, such as the leaping tenths of the left-hand accompaniment, which received some adverse criticism when it first appeared, and the cross-handed

Ex. 120

passage-work of which Field was always particularly fond, and which was still a novelty at the end of the eighteenth century:

Ex. 121

An early portrait of Field shows him apparently in the very act of composing his Second Sonata in A major. It could be deduced from this that he held the work in higher esteem than the, presumably earlier,

204

Sonata in E flat. Yet the A major Sonata is not the better work of the two.

It begins with flourishing arpeggios and a grandiose, marching rhythm which promise a new, and interestingly concerto-like approach to sonata form, but unfortunately the young composer was unable to sustain

Ex. 122

the promise of this dashing opening. The melodic material proves to be as disappointingly empty of real substance as its treatment is conventional. There are a few interesting features, such as the use of extended tonic pedals (always to be a Field 'finger-print'), and the 'snap' which is a characteristic of the second subject (perhaps a reflection of the contemporary craze for 'Scottish' airs), but as a whole this movement is the weakest in all the sonatas. The most noteworthy passage in the work

Ex. 123

occurs when, for a brief moment, the music sideslips from E to C major, an effect which Field was to repeat in later works, notably the Fourth Concerto (see Ex. 123).

The rondo, a kind of Scherzo-Valse, again suggests Dussek, though it is much inferior to any sonata movement by that master. It is as light and as frivolous as the rondo of the First Sonata, but it lacks a memorable theme.

The weightiest and most interesting of the three sonatas is the third, in C minor. Field evidently regarded this key as a challenge, at least as far as the first movement is concerned. The subject matter is far more pithy and symphonic than that of the other sonatas, and the young

Ex. 124

Field, perhaps guided by his master, achieves some really interesting development of his material. There is a fire and tension about the music which recurs very rarely, even in the works of his maturity. Such a passage as the following is sufficiently unusual in Field's *œuvre* to suggest the possibility that the dominating presence of Clementi was not merely breathing down his neck but actually guiding his pen:

Ex. 125

The principal theme of the rondo has a rather peculiar flavour. It seems to be the outcome of a composing session at the keyboard, since it could scarcely have come into being without the use of the sustaining pedal and of experiments with Field's favourite hand-crossing technique; nevertheless, it sounds, at times, so much like a rollicking glee of the period that one is tempted to search for its origin in some long-forgotten popular song:

Ex. 126

The figure ♪♫ which Field had already used in several of his early variations and rondos on popular airs is here used somewhat to excess—so frequently indeed that the ear tires of it, despite the relief of some brilliant episodic passages which, in themselves, are often as vital and inventive as the best parts of the first movement. For all its good intentions this sonata betrays Field's still unpractised hand too often for it to be a wholly satisfactory work, and of the three which form his Op. 1 it is the unpretentious little Sonata in E flat which, within its modest limits, is the most successful.

Field wrote one more piano sonata. This work, in B major, was composed during his earlier years in Russia, and first published in 1813. It is a considerable advance on its predecessors. Though containing no new structural developments (like the other sonatas, it has no slow movement),

Ex. 127   Moderato cantabile

its pianistic style is more expansive and romantic. Field seems quite at his ease here, and there is no sense that he is striving for something beyond his powers. The *Sturm und Drang* of the C minor Sonata is replaced in this work by easy-going charm and good humour: it might be a portrait of Field himself during the happy years of his young manhood in St. Petersburg and Moscow.

The little semiquaver figure which occurs in the first bar of the principal theme (Ex. 127) recurs in the second subject (Ex. 128), and, in a slightly altered form, is the basis of the whole of the development section. This kind of unity was evidently something on which Field set much store, for we find it in most of his more extended pieces, including all four of the sonatas.

Ex. 128

The rondo starts on a dominant seventh chord:

This was no longer a complete innovation in 1813, but it was still rare
enough to add a touch of spice to the beginning of a piece which is full of
wit and unconventionality. A more interesting feature is the distinctly
Russian flavour of some of the later material. In his use of Russian folk
songs and dances as subjects for variations Field was already a pioneer
(this area of his work is of great interest to students of early Russian
musical history), but the introduction of a quasi-Russian dance tune, such
as the following, into a sonata movement is even more original, if not
entirely without precedent:[1]

Ex. 130

The Sonata in B major attempts less than its predecessor in C minor,

[1] Some of Bortnyanksy's (1751–1825) piano sonatas contain themes which are slightly
influenced by Russian folk music.

but achieves more. Sonata form, however, was fundamentally uncongenial to Field, and though in later years he frequently found it necessary to add to his stock of concertos, he never wrote another sonata. He preferred to devote his creative energies to the poetic miniatures which he had made peculiarly his own, and in which the necessary contrast and tensions of sonata form could be avoided.

XVII

Works in Variation Form

❧❦❧

Aᴘᴀʀᴛ ꜰʀᴏᴍ the seven concertos, the sonatas, the quintets and the pieces which have been discussed in the chapter devoted to the nocturnes (not all of them, as we have seen, so named by the composer himself), Field wrote other pieces which are more difficult to fit into neat categories. The majority of these are either in rondo or in variation form.

The most substantial pieces among them, four fantasias, are all, basically, variations on themes by other composers, though they differ from one another in the amount of modulatory freedom and additional thematic material which earns them their title. There are also some pieces in variation form, most of them dating from Field's earliest years, which, for reasons which will be discussed, were published as rondos. On the other hand, there is an *Air Russe Varié*, for four hands, which is not a set of variations at all, but a miniature fantasia in which Field uses not one but three Russian themes. Naturally some of the pieces entitled variations or rondos are what their first editions claim them to be, though there are some among them which were given new titles in later editions, as were certain of the nocturnes.

Such confusion of nomenclature makes it necessary to group these pieces, as far as possible, according to the forms in which they are composed, without regard to their original titles. It is intended, therefore, to consider under one heading all those pieces which, to a greater or lesser degree, are based on variation form, and among which the fantasias form the principal group.

With the exception of the Three Sonatas, Op. 1, Field's *Fantasia on a theme of Martini*, Op. 3, is the only work to which he allotted an opus number.[1] The theme upon which it is based is not, in fact, by the once-

---

[1] It is not known which of Field's works he considered to be his Op. 2.

famous Italian composer, Martini, but by the Spanish composer, Martin y Soler: it is an air from the latter's opera, *La Scuola dei Maritati*, which was produced in St. Petersburg in 1794. In spite of the decline of Russian interest in Italian opera in favour of the French variety, which took place from about 1801, this operatic 'hit' retained its popularity in St. Petersburg during the first years of the nineteenth century. It would seem, therefore, that Field's fantasia was composed, primarily, for his Russian public, and it is likely that there was an earlier Russian edition of it than that published by Kühnel, of Leipzig, in 1812. If there was such an edition, all trace of it has disappeared.

Though an early work, it is the most interesting of the four fantasias. As we know it today, the piece is not the original version but a revision made some time after its first publication. But it remains unchanged in essence, and it may be regarded as the earliest of Field's works to reveal his mature musical personality.

It is a remarkably forward-looking piece, its decorative ornamentation being prophetic of the so-called 'Chopinesque' style which Field was to develop more completely in his nocturnes. There is even a striking anticipation of the Fourth Nocturne in the following passage:

Ex. 131

The fantasia opens with a gentle, hesitant introduction (Ex. 132), which,

Ex. 132

though it hints already at Martin y Soler's aria, is extremely unlike the crude orchestral passage which precedes it in the opera:

Ex. 133

Field's presentation of the air itself is given a new, and aptly pianistic setting, and is immediately followed by a long, rhapsodic improvisation, in which fragments of the theme are used as starting points for many new and beautiful ideas (see Ex. 134).

Then follow two variations on Martin y Soler's theme, the first

Ex. 134

[*Continued overleaf*

Ex. 134—*contd.*

elaborately ornamented in a manner which makes it difficult to remember that Chopin was but two years old when this music was first published in Germany and probably unborn when it was composed:

Ex. 135

The second, much more brilliant, allows the outline of the theme to be heard through a haze of scale passages:

Ex. 136

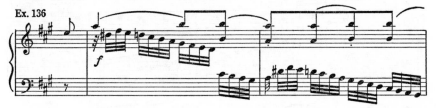

The tempo now increases, the passage-work becomes more animated and the music erupts into a brilliant A major arpeggio which suddenly overflows into C sharp major. Here there is a pause, and a brief recitative which acts as a link to the beautiful coda. The coda deserves quotation at length:

Ex. 137

[*Continued overlea*

Ex. 137—*contd.*

Field's original intention has been to separate the recitative from the coda by a brusque interruption in F sharp major:

Ex. 138

Fortunately this inept passage, along with some other roughnesses, was eliminated in the revised version, and the final result is a charming piece in which Field seems to be discovering, for the first time, a truly personal idiom.

During his visit to St. Petersburg, in 1802, Louis Spohr attended performances of Boïeldieu's opera *Le Calife de Bagdad*, in which the star attraction was the singing and acting of the soprano, Phyllis Andrieux. Spohr noted in his diary that the principal success of the evening was invariably this lady's singing of a charming polonaise, from which he quoted the opening phrase:

Ex. 139

At that time Boïeldieu himself was the director of the French opera company in St. Petersburg, and though this polonaise does not appear in the score of his *Calife* it was almost certainly he who composed it for *Mademoiselle Phyllis* (as she was known to her St. Petersburg fans). There was a 'family connection' between them: her sister, who was also a member of the company, was Boïeldieu's mistress. The polonaise was issued by the St. Petersburg publisher, Dalmas, under the name of Boïeldieu (reasonably conclusive evidence of his authorship), and it is upon this melody that Field composed his *Nouvelle Fantaisie sur le motif de la Polonaise, 'Ah Quel Dommage'*.

The fantasia begins with a tiny, two-bar introduction, after which the polonaise melody is given in full. At first Field contents himself with pulling it into pianistic shape and adding a short coda; otherwise he leaves it exactly as it was known to St. Petersburg opera-goers. Then follows an extremely elaborate variation, principally interesting for its use of accented passing notes:

Ex. 140

[*Continued overleaf*

Ex. 140—*contd.*

The music, which has, so far, remained firmly in G major, now changes to the sub-dominant for the introduction of a new theme:

Ex. 141

This, however, is no more than the beginning of a long modulatory section of which the most interesting passage starts in B major. For a startled moment one seems to be hearing a pre-echo of a certain well-known melody by Chopin, but the impression is fleeting. This part of

Ex. 142

the fantasia is remarkable for its melodic and harmonic freedom, and for the delicate sonority of its piano writing:

Ex. 143

A return to the music of the opening, quite unvaried, suggests that the work is to be rounded off with a disappointingly exact recapitulation; but after only a few bars the music breaks off abruptly, there is a brief pause, and then Field embarks on a new and brilliant variation in which the left-hand part is of considerable difficulty:

Ex. 144

Extensions of this kind are rarely to be found in Field's music, though something similar occurs in the rondo of the Fourth Concerto.

Despite many charming moments, the fantasia is less interesting than that on Martin y Soler's theme, partly because the polonaise melody is too long and too complete in itself to be suitable for variation treatment, but also because Field's musical personality remains too discreetly in the background: only in the codettas and the long central section does he allow his inspiration complete freedom.

The Third Fantasia, in A minor, is based on a popular Russian melody (quoted by Glinka in his memoirs) of which several variants exist. The tune is known to Russians by words which translate rather awkwardly into English as 'In the garden, in the vegetable garden'; but Field's title for his work is *Fantaisie sur un air favorit de mon ami N. P.* Speculation about the identity of N. P. is useless: the initials could stand for a Russian given-name and patronymic (Nikolai Petrovitch, for instance) and are as likely, perhaps more likely, to be those of Field's manservant or his coachman than of anyone more exalted. Though N. P. is mentioned in the title, the piece is actually dedicated to one of Field's aristocratic pupils, Madame Catherine de Hitroivo (*neé* Lapoukhin).

This fantasia was originally provided with an orchestral accompaniment, but the orchestral parts were never published, the manuscript has disappeared, and all that now remains is the solo part. However, the accompaniment was optional, and can have added little to the piano part, which is complete in itself. The work is long and repetitive and in parts extremely florid. Field later made a shortened version of it, for which he dropped the title *Fantaisie* in favour of *Thème Russe Varié*. In both of the two printed versions the Russian theme is stated immediately, in the simplest terms (see Ex. 145), and is followed by several continuous varia-

Ex. 145

tions in strict tempo—a treatment of variation form which Field had already used with great success elsewhere.[1]

In the later version of the work there is an additional variation placed immediately after the theme. This afterthought is worth preserving:

Ex. 146

The fantasia earns its title by the introduction of new ideas and by adventurous modulations; but it lacks poetry and spontaneity, and in this respect it is inferior to the earlier fantasias.

A return to A minor brings a restatement of the Russian theme, followed by a long variation in A major. This contains much busy passage-work for the right hand in the highest register of the keyboard:

Ex. 147

[Continued overleaf

[1] See page 226.

Ex. 147—*contd.*

Field eliminated the whole of the A major variation in his shortened version.

Like its predecessors, the fantasia ends without concert-piece heroics. In place of applause-catching octaves, trills and arpeggios, *à la* Hummel, the Russian melody briefly reappears, and the music then fades into silence. Field wrote three versions of this ending which may be compared below:

Ex. 148

The Fourth Fantasia is less interesting than its predecessors. Published shortly after Field's visit to London in 1832, it gives the impression of having been quickly thrown together to make a few urgently-needed guineas for its composer: in other words, it is a mere pot-boiler, like the so-called *Troubadour* Nocturne of the same year and the *Cavatine, Reviens, reviens*.

The theme on which it is based is a third-rate ballad by Thomas Bayley, who, in 1825, published a set of *Songs of the Boudoir*, of which it is one. Bayley's song won great and quite undeserved popularity which it retained for many years.[1] This can have been Field's only reason for making use of it, for it is poor stuff in itself, and also an unsuitable choice of a theme for variations. Field gives Bayley's melody in full, and follows it by five superficially brilliant variations, the last in waltz rhythm. Unlike the other fantasias, this one contains no modulatory section in which Field might have escaped for a while from the confines of his chosen theme. Only Bayley's little ritornello seems to have momentarily

Ex. 149

awakened Field's drowsing muse (see Ex. 150).

The dedication of this rather unsatisfactory production to the Emperor of Russia is curious. The Emperor Nikolai I was not a patron of the arts,

[1] Her Excellency, Sinead Bean de Valera, the wife of the President of Ireland, who is now in her nineties, well remembers her mother (born in 1839) singing Bayley's air on numerous occasions; and she is still able to recall both the words and the melody of the song. This proves that 'We met' was still a popular ballad in the 1860s, and probably much later.

and it will be recalled that Field had refused a court appointment during the reign of Alexander I. Now that he had left Russia, and had no immediate plans for returning there, one wonders why he should, for the first time, have decided to offer a tribute (and such an indifferent one) to the Tzar. It is possible that the dedication was added by the publisher without Field's concurrence, and was in some way connected with the mistaken idea, widely held in Western Europe, that he held the post of *Maître de Chapelle* to the Russian court: not that the illustrious name of its dedicatee did anything to save the fantasia from immediate oblivion. Though the fantasia on *Un Air favorit de mon ami N. P.* and the fantasia on the polonaise *Ah quel dommage* deserve an occasional hearing, and that on a theme by 'Martini' is among the best of Field's works outside the nocturne genre, the last fantasia probably has less claim for revival than any other work by Field.

Field's other works in variation form fall into two categories: those composed during his prentice years in London, and those dating from the period of his greatest successes in Moscow and St. Petersburg.

The first of them, 'Fal lal la, the much admired air in *The Cherokee*, with variations for the grand or small pianoforte by Master Field', dates from about 1795, when Field was still an infant prodigy, and generally believed to be two years younger than his real age, which was thirteen. The air in question is said to be a 'Welch' tune, though it is quite untypical of Welsh folk music. It was introduced into a three-act opera, *The Cherokee*, put together from various sources by Stephen Storace, who also composed some of the music. It had been popularised by the singing of Mrs. Bland, one of the most admired vocalists of her day, and a great favourite at Vauxhall.

Too much should not be expected from a child of thirteen, however extraordinary his piano playing (Field was no Mozart), and the most that can be said of these variations is that they are rather better than the bulk of the trivia that poured from the music printing presses of the time. They contain no prophetic hints of future developments—fewer indeed than some variations on another Welsh air, 'Ar hyd y Nos', or those on the Scottish air, 'Logie of Buchan' (published as a rondo), which, though both were printed anonymously, have been convincingly attributed to Field by Alan Tyson. The temptation to give space to a consideration of these anonymous pieces (and to another rondo based on the Irish air, 'Geary Owen', also attributed to Field by Dr. Tyson) must be resisted until conclusive evidence of their authorship becomes available. As for 'Fal lal la', though it contains a fingerprint of early Field in its second bar, where the figure ♪♪ of the original song is altered to ♪♪♪ ♪, it is unremarkable other than as an illustration of the young composer's pianistic dexterity.

The only other set of variations which, from internal evidence, appears to date from Field's early teens, is that on the air 'Since then I'm doomed', which is first mentioned in Gerber's Lexikon of 1812, where Clementi is named as its earliest publisher. The air, wrongly attributed by Gratton Flood to Giordani, is by Antoine Laurent Baudron, and is identical with the theme of Mozart's splendid variations on 'Je suis Lindor'.[1] Beside Mozart's masterly work Field's five variations sound sadly insignificant, and it is difficult to accept the fact that anything so characterless could be contemporary even with the anonymous pieces on Welsh, Scottish and Irish airs, to say nothing of the charming variations on 'Edinboro' Town' which form the slow movement of Field's piano concerto of 1799. The

---

[1] Baudron's melody was a setting of the song 'Je suis Lindor', in Beaumarchais' *Barbier de Séville*. In England it became well known, but to quite different words.

fact that Breitkopf & Härtel reprinted this piece as late as 1818 has misled some students of Field's work to assign it a much later date than the 1790s; but Breitkopf's action can be explained by the firm's anxiety to flood the market with as much of Field's music as possible while the demand for it was at its height: the source from St. Petersburg having temporarily dried up, it was necessary to search for new material, even early and inferior material, from elsewhere.

Clementi's mention of a *quintetto* in his letter to Collard of 1806 proves that Field was not entirely inactive as a composer during his earlier years in Russia, but it was not until 1808 that his first publication since the Three Sonatas, Op. 1, was on sale in Russian music shops. In that year a Moscow music publisher, C. F. Schildbach, brought out the so-called *Air Russe Varié*, for four hands; but this work, since it is not really in variation form, must be discussed elsewhere.

The following year, Schildbach issued another *Air Russe Varié*, this time for two hands, which (despite the fact that a later, English, edition describes it as a rondo) is a genuine set of variations, though of an unusual kind.

Field's *Kamarinskaya* variations are based on one of the many short, open-ended Russian dance tunes which can be repeated *ad libitum*, and which positively demand the sort of impromptu variation treatment they received from gypsy bands at rustic festivities in Russia.[1] A variant of the *Kamarinskaya* tune, included by Wranitsky in his ballet, *Das Waldmädchen*, had already been used by Beethoven for a very fine set of variations, published by Artaria in 1797; but Field's treatment of the theme, quite unlike Beethoven's, is obviously inspired by the authentic performances of Russian dance music which he would have heard when he went 'gypsying'.[2]

Ex. 151

---

[1] The *Kamarinskaya* (lit. chambermaid) tune is traditionally played at Russian peasant wedding festivities.

[2] An evening visit to the gypsy encampments outside Moscow and St. Petersburg was a popular Russian diversion (for men) throughout the nineteenth century.

The short introduction, which returns as a coda, is already a kind of preliminary variation (see Ex. 151), and sets the feet tapping even before the six-bar tune is heard:

Ex. 152

The unbroken chain of fifteen variations in tempo which follows is of considerable historical importance, since it provided Glinka with a model for the dance section of his own *Kamarinskaya* fantasia, a work which Tchaikovsky regarded as the foundation stone of Russian national music. How near Field approaches to Glinka's own method of treating the tune can be seen in the following passage:

Ex. 153

[*Continued overleaf*

Ex. 153—*contd.*

The most surprising fact about this remarkable little piece is that it is never performed. Perhaps its neglect is due to the extreme difficulty of its final variations, in which the player is required to perform wide leaps with both hands, in opposite directions, at a fast tempo:

Ex. 154

On March 31st, 1814, the Emperor Alexander I of Russia, accompanied by the King of Prussia, rode into Paris at the head of a long procession of allied troops, watched by large and anxious crowds. Some days later, having finally decided to restore Louis XVIII to the throne of France, the Tzar attended a gala performance at the Théâtre de l'Opéra, where he was greeted by a choral eulogy written specially for the occasion. 'Vive Alexandre, modèle des Rois,' chanted the singers, 'Sans rien prétendre, sans nous donner les loix, ce Prince auguste a le triple renom de grand, de juste de nous rendre un Bourbon.' There had been no time for special music to be composed for the occasion (so it was claimed) and the verses had been hurriedly fitted to an old French air, *Vive Henri Quatre*, which doubtless sounded suitably solemn and impressive. But one wonders if the Emperor was aware of the rather ribald words with which this air has always been associated in French minds: 'Vive Henri Quatre, vive ce Roi Vaillant, Ce diable à quatre, A le triple talent, De boire et de battre, Et d'être un vert galant.' Was there perhaps a subtle touch of Gallic mockery in the choice of *Henri Quatre* for a hymn of praise to the conquering Russian Emperor? It is at least a possibility.

For a time *Vive Henri Quatre* became a first choice among virtuosi as a subject for improvisations and variations. Field was among the earliest to make use of it, possibly as the result of a commission from Dalmas, and his variations on the theme were published during the winter of 1814, together with the words sung in Paris and also some much more fulsome verses added later in St. Petersburg.

As a subject for variation treatment the French tune is rather intractable,

Ex. 155

so Field used it merely as a bass for a new theme of his own, and it is this charming melody which is the real subject of the variations.

Ex. 156

Thus the work is, in a sense, a set of charming variations on an original theme, and the only work of this type which Field composed. It is among the most refined and attractive of his pieces. The variations contain none of the brilliance and grandeur appropriate to music written ostensibly in honour of a victorious monarch: on the contrary they are delicate and restrained, and not without an occasional touch of pathos:

Ex. 157

Only in the fourth variation is there a little of the glitter which usually characterises such politically expedient compositions:

Ex. 158

So muted in tone is the final variation that Field might almost be lamenting the defeat of the French (he was indeed a great admirer of French liberal ideas and of all aspects of French culture) rather than celebrating the victory of Russia and her allies:

Ex. 159
(Molto moderato)

This charming work is the most individual and musically satisfying of all Field's works in variation form, and, like the *Kamarinskaya* variations, it well merits revival.

Field wrote one other set of variations, for which he again used a Russian theme. This tune has many of the characteristics of a dance, but it is in fact one of the many Russian 'town' folk songs, and is known to Russians as 'My dear bosom friend'. It is, or used to be, sung on convivial occasions (Glinka relates how carousing students once kept him awake all night by bawling it in the room below him) and it is not unlikely that Field first became acquainted with it in similar circumstances. Its dance-like

character (Ex. 160), might easily have suggested the 'continuous variation in tempo' technique which Field had invented for the *Kamarinskaya* tune, but here he reverted to a more conventional treatment and wrote seven separated variations, none of them of great originality. The little *Adagio* variation is interesting in that it features a motif from the second part of the theme as an accompaniment to chromatic passage-work of a type which Field usually reserved for his concertos (Ex. 161), but though the

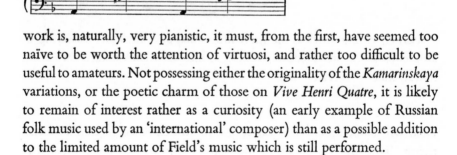

work is, naturally, very pianistic, it must, from the first, have seemed too naïve to be worth the attention of virtuosi, and rather too difficult to be useful to amateurs. Not possessing either the originality of the *Kamarinskaya* variations, or the poetic charm of those on *Vive Henri Quatre*, it is likely to remain of interest rather as a curiosity (an early example of Russian folk music used by an 'international' composer) than as a possible addition to the limited amount of Field's music which is still performed.

XVIII
Works in Rondo Form

~❧~

No concert given by Field would have been complete without one or more of his rondos. He usually billed a nocturne paired with a rondo in the second, lighter part of his programmes, leaving the exact choice of these items to be decided at the last minute.

Contemporary publishers' lists of Field's work include many a piece called 'rondo', though, as has been pointed out, not every one is a genuine example of rondo form. In Field's day the word 'rondo' could suggest not merely a particular musical structure but also the use of a special type of theme—light, buoyant, rhythmic, not too slow, but not so fast that it would prevent the inclusion of elaborate passage-work. Sometimes the rondo character of a piece could outweigh the fact that it was not really a true rondo: thus it was possible, in 1798, to publish Master Field's arrangement of 'The two favourite Slave Dances from *Blackbeard*' as a rondo, simply because it contained an element of repetition; and even, fourteen years later, to bring out an English edition of the *Kamarinskaya* variations as a rondo merely because the rhythmic, dancing character of the theme suggested the rondo style.[1]

Unfortunately some of the pieces published during Field's earliest years are not presently available, though a copy of the elusive Rondo in A major, based on a hornpipe (composer unknown) popularised in London by the dancing of Signora Del Caro, an admired ballerina of the 1790s, has recently come to light. According to Gratton Flood, Field, while still a boy, also wrote a rondo on a song by his first master, Giordani: but it seems likely that Flood merely assumed the *Slave Dance* Rondo, mentioned above, to be based on Giordani's air 'Slave bear the sparkling goblet

[1] It is more difficult to follow the reasoning behind the issue of the anonymous 'Logie of Buchan' variations, which have been attributed to Field, as a rondo.

round': for apart from Flood's mention of it, no trace of a publication or a performance of this piece can be found.

One other rondo by Field dates from his early youth: it is based on a lively dance tune by John Moorehead, a contemporary and compatriot of Field's father, and, like him, an orchestral player in the London theatres. Moorehead's tune won him a small success in *Speed the Plough*, one of numerous Covent Garden productions for which he provided music during the 1790s. Field's 'Speed the Plough' Rondo (it took the name of the play) contains a little more invention than some of his very early pieces, but hardly enough to suggest a genuine creative talent. However, he was to put Moorehead's tune to better use some years later.

Of the many piano solos by Field issued by him, or his publishers, with titles such as Rondo, Rondo favori, Rondeau, Airs en rondeau, etc., most were either reissues of very early pieces or adaptations of movements from concertos and pieces with string quartet accompaniment. The single exception—a *Rondo Ecossais*, published about 1810—turns out to be Field's second working-out of Moorehead's dance tune. Despite its frivolity this new version is not without interest and merit.

Field's early *Speed the Plough* Rondo is in B flat major. The *Rondo Ecossais* is in B, and is a much more accomplished piece of work. The Scottish flavour, such as it is, reflects the general enthusiasm for what was considered to be the quaint exoticism of Scottish folk music, the fashion for which had spread throughout Europe and reached Russia some years before. A few drone basses and 'Scotch Snaps' were enough to enchant the high-society ladies of Moscow and St. Petersburg, most of whom

Ex. 162

despised the folk songs and dances of their own country as mere 'coach-men's music'. Field includes both drones and snaps in his *Rondo Ecossais*, though the sprightly rhythm of its main theme is not essentially Scottish: Moorehead was, after all, an Irishman (Ex. 162). Field's own second subject, with its drone bass and sliding inner voice, is more in keeping with the title of the piece (Ex. 163), though the unusually long coda,

Ex. 163

marked *Presto*, introduces a new motif which might have been suggested by a memory of some Irish reel, heard in Field's far-off Dublin boyhood:

Ex. 164

The piece ends with a typically Field-ish tonic pedal and a final touch of local colour:

Ex. 165

As all Field's other rondos are discussed in the chapters on the concertos and the chamber music, it is only necessary here to mention the manner and extent to which their unaccompanied versions differ from the original texts.

The *Divertissement* for piano and strings in E major and the second movement of the one in A major are the originals of the well-known rondo called *Le Midi*, and of the Rondo in A major (published at various times as Rondeau no. 2, Rondeau favori and Rondo brilliante). Both pieces underwent minor surgery when their string accompaniments were pared away from them; even so, they remain, in their solo versions, much as the composer first conceived them. The most important difference in the E major rondo is the afterthought which led Field to increase the repeated 'bell' notes of the coda from nine to twelve, thus earning for the piece its sobriquet, *Le Midi*. To have called it *Les neuf heures du matin* would hardly have had the desired effect. As for the Rondo in A major, it was necessary to incorporate a few bars of the string accompaniment in the piano arrangement, but otherwise the piece remains substantially un-changed. This rondo also contains a few touches of 'Scottish' local colour:

Ex. 166

The Rondo in A flat, arranged from another piece for piano and string quartet, was subjected to more alteration, including several cuts, the most important being the introductory *Andantino*, for strings, and a much longer cut (some seventy bars) just before the coda. In adapting this piece for piano solo Field was really reverting to an earlier intention, for one of the first of his few surviving manuscripts is a rough sketch for a piano piece of which these are the opening bars:

Ex. 167

Field worked over this subject until it had gained much more rhythmic interest and vitality (Ex. 168), but even after completing the rondo he

Ex. 168

kept it by him for some time, and published only its coda, in which he metamorphosed the same theme into waltz rhythm:

Ex. 169

The complete rondo was published in 1813, and by that time it had been entirely recast as a quintet for piano and strings: this quintet version was then rearranged for piano solo and published five years later as Rondo no. 3. It is one of Field's most brilliant solo pieces and it must have brought to an effective conclusion many a concert in the salons of his aristocratic patrons.

All Field's seven concertos end with brilliant rondos. When no orchestra was available, he would play these pieces unaccompanied, making cuts in the tuttis and such changes to the solo part as were necessary. Only three of these rondos were published in revised versions during his lifetime, those from the Third, Fourth and Fifth Concertos, though most of the others were published separately, out of their proper context.

The rondo from the First Concerto can be played unaccompanied without being altered in any way. The tuttis are extremely brief and sound quite well on the piano. The rondo of the Second Concerto does not adapt quite so easily. Field wrote out a solo arrangement of it for his own use, but the manuscript has not yet been published. Apart from cuts and some compression of the solo passages it does not contain any drastic re-writing. A pause which occurs before the central, B major section receives a decorative flourish which is worth quoting, since it illustrates the type of impromptu ornamentation favoured by Field. He must have introduced many such decorations on the spur of the moment during his performances:

Ex. 170

The rondo from the Third Concerto needed more alteration to make it fit for playing without orchestra. This rondo, in Polonaise rhythm, was always a favourite with Field's audiences, and he made several versions of it to suit different circumstances. The Leningrad Conservatoire owns an interesting early Russian edition of the concerto which contains not only Field's pencilled fingering and editing, but also a manuscript page, in his own hand, which is intended as a substitute for the long *Moderato* interlude in the rondo. This previously unpublished page is given below:

Ex. 171

In 1816 Field published an even more drastic condensation of the piece with the new title *Polonaise en forme de Rondeau*. In this, not only is every bar revised, but an enormous cut of 175 bars reduces it to quite modest proportions.

The Fourth Concerto is the only one which Field republished with all its movements trimmed and rescored for playing without accompaniment. The rondo movement is the least altered of the three and, curiously enough, most of the cuts occur in its solo part, some of the tutti passages being left unchanged.

The rondos of the Fifth and Sixth Concertos also exist in manuscript versions which require no accompaniment. It is evident that, when playing these pieces without orchestra, Field treated them in his usual way, either eliminating the purely orchestral passages or replacing them with entirely different music. The first tutti in the rondo from the Fifth Concerto is a case in point. Its orchestral form

Ex. 172

is replaced, in the unpublished solo version, by this passage:

Ex. 173

There exists, however, a third version of this piece, published in London during Field's visit of 1832. This is practically a recomposition of the entire rondo, some of it, though by no means all, being an improvement on the original. It begins with some introductory bars, almost identical with the sketchy version of the main theme which appears (though crossed out) in the unpublished version—the very bars which Field was to use yet again in his Fifteenth Nocturne of 1836. The theme itself, however, is presented in a manner which changes its character, though scarcely for the better:

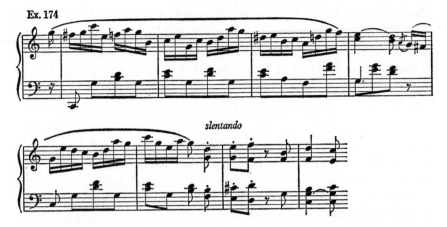

Only the rondo from the Seventh Concerto was never published separately, or subjected to any revision for solo playing.

In 1832 Collard published an *Introduction and Rondo* by Field based on a well-known drawing-room ballad of the day: Jonathan Blewitt's *Cavatina* 'Come again, come again'.[1] Field's attitude towards such potboilers, of which he produced several at this time, must have been quite cynical. His own creative urge, never a resistless, driving force in his life, had, by this time, lain dormant for some years (it was later to have a brief reawakening) but evidently, if driven by need, he was still able to undertake the hack-work of turning some of the fashionable if evanescent drawing-room airs of the time into saleable piano music.

There is not very much to be said for Field's treatment of Blewitt's sentimental ditty, though it is a degree more interesting than his fantasia on Bayley's 'We met'. The introductory *Adagio*, which presents Blewitt's air *à la nocturne*, has a few typically Fieldish passages, but the long, fantasia-like rondo which follows, based on a variant of Blewitt's theme, could be by any third-rate composer of the period. The piece is rounded off by a brief return to the music of the opening *Adagio*.

It is interesting to note that Field's international celebrity was still great enough for foreign editions of this inferior piece to be brought out as a matter of course. French and German editions appeared within a year, and in Germany it was reissued, from time to time, until as late as 1890. As

---

[1] Jonathan Blewitt (1780–1853), composer and organist: wrote numerous successful operas, produced at Drury Lane and Sadler's Wells, and a number of popular ballads, particularly in the Irish style. He was for a time one of the successors of Giordani as director of music at the Theatre Royal in Dublin.

Blewitt's name meant nothing on the continent, it was quickly dropped from the title, and the piece was simply called '*Reviens, reviens*', *Cavatine pour le pianoforte*.[1] However, Field rightly considered it to be a rondo, and it finds a place, therefore, in this chapter. It is the last of his publications to make use of the word in its title.

It may be interesting to note here that shortly after Field's arrival in England in 1831, a writer in *The Harmonicon*, for December of that year, reviewed (unfavourably) a Rondoletto in E flat which had been submitted to him as a composition by John Field. This piece was almost certainly the Rondoletto by Field's young son, Adrien, which had been published in St. Petersburg that year under the editorship of Glinka. A French edition of the piece had appeared subsequently, with a dedication to the Countess Vorenzov, but the original Russian edition, of which a copy is preserved in the library of the Moscow Conservatoire, states that it is '*composé et dedié a son père, par Adrien Field*'. As the work of a very moderately gifted child of twelve, it is only as good (or as bad) as could be expected; it is difficult to understand how it could ever have been attributed to Field *père*, for the French edition (presumably the one reviewed by the writer in *The Harmonicon*) states quite clearly that it is by A. Field.

[1] The most recent English edition (Oxford University Press, London, 1954) retains the title *Cavatina*.

XIX

Pieces for Four Hands

⚜

Fɪᴇʟᴅ ᴡʀᴏᴛᴇ five pieces for four hands on one keyboard. They are not equally interesting, but they are all, in their different ways, curiosities.

The most valuable is the earliest, to which reference has already been made. It is the so-called *Air Russe Varié*, in A minor, published in Moscow in 1808. However one considers it, one can find practically nothing in this piece which is in accord with the basic principles of variation form: indeed, Field might as easily, and perhaps with more justification, have called it a rondo, since it does contain an element of straightforward repetition. The first English edition, of 1811, sensibly evaded the question of its form by calling it simply 'Duet on a Favourite Russian Theme'.

The Duet, which is dedicated to, and no doubt specially written for, two of Field's pupils, the sisters Irene and Agathe Poltoratska, begins with an immediate presentation of its principal theme, which is based

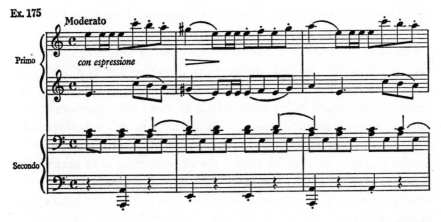

[*Continued overleaf*

Ex. 175—*contd.*

upon, but not identical with, a popular Russian air, 'How have I grieved you?' (see Ex. 175).

One of the young ladies must have been considerably more advanced than her sister, for throughout the work the *primo* part is much more florid and testing than the *secondo*. A Russian critic has pointed out that the repeated note figure in bar nine, which increases in importance as the music develops, derives from the technique of the balalaika. Perhaps only a Russian could have recognised the interesting origin of this detail. Field juggles capriciously with his chosen theme, subjecting it to some quite elaborate ornamentation, but never varying the simple pattern of the accompaniment figure. The middle section, in A major, introduces a new theme, also strongly Russian in character, though it has yet to be identified as a genuine folk tune: the balalaika figure remains much in evidence:

Ex. 176

On the return of the minor tonality it is the *secondo* part which takes the lead in introducing yet another melody. This is a variant of the famous Russian air, 'The Birch Tree', now familiar the world over because of Tchaikovsky's use of it in the finale of his Fourth Symphony:

Ex. 177

[*Continued overleaf*

Ex. 177—*contd.*

The very brief quotation of this theme suggests that it was perhaps included at the request of its dedicatees (one of their favourite airs, maybe) for it immediately gives place to an interesting bridge passage in which both the balalaika figure and a reference to the first theme are mingled with some unavoidable and visually entertaining interlocking of the players' arms:

Ex. 178

The concluding section of this effective duet returns to the material or the opening, but it is by no means a straightforward recapitulation of the first part. Field continues to find new decorations for 'How have I grieved you?' as well as new uses for his balalaika figure. The closing bars of the long coda slide gently into the major tonality of the central episode.

This little work is one of the most interesting and original of Field's earlier pieces and it deserves the attention of present-day duettists.

In 1811, Field published two small compositions for piano duet in separate issues of the St. Petersburg magazine called *Variétés Lyriques pour les Dames*. The first of these, a simple *Andante* in C minor, is plaintive and resigned in mood, with a touch of the Slavonic *Doumka* about its melodic line, which also curiously anticipates the narrow intervallic structure of certain characteristic melodies by Rakhmaninov (3rd Concerto, 2nd and 3rd Symphonies, etc.).

The second of Field's contributions to the repertoire of the duet-playing ladies of St. Petersburg, entitled *La Danse des Ours*, is a much odder production. It seems to have been the joint work of Field and W. Aumann, the editor of the *Variétés Lyriques*. Field was responsible for the *primo* part, which contains all the melodic and harmonic essentials of the piece, while Aumann added a drone bass in imitation of the hurdy-gurdy, the traditional accompaniment for the 'dancing' of the tame bears which were a familiar sight in Eastern Europe during much of the nineteenth century. Legend relates that Field, watching one day the listless dancing of a bear in a Moscow street, seized a flute from the bear-leader and improvised a lively air in the hope of making the animal move faster, and that *La Danse des Ours* was the outcome of the episode. The story, though doubtless apocryphal, suggests the kind of scene which the piece is meant to evoke.

Field can have attached no importance to this trifle; nevertheless, certain phrases from it returned to his mind while he was composing his Fifth Concerto, in 1815, and they found their way into the *Allegretto* episode of the rondo movement.

Field's next composition for piano duet, published in 1813, though of larger proportions than the little pieces written for Aumann's magazine, was probably begun with an equally frivolous intention. However, what might have been merely a piece of ephemeral dance music developed into an extended work (a forerunner of Glinka's *Valse-Fantasie*) with a contrasted middle section containing several interesting and prophetic touches of melody and harmony. During his years in Russia Field wrote a good many small ballroom dances, and the opening theme of his *Grande Walse* has much in common with those trifles (Ex. 179): but the middle section,

Ex. 179

which begins in F major, is in an altogether freer style. Not that it contains any very striking melodic ideas: its interest lies more in such characteristic touches as the use of an internal pedal in a passage very suggestive of the beautiful A flat nocturne. At one moment, indeed, the *secondo* part actually turns to A flat major for what might easily be a preliminary sketch for the opening of the nocturne, though attention is soon diverted to the *primo* part, which recalls the opening theme of the *Walse*:

Ex. 180

Only a few bars later there is a further anticipation of the nocturne in the following bars:[1]

Ex. 181

[*Continued overleaf*

---

[1] It is mentioned elsewhere (see p. 141) that in 1836, when desperately turning to old material for the completion of his penultimate nocturne (no. 15 in C) Field quarried a little figure from the central section of his *Grande Walse* and made good use of it in the Nocturne.

Ex. 181—*contd.*

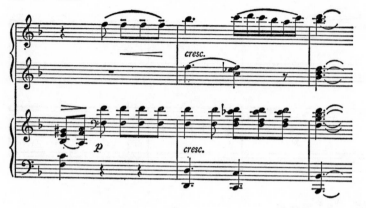

It will be noted that the 3/8 time signature of this duet is abandoned in the middle section for 6/8, though there is no audible rhythmic change in the music, which remains throughout in a slowly gyrating waltz time, marked *Molto Moderato*. Because of its inclusion in Hamilton Harty's *John Field Suite* for orchestra, the *Grande Walse* has become more widely known than most of Field's music written prior to his invention of the nocturne. It would be interesting to hear it occasionally in its original form as a piano duet.

The last of Field's piano duets, first published in 1819, is, in some respects, the most curious of all. This long, elaborate and, in places, difficult *Rondeau* in G major proves to be nothing more than an entirely new version of the rondo from Field's own Second Concerto. Yet it is by no means a mere arrangement of that piece, but rather a complicated variation upon it. Throughout its 253 bars there is not one in which the music is identical with its equivalent in the concerto movement, yet nowhere is there any new development of the material. Everything essential may be found much more simply and effectively expressed in the original piece, and the time and thought which obviously went to the making of the duet version were only so much wasted effort. One feels that the composition of an entirely new work for the duet medium could hardly have given more trouble than (perhaps not so much as) the tortuous remoulding of so much passage-work, to say nothing of the constant and pointless thickening of the texture.

The Second Concerto's rondo, while not faultless, has always been admired for its delightful melodic ideas and the luminosity of its piano writing. It is these very qualities which are obscured in the duet by a texture overloaded with fussy detail. There is something almost shocking about the conversion (perhaps 'perversion' is not too strong a word) of the sweet, clear-eyed charm of the original piece into the stiff and laboriously-worked-out re-writing of the duet. It is significant that Field evidently felt the indication *Moderato innocente* which he had placed at the head of his first version of the music to be no longer appropriate. The duet has no tempo or expression markings of any kind.

XX

Miscellaneous Pieces

❧

IN ADDITION to the works already discussed Field wrote a few miscellaneous pieces. With one exception—an *Andante* in E flat—they are all very slight: a handful of studies, some dances (Valses, Allemandes, Ecossaises, a Quadrille, an Anglaise and a Polonaise), a *Marche Triomphale*, a *Preludio* and a few little album leaves.

The largest of the studies, the *Exercice modulé dans tous les tons majeurs et mineurs*, published in 1816, is the work which Field is said to have played every day of his life, even after he had given up the compulsive practising of his early years. It is a valuable piece of pianistic 'hygiene', which can do much to promote the fluency and finger independence which are the basis of *jeu perlé*. Another study, which also modulates through all keys, appeared in 1823 as a *Nouvel Exercice*, dedicated to Field's pupil, Rheinhardt. In this piece, both hands play the same rapid passage-work an octave apart, and with the same object as the early study, of promoting finger agility. Some years later, Field wrote down, but did not publish, a variation of this exercise in which all the single notes are replaced by thirds. The manuscript, which still exists, bears a note in the hand of J. C. Kessler which tells us that it was received by Madame Caspari, a pupil of Field's, in Breslau, on April 6th, 1834.[1] Presumably, Field sent it to her by post. The date is interesting, since at that time Field's fortunes were at their lowest ebb: he was then in Naples, and in dire physical and financial distress. Yet he was apparently still capable of the troublesome task of writing down streams of thirds, all liberally supplied with fingering. We know nothing of Madame Caspari, but she can have had no excuse for neglecting this aspect of her piano playing.

---

[1] J. C. Kessler was a successful pianist and teacher living in Warsaw during the period of Chopin's youth; the latter frequently attended his soirées. In 1830 he moved to Breslau.

Field's three remaining studies possess a little more musical interest. One of them, bearing the title *Exercice Nouveau*, was first published in 1821, and Field evidently thought sufficently well of it to dedicate it to one of his aristocratic patronesses, the Princess Marie Dolgoroukaya. A study for the development of trills by the weaker fingers of the right hand, it is quite anonymous in style; it could be by Cramer, Czerny or any other efficient practitioner in the field of 'educational' music. It is well suited to its purpose, but one can sympathise with Schumann's evident bewilderment when it fell to his lot to review it for the *Neue Zeitschrift für Musik* in 1833. An enthusiast for the romantic beauty of Field's nocturnes and concertos, he found it hard to believe in the authenticity of this utilitarian music.

Schumann might have discovered more poetic feeling in the two studies by Field (in A flat and C) which the St. Petersburg publisher, A. Büttner, included in a collection of *Etudes et Exercices*, published in 1822. The study in A flat proves to be a cunningly adapted passage from Field's quintet in

Ex. 182

the same key, with the original right-hand passage-work transferred to the left hand, and a new right-hand part skilfully added, plus an occasional supporting bass note. The result is a charming little miniature, which is more of a genuine *étude* than any of Field's other *exercices* (see Ex. 182).

The last study, in C major, is also related to one of Field's major works, in this case the Fourth Concerto, though it contains no direct quotation from it. The C major episode in the first movement of the concerto obviously prompted the composition of this study, but the piece is not quite in the same class as the study in A flat.

A number of tiny ballroom dances from Field's pen have endured the passing of a hundred and fifty years. They include two sets: the *Six Danses*, published by Hofmeister, in 1820, and a collection of valses and ecossaises, published by Probst of Leipzig about 1825. These, with a few isolated dances, among them a polonaise, of which two versions exist, and several more valses, one of which appeared in Germany, soon after Field's death, with the title *Sehnsuchts-Walzer* (it is likely that there had been an earlier Russian edition), contain some unpretentiously charming music. Too slight to stand alone, these trifles can, when grouped as suites, survive comparison even with the dance suites of Beethoven and Schubert.

The *Marche Triomphale* of 1812, written in honour of General Wittgenstein, may also be mentioned here.[1] It is no masterpiece; nevertheless its attractive, springing gait and the use of tonic and dominant pedal effects in its Trio section give it an authentically Field-ish sound.

Like most famous artists of his day Field contributed, on several occasions, to the autograph albums of his friends, pupils and colleagues. Sometimes he added to his signature a few bars of music, usually the opening of one of his two pastorals. But in the case of his celebrated pupil, Maria Szymanowska, he took the trouble, as we have seen, to compose something entirely new—a short *Adagio* in C minor which contains the germ of one of his most striking ideas—the opening theme of his last concerto.

Another miniature, also in C minor, which remains in manuscript, though it has been reproduced in facsimile, bears the (for Field) unusual title *Preludio*. Though extremely short, it is sufficiently interesting to be quoted here in full:

---

[1] An impromptu on the theme by Handel, dedicated to Marshal Kutuzov and the victorious Russian army, sometimes attributed to Field, is the work of J. B. Cramer.

Ex. 183

It is not known what Field intended to do with this fragment. It is obvious that it cannot stand alone. If he had any idea of emulating Hummel in the composition of twenty-four preludes through all the keys, his single example of the form not only suggests that he would have far surpassed his famous confrère, but that he might have approached near to the masterly Op. 28 of his great successor, Frederick Chopin.

One work remains to be discussed, but it is important and there is reason to believe that it may be Field's last composition.

In 1851, his legitimate son, Adrien, who had been with him during the last months of his life, sold to the Moscow publisher, Bernard, the manuscript of a long *Andante* in E flat major. Bernard made Adrien Field provide him with a note vouching for the authenticity of the work, and this was included in the first edition. The piece was later republished by Jurgensen, but after that it went into no further editions and it soon dropped out of sight.

The tempo indication, *Andante*, may not have been intended as a title. Field's later nocturnes are sufficiently varied in character for this piece to have been meant as a possible addition to the series, though it lacks the typical wavy accompaniment which one associates with the nocturne style. But, for that matter, so do several of the others. The opening theme, however, is certainly very unusual—quite unlike anything else by Field. Its character is resigned and seraphic: appropriately transposed, it might almost be a piece of Russian 'sacred' music, perhaps part of a sacred concerto by Bortnyansky:

Ex. 184

The second section of the work is closely linked with the first by the initial repeated-note figure, which is used both as a springboard for the freely developing *cantilena* and for its chordal accompaniment. There is a momentary harmonic adventure into other keys (Ex. 185), but it is soon over, and then begins what at first seems to be a straightforward recapitulation. This, however, quickly gives way to continuous improvisatory ornamentation in the right hand which is really a variation of the opening theme. Quite an intense climax is reached before the piece ends with a

Ex. 185

coda on a dominant pedal, in which the restless demi-semiquaver movement gives place to the satisfyingly homophonic ending which rounds
the work off in the seraphic mood of the opening:

Ex. 186

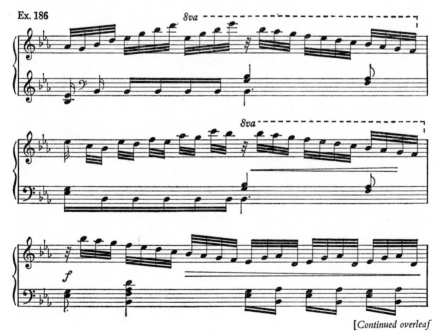

[*Continued overleaf*

s

Ex. 186—*contd.*

The *Andante* in E flat is finished in every detail and is a work in Field's most mature style. Its size and its intrinsic value set it in a place far removed from his other miscellaneous pieces, while its mood of serene, almost religious resignation makes it unique among his works. The fact that the manuscript fell into the hands of Adrien is some support for the idea that it is Field's last work. It is, therefore, an appropriate piece with which to end a consideration of his complete *œuvre*, not only because of its valedictory emotional feeling, but also because it shares with the nocturnes, his finest works, that poetic, singing quality which is the hallmark of all Field's best and most characteristic music.

APPENDIX I

Zwei Gesänge

Field's propensity for drastically revising his pieces, and even for making use of old material for quite new purposes, is nowhere more evident than in the two songs which were first published in 1825. These, his only extant vocal compositions, are far from being mere arrangements of the piano pieces with which they share common themes. They are separate works in which the initial ideas, originally conceived pianistically, are used as starting points for new and appropriately vocal thematic development.

It has sometimes been assumed that these songs are not Field's own work, and it is easy to understand why this should be so. Their very uniqueness in his output is enough to raise a doubt about their authenticity. But the first German edition, published by Breitkopf & Härtel, in 1828, states that the songs were 'in Musik gesetzt und den/Fraülein Lise und Annette Schepeleff/gewidmet/von/J. Field'. Since Breitkopf & Härtel were Field's preferred publishers from 1815 until the year of his death it is very unlikely that they would have published the songs in this way unless they knew them to be his own work. Furthermore, the dedication to the sisters Schepeleff, who are known to have been pupils of Field during his Moscow years, is an additional proof of their authenticity. But the songs are so typically 'Field-ish' in all their details that they can easily be accepted as interesting and charming revelations of the essentially vocal basis of his melodic style.

The first song, 'Levommi il mio pensiero', to words by Petrarca, is based on the First Nocturne, here transposed into B flat. It is twenty-two bars longer than the nocturne, and it includes an eight-bar introduction, a short recitative and much reshaping of the familiar melodic contours. The second song, 'La Melanconia', to words by Pindemonte, makes use only of

259

the first eight bars of the Fifth Nocturne, transposed into F, and the repeated chord motif of its coda. The whole of the second half of the melody is entirely new. A further proof of the authenticity of this song is to be found in its seventeenth bar: here a melodic variant of a phrase from the nocturne's coda is identical with the same passage as it appears in an extended version of the nocturne (the one entitled 'Serenade') which was not published until many years after Field's death. Unlike the first song, which is '*durch-komponiert*', 'La Melanconia' is a strophic song. It is curious that the Breitkopf edition gives only the first of Pindemonte's three verses in praise of melancholy.

The only other vocal work which appeared under Field's name is a duet, 'The Maid of Valdarno', which was published in London, in 1821, by the firm of Clementi, Collard & Collard, with words by W. F. Collard himself. This piece (whether an original composition or the work of an arranger must be a matter of speculation, since no copy of it survives) was probably, like the two solo songs, based on one of Field's nocturnes: this is suggested by the subsequent publication, by the Paris firm of Pacini, of a *Nocturne à deux voix* (also lost), which may well have been a French version of 'The Maid of Valdarno'.

Subscribers to the cost of Field's tombstone

The National Historical Museum in Moscow owns a piece of Fieldiana of exceptional interest. It is a list of those of his pupils, friends and colleagues who subscribed to the cost of the erection of the Field memorial monument in Moscow's Vedensky Cemetery. This valuable document must eventually be given detailed analysis. Here it can receive only a brief consideration.[1]

The list includes not only the names of the fifty-seven subscribers, but also the amounts which they gave. The first forty-seven names are all written in the same hand; the remaining subscribers appear to have signed their own names. The writer of the principal part of the list was evidently equally at home with the Cyrillic and Latin scripts. Indeed on occasion he changed from one to the other, following no consistent plan, thus adding to the difficulties of anyone trying to decipher his handwriting.

The first word—*kopiya* (copy)—is written in Russian. This is followed by a heading in French: *Souscription/pour ériger un monument funèbre/à la memoire de John Field*. The list of names begins impressively with that of Prince Dmitri Vladimirovitch Galitzin (here spelled Golitzin) who was, at that time, the Governor of Moscow. He is the only subscriber whose Christian name and patronymic are given in full, and the reason for this soon becomes apparent: it is to distinguish him from another Prince Galitzin who appears farther down the list. The Galitzins, whose name can be transliterated from Russian into various spellings, were an enormous princely clan, and among the wealthiest nobles in Russia. Next there are the names of two ladies, A. P. Tuchkova and A. N. Khomakova, and they are followed by another famous aristocratic name—M. F. Orlov. No title is given here, but this was certainly Count Mikhail Fyodorovitch Orlov, in

---

[1] A photograph of it appears facing page 193.

whose house Field was always a welcome guest, and whose wife was one of his most gifted pupils. After Orlov come two names which are difficult to decipher (probably Nacitkoi and Kriger), and then, more clearly written, Gurko. An abbreviated name, 'Our', is the first of six subscribers whose names are represented either by a single initial letter or by such an abbreviation. My conjecture is that these were the members of the committee responsible for organising the collection of the donations. Certainly it is fairly safe to assume that one of them, who appears as 'Gr. V.', is the musician, Count Vielhorsky, who had busied himself two years previously with a project to raise money for Field's assistance during his illness in Naples, and who would have been a leading spirit in any plan to honour Field's memory. Next comes Den. Davidov, undoubtedly the celebrated poet-patriot, Denis Davidov, one of the heroes of what Russians call The Great Patriotic War of 1812; and following Davidov are the names Vatnikov, Burnov, Skarytin and Savin (grandfather of the future famous actress, Maria Savina). 'N' (another committee member?) and G. Neidlard precede the more familiar names of Bulgakov and Rakhmanov. Andrey Bulgakov is known to Field scholars from his interesting correspondence with his brother Konstantin, who lived in St. Petersburg: the Rakhmanovs were, of course, those Russian aristocrats who rescued Field when he was said to be *in extremis* in Naples. One would expect to find the names of these two subscribers in the list but it is surprising that they contributed no more than ten roubles each. The remaining names on the first page include, as well as Natokin, Aldvin, 'Gr. V.', Narkov, 'P.', 'N.'. 'Our', and a Doctor Markus (was he Field's last doctor?) the famous names of Prince Gagarin and Count Tolstoy. According to the most recent Soviet research it was at this very time that Prince Gagarin (here mis-spelled Gararin) was deeply involved in the plot that was to lead to the death of Pushkin little more than a fortnight after Field's funeral took place. The Gagarins, one of Russia's oldest and most illustrious families, have left many marks on their country's history, the latest being the exploits of the first cosmonaut, Yuri Gagarin, who was directly descended from the aristocratic Gagarins of Field's day. As for Tolstoy, one cannot be sure which of the several branches of that family is in question, but there is reason to believe that the Count Tolstoy mentioned here was the father of the great novelist and social reformer, L. N. Tolstoy, whose wife's memoirs mention that the novelist's mother had been a pupil of Field's in her youth.

The second page of the list begins with the names of six members of one family, the Mukhanovs, four of them women and two men. Most of these people subscribed twenty-five roubles, but one lady, Ekaterina Mukhanova, put the others to shame by giving a cool hundred. This suggests that she was probably a favourite pupil of Field's, a supposition which is supported by his dedication to her of the so-called 'Troubadour' nocturne. She is the Mademoiselle Catherine de Moncanoff [*sic*] whose name appears on the title page of the first English edition of 1832.[1] The six Mukhanovs are followed by Marie Kayedinokov (Christian name written in Latin script and family name, without the usual feminine ending, in Cyrillic), and then three foreigners—C. (or possibly S.) Dammann, Mme Scalon and Mme Mulhausen, whose names are written in Latin script, which is also used, though less suitably, for Mme Dournoff, *née* Griboyedov. Mme Dournoff (in modern transliteration of Cyrillic script this would be Durnov) will have been a connection of the well-known poet and politician, A. S. Griboyedov, who was appointed Russian ambassador to Persia in 1828. This was really a form of political exile. He was killed in a rising in Teheran some years later.

For the rest, the compiler of the list uses now one script, now the other. Thus G. Sarochnikoi, A. Kologrivova and Ekat. Andr. Mukhanova, *née* Countess Gendrika (possibly the wife of one of the two male Mukhanov subscribers) are written in Cyrillic, whereas Princesse Cleopâtre Schakowsky's name is written in Latin script. This last princess was (despite the slightly different spelling of her name) the daughter of the dramatist, Prince A. A. Schakovskoy, who provided the libretti for several early Russian operas. Two more noble ladies, Ekat. Vlad. Novosiltsova, *née* Orlova, and the Princess (the Russian word *Knyazhnya* is used here) T. M. Prozorovskaya, both of whom contributed fifty roubles, bring us to what is possibly the most interesting name on the list, the German-sounding Eltzner, which could easily be a transliteration into Russian of Elsner. The capital E which begins the name is written over another capital which, though unclear, looks more like a Latin J than anything else: J. Elsner. Józef Elsner? That Józef Elsner who is still remembered for

1 The Mukhanov family moved in high social, political and artistic spheres. They were closely related to the once-celebrated Count Nesselrode, chancellor and foreign minister to Alexander I, and Russia's representative at the Congress of Vienna. One of Nesselrode's many nieces, Marie Mukhanova (later Mme Kalergis), studied under Chopin in Paris, and was one of Wagner's many benefactors during his 'Tristan' period.

having been Chopin's teacher during the latter's youth in Warsaw—could it be he? Certainly Józef Elsner visited St. Petersburg in 1839 (his oratorio *The Suffering of Jesus or the Triumph of the Gospel* was performed there during that year), but there is no evidence that he was ever in Moscow. Nevertheless the interesting possibility that Chopin's old teacher may have contributed the rather odd sum of twenty-one roubles towards Field's memorial monument demands close investigation.

The rest of the subscribers appear to have signed their own names. They were Catherine Rickter (or Richter), Du Vernoy, Jakolef (M. L. Yakovlev, a talented amateur singer and composer), 'K', Zaikine, Gertman, G. L. Povoubetz, Elizabeta B. Cherkasova, Gavriel S. Cherkasov and Ekaterina Khitrivo. The last-named lady was the only one of Field's dedicatees, apart from Ekaterina Mukhanova, to contribute to the monument. In 1823 he dedicated to Madame Catherine de Hitroivo [*sic*] his Fantasia for piano and orchestra *sur un air favorit de mon ami N.P.*

The contributions range from one hundred, the highest figure, to five roubles, and except for those of Eltzner and Mme Hirsch they are all in multiples of five. The total amount, one thousand, four hundred and sixty-seven roubles, was quite large enough to pay for the simple but impressive monument which was erected early in 1838: yet one feels that the list is incomplete. The first page is totalled but the second page is not; furthermore, there are many names missing which one would have expected to have found associated with such a project. Perhaps more information will come to light. Meanwhile we have a valuable document which tells us, among much else, how secure was Field's hold on the affections of Moscow's music-lovers, and how greatly they revered his art even after it had become no more than a beautiful memory.

APPENDIX III

Works

Piano and Orchestra

1. Concerto No. 1 in E flat
2. Concerto No. 2 in A flat. Cf. 13, 57
3. Concerto No. 3 in E flat. Cf. 58
4. Concerto No. 4 in E flat. (Two versions.) Cf. 80
5. Concerto No. 5 in C, l'Incendie par l'Orage. Cf. 59
6. Concerto No. 6 in C. Cf. 23, 60
7. Concerto No. 7 in C minor. Cf. 29
8. Fantaisie sur un air favorit de mon ami N.P. (orchestral accompaniment lost). Cf. 43, 50
9. Sérénade (based on a variant of Nocturne No. 5). B flat. Cf. 22b

Chamber Music

10. Divertissement avec Quatuor. No. 1. E major. Cf. 17, 54
11. Divertissement avec Quatuor. No. 2. A major. Cf. 17, 25a, 25b, 55
12. Rondeau avec Quatuor. A flat. Cf. 61, 73
13. Sérénade, avec accompagnement de 2 violons, 2 altos, violoncelle et basse (an early version of the Poco Adagio from the 2nd Concerto)
14. Quintet for piano with string quartet. A flat. Cf. 66, 79
15. Nocturne No. 16 in F. Piano with string quartet (ad lib.). Cf. 33
16. Grande Pastorale. E major. See page 198. Cf. 34a, 34b, 81
17. Midi, Rondeau pour le Piano Forte avec accompagnement de quatuor (ad. lib.), précédé d'une Pastorale. (Revised versions of 10, and the first movement only of 11.) Cf. 25b, 54

Piano works (solo)

Nocturnes

18. No. 1 in E flat (2 versions). Cf. 89
19a. Romance in C minor. Cf. 19b
19b. No. 2 in C minor. Cf. 19a
20. No. 3 in A flat
21. No. 4 in A
22a. Serenade in B flat. Cf. 22b
22b. No. 5 in B flat. Cf. 22a, 90
23. No. 6 in F (two versions). Cf. 6, 2nd movement
24. No. 7 in C
25a. No. 8 in A. Cf. 11, 17, 25b
25b. Pastoral in A. Cf. 11, 17, 25a
26. No. 9 in E flat. (Romance)
27. No. 10 in E minor (two versions)
28. No. 11 in E flat (two versions)
29. No. 12 in G (extracted from 7th Concerto). Cf. 7
30. No. 13 in D minor
31. No. 14 in C (two versions, one in MS)
32. No. 15 in C
33. No. 16 in F. Cf. 15
34a. Grande Pastorale (Nocturne no. 17 in Breitkopf & Härtel edition.) Cf. 16, 34b, 82
34b. Pastoral. E major. (Nocturne no. 10 in Schuberth Edition.) Cf. 16, 34b, 82
35. Nocturne in B flat. Unnumbered
36. The Troubadour, Notturno. C

Sonatas

37. No. 1 in E flat. Op. 1 No. 1
38. No. 2 in A. Op. 1 No. 2
39. No. 3 in C minor. Op. 1 No. 3
40. No. 4 in B

Appendices

Fantasias

41. Fantaisie sur l'Andante de Martini. Op. 3
42. Nouvelle Fantaisie sur le motif de la polonaise *Ah quel dommage*. G major
43. Fantaisie sur un air favorit de mon ami N.P. A minor. Cf. 8, 50
44. Nouvelle Fantaisie. G major. Cf. 73

Variations

45. Fal lal la, the much admired air in *The Cherokee*, with variations. A major
46. Air avec variations, 'Since then I'm Doomed'. C major
47. Air du Bon Roi Henri IV, Varié. A minor
48. *Kamarinskaya*, Air Russe Varié. B flat
49. Chanson Russe Varié. D minor
50. Variations on a Russian National Song. A minor. Cf. 8, 43

Rondos

51a. The two Favourite Dances in *Blackbeard*, arranged as a Rondo
51b. Deux Airs en rondeau (identical with 51a)
52. 'Signora Del Caro's Hornpipe', arranged as a Rondo.
53. Rondo on the air 'Logie of Buchan'. (Issued anonymously but attributed to Field.) Missing, but cf. 91
54. 'Speed the Plough', arranged as a rondo. B flat. Cf. 62
55. 'Le Midi', Rondeau. E major. Cf. 10, 17
56. Rondeau (also as Rondo brillant and Rondo Favori). A major. Cf. 11
57. Rondeau. A flat. Cf. 12, 74
58. Rondo from the 2nd Concerto. MS. A flat. Cf. 2
59. Polonaise Favorite en forme de Rondeau (two versions, one MS). E flat. Cf. 3
60. Rondo from the 5th Concerto. C (two versions, one in MS). Cf. 5
61. Rondo from the 6th Concerto. C. MS. Cf. 6
62. Rondo Ecossais. B (on the same theme as 54)
63. Introduction & Rondo on Blewitt's Cavatina, 'Return, return'. E major

Studies

64. Exercice modulé dans tous les tons majeurs et mineurs
65. Exercice Nouveau. C major
66. Nouvel Exercice
67. Etude. A flat (based on a passage in the Quintet). Cf. 14
68. Etude. C major
69. Exercise for double thirds. MS

Dances

70. Six Danses.
    1. Walzer in G: Trio in D   2. Walzer in A: Trio in A
    3. Walzer in A: Trio in A   4. Quadrille in F
    5. Quadrille in E flat: Trio in E flat   6. Anglaise in E flat
71. Quatre Danses.
    1. Valse Brilliant (*sic*) in E flat   2. Ecossaise in D
    3. Valse in C   4. Ecossaise in D
72. Sehnsuchts-Walzer. E major
73. Valse. G. Cf. 44
74. Walze, tirée d'un Rondo. A flat. Cf. 12, 57
75. Polonaise. E flat (two versions)

Miscellaneous Pieces

76. Marche Triomphale. E flat: Trio A flat
77. Andante. A flat (after the Quintet, MS). Cf. 14, 67
78. Andante. E flat
79. Preludio in C minor
80. Album Leaf. C minor
81. Siciliano. G minor (transcription from the 4th Concerto). Cf. 4/2
82. Pastoral. E, MS. Cf. 16, 34a, 34b
83. 'Ein Bärentanz', Allegretto. C (published as an appendix to J. Dessauer's *John Field: sein Leben und seine Werke*)

Duets

84. Air Russe Varié à Quatre Mains. A minor
85. Andante à Quatre Mains. C minor
86. La Danse des Ours (with W. Aumann). E flat. Cf. 8/2
87. Grande Walse à Quatre Mains. A

88. Rondeau à Quatre Mains. G (based on the rondo of the 2nd Concerto)

Songs

89. 'Levommi il mio pensiero' (words by Petrarca). B flat. Based on Nocturne no. 1. Cf. 18
90. 'La Melanconia' (words by Pindemonte). F. Based on Nocturne no. 5. Cf. 22b

Pieces attributed to Field

91. Rondo, 'Logie of Buchan'. B flat. Published anonymously. Cf. 53
92. Welsh Air, 'Ar hyd y nos', with variations. Published anonymously
93. 'Gary (Geary) Owen', arranged as a Rondo. Published anonymously
94. Etude in D, MS. Unidentified étude written on a spare page of an authentic Field manuscript, though not in Field's hand.

Doubtful and wrongly attributed works

95. 'The Maid of Valdarno', duet for two voices and pianoforte. Lost. Likely to have been an adaptation of a Field Nocturne
96. Frühlings-Walzer. E. Really by Weber
97. Rondoletto. E flat. Really by Adrien Field
98. Impromptu on a theme by Handel. Really by J. B. Cramer
99. Quadrilles on themes from Weber's operas. Really by L. Field

Arrangement

100 Concertante in F, by Pleyel, arranged for pianoforte solo.

SELECT BIBLIOGRAPHY

ANDREWS, HILDA, 'Sidelights of Music History—John Field, Pianist-Composer, the Herald of Chopin and Liszt', *The Music Teacher*, Vol. 8, London, 1929.

BENITEZ, SISTER M. SCHOLASTICA (C. S. B.), 'The Nocturnes of John Field', unpublished M.A. dissertation, Catholic University of America, Washington, D.C., 1957.

BLOM, ERIC, 'John Field', *The Chesterian*, no. 11, London, 1930, 201–7 and 233–8.

BULGAKOV, Correspondence between A. Y. Bulgakov and K. Y. Bulgakov, 'Russki Arkhiv' (Russian archives), St. Petersburg, 1902 and 1903.

CAREY, MARTIN C., 'John Field (1782–1836), a medical portrait', unpublished address given to the Historical Section of the Royal Academy of Medicine in Ireland, Royal College of Physicians, Dublin, February 15th, 1957.

CLEMENTI, MUZIO, 'Memoirs of Clementi', unsigned article in the *Quarterly Musical Magazine*, Colburn & Bentley, London, 1830.

COX, JOHN EDMUND, *Musical Recollections of the last Half-Century*, Tinsley Brothers, London, 1872.

CRAIG, MAURICE, *Dublin, 1660–1860; a social and architectural history*, Allen Figgis Ltd., Dublin, 1969.

CURTIN, J. McAULIFFE, 'James Quinlan, Formerly Surgeon-General to the Czar of Russia, 1826, an historical note', address given to the Historical Section of the Royal Academy of Medicine in Ireland, January 29th, 1964, *Irish Journal of Medical Science*, Dublin, 1967.

DALE, KATHLEEN, *Nineteenth-Century Piano Music*, Oxford University Press, London, 1954.

DALE, KATHLEEN, 'Rediscovering John Field', *The Listener*, no. 64, London, 1960, 600.

DAVIES, JOAN, 'John Field, the father of Romantic Music', *The Consort*, Vol. XXI, London, 1964, 299.

DESSAUER, HEINRICH, *John Field, sein Leben und seine Werke*, Beyer & Söhul Langensalza, 1912.

DOSCHER, DAVID, 'John Field, The Pianoforte's First Modern Composer', *International Piano Library Bulletin*, Vol. II (special John Field issue), New York, 1968.

DUBUK, ALEXANDER, 'Memories of John Field, with an introduction by M. Balakirev', *Knizhka Nedeli* ('Weekly Booklets'), Moscow, 1898.

EWEN, DAVID, 'The Centenary of a neglected composer: John Field', *The American Music Lover*, Vol. XI, 1937, 287.

FÉTIS, FRANÇOIS-JOSEPH, *Biographie Universelle des Musicians et Bibliographie de la Musique*, Firmin-Didot Frères, Paris, 1867–70.

FÉTIS, FRANÇOIS-JOSEPH, Revues des Concerts, *La Revue Musicale*, Paris, 1832 and 1833.

FLOOD, WILLIAM H. GRATTON, *John Field: inventor of the Nocturne*, William Lester Ltd., Dublin, 1920.

FUSIL, LOUISE, *Souvenirs d'une Actrice*, Hauman, Brussels, 1841.

GARDINER, WILLIAM, *Music and Friends*, Longman, London, 1838.

GEBHARD, FR. ALB., 'John Field: a Biographical Sketch', *Severnaya Pchela* ('The Northern Bee'), St. Petersburg, 1839, 12. VIII no. 180/14. VIII no. 181.

GLINKA, M. I., *Memoirs*, trans. from the Russian by R. B. Mudge, University of Oklahoma Press, Oklahoma, 1963.

GORER, RICHARD, 'John Field and his Storm Concerto', *The Listener*, London, January, 1956, 33.

GORER, RICHARD, 'The Mystery of John Field', *Monthly Musical Record*, Vol. LXXV, London, 1945, 220–32.

HALLÉ, SIR CHARLES, *Life and Letters of Sir Charles Hallé: being an Autobiography (1819–1869) with Correspondence and Diaries*, Smith Elder, London, 1896.

HALSKI, CZESLAW R., 'Musical Europe in Retrospect', *Music & Letters*, London, October, 1958, 372–7.

HAYDN, JOSEPH, *Collected Correspondence and London Notebooks*, edited by H. C. Robbins Landon, Barrie & Rockliff, London, 1959.

HAZLITT, WILLIAM, *Memoirs of the late Thomas Holcroft*, Longman, London, 1852.

HEDLEY, ARTHUR, *Selected Correspondence of Fryderyk Chopin*, Heinemann, London, 1962.

HIBBARD, TREVOR, 'John Field's Rondeaux on "Speed the Plough"', *Music Review*, Vol. XXIV, Cambridge, 1963, 139–46.

HOGARTH, GEORGE, *Musical History, Biography and Criticism*, J. W. Parker, London, 1836.

HOPKINSON, CECIL, *A Bibliographical Thematic Catalogue of the Works of John Field, 1782–1837*, printed for the author, London, 1961.

JAL, A., 'Anecdotes, (Deux Portraits)', *Le Pianiste*, No. X, Paris, 1835, 75–7.

KAMINSKAYA, A., 'John Field's work as a performer and teacher and his piano compositions', unpublished dissertation, Moscow Conservatoire Library, 1951.

KONTSKI, ANTON, 'Outstanding Composer-Pianists of the Present Century and their influence on Musical Art', *Teatralny i muzycalny Vestnik* ('The Theatrical and Musical Herald'), No. 5, Moscow, 1858, 55–6.

LAMBURN, EDWARD, *A Short History of a Great House*, Collard & Collard, London, 1938.

LEHMAN, EVANGELINE, 'John Field, an Irishman, the grandfather of Russian Music', *The Etude*, Vol. LVIII. Philadelphia, 1940, 154 and 204.

LISZT, FRANZ, *Ueber John Fields Nocturne*, Schuberth, Leipzig, 1859.

MARMONTEL, ANTOINE, *Les Pianistes Célèbres*, Paul Bousrez, Tours, 1877.

MAXWELL, CONSTANTIA, *Dublin under the Georges: 1714–1830*, G. Harrap & Co. Ltd., London, 1946.

MONTAGU-NATHAN, M., 'Russian Field', *Monthly Musical Record*, Vol. XLVIII, London, 1918, 106–17.

MOSCHELES, IGNAZ, *Aus Moscheles' Leben: nach Briefen und Tagebüchen*, *hrsg. von seiner Frau*, Duneker & Humbolt, Leipzig, 1872–3.

NEIGHBOUR, OLIVER W., 'Early Editions of John Field', *British Museum Quarterly*, Vol. XIX, London, 1954.

NIKOLAYEV, A., 'John Field', *Gosudarstvennoye Muzykalnoye Izdatyelstvo* ('State Music Publications'), Moscow, 1960.

OLIVIER, DARIA, *The Burning of Moscow*, 1812, Allen & Unwin, London, 1966.

ORTIGUE, JOSEPH LOUIS D', *Le Balcon de l'Opera*, Librarie E. Renduel, Paris, 1830.

PARKE, WILLIAM T., *Musical Memories*, Colburn & Bentley, London, 1830.

PAUER, ERNST, 'Two Pupils of Clementi—Field and Cramer', *Monthly Musical Record*, London, I/1, 1871, 20.

PIGGOTT, PATRICK, 'Field and the Nocturne', *The Listener*, no. 68, 1746, London, 1962, 409.

PIGGOTT, PATRICK, *John Field and the Nocturne*, Proceedings of the Royal Musical Association, London, 1968–9.

PLEASANTS, HENRY, *The Musical World of Robert Schumann: a selection from his own writings*, St. Martin's Press, New York, 1965.

SCHUMANN, ROBERT, *Gesammelte Schriften über Musik und Musiker*, Leipzig, 1891.

SOCCANNE, PIERRE, 'Les Inspiratrices, XII, John Field, ou Mlle Charpentier et . . . l'autre', *Le Guide de Concert*, Paris, March, April, 1934, 679–81.

SOUTHALL, GENEVA HANDY, 'John Field's Piano Concertos: an analytical and historical study', unpublished Ph.D. dissertation, University of Iowa, 1966.

SPOHR, LOUIS, *Selbstbiographie*, G. H. Wigand, Cassel und Göttingen, 1860.

TIDEBOHL, ELLEN VON, 'Reminiscences of John Field', *Monthly Musical Record*, March, April, May, June 1923.

TYSON, ALAN, 'John Field's Earliest Compositions', *Music & Letters*, London, July, 1966, 239–48.

UNGER, MAX, *Muzio Clementis Leben*, Beyer & Söhul, Langensalza 1914.

Among the numerous unsigned articles about Field which appeared in English, French, German, Austrian and Russian journals and newspapers the following are of particular interest:

The Dublin Evening Post, Dublin, 27 March 1792.

The Morning Post, London, 9 February 1799.

The Harmonicon, London, 27 February 1832.

La Revue Musicale, Paris, 26 January, 9 February, 22 June, 24 August, 1833.

Semaphore de Marseilles, 2 August 1833.

Il Barbiere di Siviglia, Milan, 16 November and 7 December 1833.

Syn Otchestva ('Son of the Fatherland'), No. 15, St. Petersburg, 1834, 504–15.

Select Bibliography

Zeitschrift für Kunst, Literatur und Mode, Vienna, August 1835.

Khudozhestvennaya Gazeta ('Newspaper of the Arts'), No. 1, Moscow, 1837, 14–16.

Allgemeine Musikalische Zeitung, Leipzig, No. 29, 19 July 1837.

Russki Invalid ('The Russian Invalid'), No. 195, St. Petersburg, 1846, 777.

Nuvelist ('The Novelist'), No. 6 (literary supplement), St. Petersburg 1844.

Ilyustrirovannaya Gazeta ('Illustrated Newspaper'), Moscow, 22 January 1870, 39.

Index

Act of Union, 2
Adam, Adolphe, 95n
Alabyev, A. N., 113
Albion Tavern, London, 69
Albrechtsberger, J. G., 19, 20
Aldvin, 262
Alkan, Charles H. V., 73
Allgemeine Musikalische Zeitung, xiv, 17n, 59
Alpe, Mrs, 13, 14
Amiens, Peace of, 18
Andrieux, Phyllis ('Mademoiselle Phyllis') 217
Anonymous pieces attributed to Field, 14, 225
Apraxin, Baron, 57
Arapov's *Chronicles of the Russian Theatre*, 49n
Arsenyev, Governor, 30, 31
Artaria (Viennese publisher), 19, 226
Asafyev, B. V., 116n
Athenaeum The, 70
Aumann, W., 247
Aungier Street, Dublin, 5
Austen, Jane, 22n, 32, 145
    Pride and Prejudice, 145
    Sense and Sensibility, 145
    The Watsons, 22n
    Miss Fairfax, 32

Bach, J. C., Concertos by, 146
Bach, J. S., 114
    48 Preludes and Fugues, 18, 113
    Fugues (unspecified), 18, 102
    Concerto (after Vivaldi) for four claviers 45
Bachmetiev, Marie de (née Lvov), 153

Backhaus, Wilhelm, 45
Baillot, P. M., 79
Ball, Baron (a banker to the Russian court), 87
Baltic Sea, 61
Baltic States, 21
Barbier de Séville, Le (Beaumarchais), 225
Barbiere di Siviglia, Il (Milanese journal), 88, 89
Barthelmon, F. H., 12
Bastille Day celebrations, 18
Bath, 3, 9, 10
Bath Abbey, 10
Baudron, Antoine Laurent, 225
Bayley, Thomas, 223
    'We met' (from 'Songs of the Boudoir'), 223, 241
Beaufort Buildings, the Strand, London, 67
Beethoven, L. van, 19, 52, 53, 64, 75n, 92n, 114, 203, 254
    'Archduke' Trio, 183
    Fifth Concerto in E flat, 169
    'Kreutzer' Sonata, 53n
    Pastoral Symphony, 169
    Sonata in C sharp minor, Op. 27, No. 2, 132, 197
    Third Concerto in C minor, 53
    Variations on a Russian Dance from Wranitsky's ballet, *Das Wald-mädchen*', 226
Belge, Le, 79
Bellini, V., 64
Bennett, W. Sterndale, 66
Berlin, 19, 21, 26, 47
Berlioz, Hector, 73, 77, 95n, 114
    La Damnation de Faust, 95n
Bernard (St Petersburg publisher), 96, 255

Index

* Field's only baptismal name was John. There is no truth in A. Nikolayev's statement that his name was John Brown Field.

Index